Community Development in Canada

Jason D. Brown
University of Western Ontario

David Hannis
Grant MacEwan College

Library and Archives Canada Cataloguing in Publication

Brown, Jason, 1968-
   Community development in Canada / Jason D. Brown, David Hannis.

Includes bibliographical references and index.
ISBN-10: 0-205-46515-3
ISBN-13: 978-0-205-46515-6

   1. Community development—Canada—Textbooks.
I. Hannis, David, 1945- II. Title.

HN110.Z9C6 2008   307.1'40971   C2006-905871-7

ISBN-10: 0-205-46515-3
ISBN-13: 978-0-205-46515-6

Editor-in-Chief, Vice-President of Sales: Kelly Shaw
Executive Acquisitions Editor: Ky Pruesse
Executive Marketing Manager: Judith Allen
Supervising Developmental Editor: Suzanne Schaan
Signing Representative: Duncan MacKinnon
Production Editor: Kevin Leung
Copy Editor: Colleen Ste. Marie
Proofreader: Emma Gorst
Production Coordinator: Avinash Chandra
Composition: Laserwords
Art Director: Julia Hall
Cover Design: Geoff Agnew
Cover Image: Photodisc

1 2 3 4 5   12 11 10 09 08

Printed and bound in the United States of America.

Contents

iv Contents

Preface

Students study community development for a variety of reasons. Some come to the course with a wealth of life experience and a great deal of expertise in community development work. Others are completely new to the area, and come with an interest in how community organization and capacities impact the well-being of citizens. Our vision for this book, therefore, was to include theoretical and historical perspectives as well as a brief look at the contemporary approaches used and skills needed by community workers. We have highlighted many major contributions by Canadians to the development and practice of community development.

This book was written for a broad audience. *Community Development in Canada* is intended for related courses at community college and university, as well as in adult education and professional development environments.

There are three main themes in this book. In Chapters 1 to 4, we discuss the meanings and uses of the term *community*, as well as ways that communities change over time. We identify major influences on community development practice, as well as historical and contemporary perspectives on community work. Then, in Chapters 5, 6, and 7, we focus on the skills needed for community work. A major emphasis in this section is on relationship-building and maintenance. We also discuss a generic process model that may be used to identify issues that arise in community development work at different times. In Chapters 8 to 11, we look at Canadian community development practice. We have selected case studies from each province and territory to illustrate principles of community practice, and we also discuss development in Aboriginal and international communities, and the future of community development and social welfare in Canada. The book also includes an extensive bibliography to assist instructors and students with future study.

Community Development in Canada is accompanied by a Test Item File, which is available to instructors for downloading from a password-protected section of Pearson Education Canada's online catalogue (vig.pearsoned.ca). Navigate to your book's catalogue page to view a list of those supplements that are available. See your local sales representative for details and access.

Acknowledgments

Many people have made contributions to this book. I would like to thank my partner, Shelley, for her encouragement and support throughout the many evenings and weekends spent on this project. My children—Kaylee, Jenna, and Kobe—have been constant sources of energy and inspiration. I have also been very fortunate to have wonderful friends, colleagues, and traditional people who have been patient and kind teachers. I am grateful to David Hannis, who has willingly shared what he has learned and allowed me to benefit from his experience and expertise in this field.

Jason D. Brown

My contribution to this long overdue text is a reflection of many years' work as a community developer and adult educator. It has truly been a pleasure to collaborate on this project with Jason Brown, who shares my passion for community, and with the good folks at Pearson Education, who initially prodded me into action and remained supportive during the evolution of this publication. I owe a particular debt of gratitude to the many selfless community activists I have worked with in the past and to countless numbers of social work students at Grant MacEwan College, whose energy and critical thinking capacities have served to remind me of my own physical and intellectual limitations. I have also drawn strength from my two daughters, Katherine and Kristina, whose strong ethical perspectives on life, commitment to social justice, and unconditional love have been a valued source of inspiration for me.

David Hannis

We would also like to thank the staff at Pearson Education for their understanding and support as this project took unexpected turns during its development. The contributions of Rachel Stuckey, developmental editor, Colleen Ste. Marie, copyeditor, as well as Jessica Mosher, Patty Riediger, and Ky Pruesse, are reflected in this work.

And for their thoughtful comments and helpful suggestions, we would like to thank the following reviewers:

Pramila Aggarwal, George Brown College

Lawrence Becker, Douglas College

Lynne Brennan, George Brown College

Thomas Brenner, Renison College–University of Waterloo

Marinus Dieleman, Northern College

James M. Fulton, Fleming College

Susan Pratten, Sheridan College

Lisa Shaw-Verhoek, Algonquin College

Leo Smits, University of Guelph-Humber

Finally, we give special thanks to Leo Smits at Guelph-Humber, who, in addition to reviewing the manuscript, shared his knowledge and experience in international development, providing us with a road map for writing Chapter 10. His input was extensive; however, any errors or inconsistencies remain those of the authors.

chapter one

Importance of Community

LEARNING OBJECTIVES

After reading this chapter, you will be able to:

1. Analyze and discuss the social, physical, and political needs that communities serve.
2. Identify and discuss some definitions of *community*.
3. Define *social capital* and apply the concept to community well-being.
4. Describe different types of communities.
5. Understand the different types of functions that communities serve.

The word *community* comes from the ancient Greek word for *fellowship*. In fact, over 2300 years ago Aristotle described people coming together into communities for different reasons. More recent writers have determined that those reasons include enjoying mutual association, fulfilling basic needs, and finding meaning in life (Christenson & Robinson, 1980). And most contemporary human services professionals would agree that communities make important contributions to individual and family well-being. After all, we've all heard that "it takes a village to raise a child." However, despite increasing evidence on the benefits of community-level action to improve individual and family health and well-being, most contemporary human services in Canada target the needs of individuals and families. This book presents ways to understand and participate in community development for the purpose of enhancing collective health and well-being. In this chapter, we review both early and more recent research findings on the importance and effect of healthy communities on personal well-being. Following that, we discuss different types of communities, and finally, we turn our attention to the functions of communities.

CHAPTER OUTLINE

PHYSICAL AND MENTAL HEALTH BENEFITS OF COMMUNITY

In the nineteenth century, the sociologist Emile Durkheim observed that people who had more connections with their families and community members were less likely to commit suicide. From his research, he concluded that suicide is less common among married people and within tightly knit religious communities, rare in times of national unity, and more frequent when rapid social change disrupts the social fabric. For Durkheim, the incidence of suicide was predictable. More recently, research conducted in some Canadian boom towns during the 1990s has also investigated questions about how communities cope with crisis. In Elliot Lake, for example, which was at one time the uranium capital of the world, the closure of mines and mass layoffs in the early to mid-1990s had significant effects on residents (Mawhiny & Pitblado, 1999).

A recent analysis of the state of community in North America concluded that those who were more integrated with their communities were less likely to get colds, or have heart attacks, strokes, cancer, or depression (Putnam, 2000). The author of this analysis also cited studies from other countries, including Scandinavia and Japan, which also showed the connection between strong communities and lower levels of illness. In recent years, rates of depression, suicide, stomach upsets, migraines, and sleep disorders have all increased among young people, and social isolation among youth has become of increasing concern. Today, the average North American teenager spends about three-and-a-half hours alone each day (Putnam, 2000).

When individuals feel isolated from each other, mental and physical health problems may develop (Adler & Towne, 1999). A lack of social relationships, for example, jeopardizes heart function to a degree that rivals the dangers associated with cigarette smoking, high blood pressure, obesity, and lack of physical activity. Socially isolated people are four times more susceptible to the common cold and are two or three times more likely to die prematurely than those who have active social networks. Not surprisingly, a strong sense of belonging to a community is associated with greater physical and social health (Statistics Canada, 2005b).

Typically, we each look for a sense of purpose and sense of belonging from our families, close friends, organizations, and voluntary activities. Unfortunately, for increasing numbers of people, these sources of support are absent.

CONTEMPORARY COMMUNITIES

Western society, especially in North America, is highly mobile. Many people are forced to move away from supportive family and friends to pursue career opportunities thousands of miles away from their homes. Such people are often too physically exhausted at the end of the day to invest much time and energy in nurturing their neighbourhood networks. This problem becomes even more acute for parents who have at least one and sometimes two full-time jobs (one outside the home and one within it). And while some people may be able to maintain connections with their extended families, others may have families so dysfunctional that they provide little support or relief from stress. As well, with increasing numbers of seniors in our communities, the problem of the socially isolated elderly becomes more acute.

In Canada, the census (Statistics Canada, 1996) shows several population trends that affect communities:

- Canadians move frequently. Western Canadians are more likely to move than those from eastern Canada. Two-thirds of eastern Canadians have lived at the same address for more than five years. In Alberta and British Columbia, only 50 percent can make this claim (Kremarik, 2000).
- Recent immigrants report low social contact. Those who have moved to Canada in the past year have fewer contacts with their neighbours than people born in Canada or those who have lived in Canada for at least a decade (Kremarik, 2000).
- Easterners talk to their neighbours more. People in the Atlantic provinces talk to their neighbours more often than do people living in other parts of the country. Almost 90 percent of Newfoundlanders report some level of contact with their neighbours. Quebecers were reported to speak to their neighbours much less often (Kremarik, 2000).
- Couples have higher rates of interaction with neighbours. Two-parent families with children at home, and two-spouse families, have the highest rates of interaction with neighbours. People living alone and single parents are the least likely to have contact with neighbours (Kremarik, 2000).
- Younger people interact less than older residents with their neighbours. In fact, people in their twenties, compared to people in their sixties, have far less to do with their neighbours. Furthermore, rural residents are more likely than city people to be neighbourly (Kremarik, 2000).
- The physical layout of a community affects interaction. Housing design is believed to impact on the frequency of interaction between neighbours. Detached houses with adjoining garages, for example, are the least conducive to social interaction, while residences with porches are more likely to facilitate social contact (Kremarik, 2000).

Fostering a Sense of Community

People want and need a sense of community, but there are challenges. Growing numbers of people do not have or cannot draw on the social supports provided by close friends, families, and volunteer activities. At the same time, many communities are struggling to maintain vibrant organizations because increasing numbers of men and women are spending more time in the workplace, where they seek to meet their needs for social inclusion, rather than in their homes and neighbourhoods.

And when our communities are not strong, individuals feel weaker. Conversely, when communities are strong, individuals can feel more powerful. The relationship between individuals and their communities is, therefore, a symbiotic one; they nurture each other continuously (Lee, 1992).

But when individuals feel that they have little or no control over their environments, their self-image suffers, and they may experience a sense of hopelessness and manifest what Freire (1973) describes as a "culture of silence," or "learned helplessness." Sometimes this sense of powerlessness turns inward in self-destructive behaviours, or it may externalize and take the form of physical and emotional abuse directed toward others.

Communities are essential both to individual and collective well-being; they play a vital role in helping us meet a fundamental need to understand ourselves and make our environments comprehensible, predictable, and manageable. As individuals, we need to feel connected to each other in order to experience a positive self-image. Collectively, the strength of our democracy depends on citizens' abilities to come together around common issues, and elect, and hold accountable, politicians who represent the wishes of a broad cross-section of community members.

DEFINING *COMMUNITY*

For such a commonly used term, there are a variety of definitions for *community*. For example, in a marketing context, a "community" may well be a demographic group, without any reference to a place and without any connections or commonalities among people. And writers or researchers interested in the term as it applies to *community development* offer different kinds of definitions.

A review of over 90 definitions of **community** showed that two-thirds included social interaction, common connections, and location (Warren, 1978). Interaction and relationships within places, and commonalities in interests, beliefs, and behaviours are often mentioned. *Community* is "that combination of social units and systems which perform the major social functions having locality relevance" (Warren, 1978, p. 9). Galbraith (1990) suggested that *community* may be defined as "the combination and interrelationships of geographic, locational, and non-locational units, systems, and characteristics that provide relevance and growth to individuals, groups, and organizations" (p. 5). These definitions emphasize the community as a place.

Other definitions emphasize the interaction of members. For example, a community is "a human system of more than two people in which the members interact personally over time, in which behaviour and activity are guided by collectively-evolved norms or collective decisions, and from which members may freely secede" (Boothroyd, 1990, p. 105). In another definition, community is about making change: it is "a collection of people who have become aware of some problem or some broad goal, who have gone through a process of learning about themselves and about their environment, and have formulated a group objective" (Roberts, 1979, p.10). An important direction of contemporary research on social relationships in community context is the concept of social capital.

Social Capital

The term *social capital* was first used by L. J. Hanifan, state supervisor of rural schools in West Virginia in 1916, to stress the importance of community involvement in successful schools (Putnam, 2000). **Social capital** is a community's social fabric. It refers to the network of relationships between people. The main thrust of social capital theory is that social networks have value. They affect individual health and contribute to a sense of well-being. Social networks also affect communities. The benefits to communities of high social capital include enhanced productivity, more effective democratic processes, and reduced rates of criminal activity (Putnam, 2000).

Social capital emphasizes relationships, networks, norms, trust, and resources (Mignone, 2003). A community with a high level of social capital would have high levels of trust among residents, broad-based participation in decisions, collective action, and would share resources within its boundaries (Mignone, 2003). Adapted to a First Nations community context, the main factors of social capital include **bonding** (relations within the community), **bridging** (ties with other communities), and **linkage** (ties to institutions) (Mignone, 2003). A First Nations community with high social capital, therefore, would have good relations within its boundaries, to other nearby communities (not necessarily First Nations communities), and to institutions, such as governments and corporations. Relationships are fundamental to social capital, and strong relationships lead to strong communities.

Types of Communities

The German scholar Ferdinand Tonnies (1855–1936) distinguished between two fundamental types of community, *Gemeinschaft* (pre-industrial) and *Gesellschaft* (modern) (Plant, 1974). According to Tonnies, pre-industrial *Gemeinschaft* communities are characterized by interacting, reciprocal relationships involving relatively intimate face-to-face dealings with the whole person, rather than segmented, bureaucratized, and role-determined components. *Gesellschaft* industrial societies, on the other hand, where most of us live, are based on contract, legal/rational notions, and the achievement of individual rather than collective goals. Clearly, sustaining a sense of community becomes a bigger challenge in modern, industrial, competitive societies than in ones where a greater emphasis is placed on relationships, mutual support, and the achievement of common goals.

One of the authors of this book was involved in research examining the social impacts of boom towns. **Boom towns** are small, primarily agriculturally based communities that are transformed virtually overnight by the rapid development of some locally available resource, usually oil and gas, lumber, or coal (Hannis, 1988). While researching boom towns, it was possible to see the transformation of a community from *Gemeinschaft* to *Gesellschaft* within a period as short as five to ten years, often accompanied by disastrous social consequences. Crime rates rose and a growing depersonalization of services occurred as local governments grew and became more bureaucratic, and as small-town stores gave way to large chain stores and franchises controlled by outsiders. Indeed, these negative social impacts—including the collapse of families, substance abuse, mental illness, and increased crime—became so inevitable that it was possible to actually predict the incidence of these issues with some degree of accuracy.

A more recent definition of *community* describes three types: geographic, function or attribute, and interest (Lee, 1992). A **geographic community** is a group of people living in the same physical area. A **function or attribute community** refers to a group of people who share or possess a common and essential factor, such as gender, race, religion, or socio-economic status. An **interest community** describes a group of people who come together to address a common interest or concern. This category would include professional associations, trade unions, and social action groups, for example. These community types can overlap or operate separately. For example, some urban neighbourhoods have clear physical boundaries, such as roadways or buildings, that define it. Within such a community, there may also be a group of people who share some similarity. A seniors-only apartment is an example. The tenants of such an apartment may come together for particular events, such as ways to approach a neglectful landlord to make needed repairs. In this example, the seniors' community is a community of geography, attribute, and interest.

Functions of Communities

There are five functions of a community (Warren, 1978). The **production, distribution, and consumption** function of a community ensures some measure of meeting supply and demand for certain basic necessities, such as food, shelter, and clothing, by locally owned and run businesses, or by local governance. A **socialization** function is met through the process of transmitting, to members, prevailing knowledge, social values, and behaviour patterns. A **social control** function is met by communities that ensure conformity to group norms. The **social participation** function of communities is met by providing opportunities for members to interact with each other and to participate in co-operative activities. A **mutual support** function means that the community acts as a bridge between families and bureaucratized services by providing informal opportunities for mutual support, including care for the sick, child care, and help in times of crisis.

Given the importance that many writers and politicians have given to the notion of community, surprisingly few resources have been devoted to enhancing community networks. Typically, once a community is created, the development of mutually supportive social networks tends to be left to chance. Initiatives that challenge the unplanned approach to building communities are called **intentional communities,** which are defined as the following:

> . . . a group of people who have chosen to live or work together in pursuit of a common ideal or vision, [of whom] most, though not all, share land or housing. Intentional communities come in all shapes and sizes, and display an amazing diversity in their common values, which may be social, economic, spiritual, political and/or ecological. Some are rural; some urban. Some live all in a single residence; some in separate households. Some raise children; some don't. Some are secular, some are spiritually based, and others are both. (Kozeny, 2000)

Intentional communities are not a recent phenomenon, although interest in them has grown over the past few decades. Kozeny (2000), for instance, has dated one of the earliest intentional communities to the sixth century BC when Buddha's followers rejected wealth, turned to meditation, and joined together in ashrams to model an orderly, productive, and spiritual way to live. Common themes in intentional communities are living co-operatively, solving problems nonviolently, and sharing experiences with other members. Recent examples include the **ecovillages**, based on this concept, founded in Ithaca, New York; Los Angeles, California; and St. Petersburg, Russia in the 1990s.

SUMMARY

- Illness is more common among people who don't have a sense of belonging to a community.
- Community life in Canada is changing due to residential mobility, changes in family, and economic factors.

- Communities are defined in a variety of ways, based on location, function, or connections.
- Social capital refers to the networks between people in a community as well as between the community, other communities, and institutions.
- Communities serve several functions, including production, socialization, control, participation, and support.

DISCUSSION QUESTIONS

1. What is the ideal community to you? Consider the following: demographics, location, employment, government, recreation, law and order, health needs, social needs, education, spiritual needs, commerce, and transportation.
2. In communities, what processes are at work to prevent illness? What is it about a community that promotes well-being?
3. How can you foster a sense of belonging within a diverse community? Consider diversity in terms of ethnicity, economics, and age.
4. Think of the community you grew up in. Did the community have high, medium, or low social capital? Why?
5. Which functions of community are most important to you? How can you nurture them in the communities you currently live, learn, and earn in?

WEBLINKS

www.well.com/~bbear/hc_articles.html Healthy Cities/Healthy Communities

www.phac-aspc.gc.ca/vs-sb/voluntarysector/benefits/benefits2a.html Social Capital and Health

www12.statcan.ca/english/census01/home/index.cfm Statistics Canada–2001 Census

www.scn.org/cmp/whatcom.htm What is community?

KEY TERMS

Bonding (social capital), p. 5

Boom towns, p. 5

Bridging (social capital), p. 5

Community, p. 4

Ecovillage, p. 6

Function or attribute community, p. 5

Gemeinschaft, p. 5

Geographic community, p. 5

Gesellschaft, p. 5

Intentional communities, p. 6

Interest community, p. 5

Linkage (social capital), p. 5

Mutual support function, p. 6

Production, distribution, and consumption function, p. 6

Social capital, p. 4

Social control function, p. 6

Social participation function, p. 6

Socialization function, p. 6

chapter two

Introduction to Community Development

LEARNING OBJECTIVES

After reading this chapter, you will be able to:

1. Distinguish between top-down and bottom-up approaches to community development.
2. Identify the main features of community development process and practice.
3. Apply factors that can have a negative effect on communities.
4. Apply factors that can have a positive effect on communities.
5. Understand different perceived roles of a community developer.
6. Understand that there is a range of initiatives across Canada that exemplify community development.

The wide range of definitions for *community* and *community development* shows that no two communities or processes are exactly alike. Yet there are some challenges that many communities face, as well as strengths they possess, that can be relevant in community development efforts. While communities are of central importance to individual and family well-being, human services and health professionals often pay little attention to working at the community level. There are several reasons why community development work is difficult for these professionals and their employers to understand and appreciate, which we will discuss in Chapter 7. However, the results of community development work can have multiple and significant positive effects on an entire community. In this chapter, we review some definitions of community development before turning attention to factors that weaken and strengthen communities. We identify some perceptions about community development practice, and provide examples of how community development addresses basic needs in different locations across Canada.

CHAPTER OUTLINE

What Is Community Development?

Nurturing Community
> *Factors That Weaken Communities*
>> *Lack of a Sense of Collective History*
>> *Stigma*
>> *High Mobility*
>> *Fragmentation*
>> *Lack of Services*
>> *Lack of Local Decision-Making Authority*
>> *Lack of Boundaries*
>
> *Factors That Strengthen Communities*
>> *Active Voluntary Organizations*
>> *Identity*
>> *Community Centre*
>> *Common Need or Enemy*
>> *Good Transportation Systems*
>> *Balanced Land-Use Plans*

Some Myths About Community Development Work
> *Myth 1: Community Work Is Easy*
> *Myth 2: Anyone with a Professional Credential or a Big Heart Can Be Effective*
> *Myth 3: Community Services Are Well Funded*
> *Myth 4: All Communities Are Democratic*
> *Myth 5: All Communities Speak with One Voice*
> *Myth 6: Outcomes Are Easy to Measure*
> *Myth 7: Solutions Are Easy to Find and Implement*
> *Myth 8: Community Development Is the Same in All Communities*

Examples: Meeting Basic Needs
> *Food*
> *Shelter*
> *Employment*
> *Safety*
> *Sense of Place*

Summary

Discussion Questions

Weblinks

Key Terms

WHAT IS COMMUNITY DEVELOPMENT?

There are many definitions of *community development*, and they vary considerably, based on their goals and approaches. One way to distinguish definitions from one another is to recognize the differences between those that imply a top-down versus a bottom-up approach. **Top-down** approaches impose a goal and often a process on a community. From a top-down perspective, the goal of community development and the way that goal will be achieved are already defined. For example, let's say a developer wants to purchase land in a community for commercial interests. She or he may organize a community meeting to discuss the matter with local residents. Attendees at such a meeting may include high-ranking political officials who support the initiative, which may lead to an increase to the civic tax base. The developer's purpose, in this example, is to get community support for the idea by persuading community members that the proposed project would be good for them in the long run. In this example, the community does not determine the goal and approach; rather, the developer imposes both. Sometimes these kinds of initiatives are characterized as community development or community-building activities. But few contemporary community workers with grassroots connections would support this approach.

Instead, the bottom-up approach has received most of the attention and support of scholars and activists as well as grassroots leaders and community members. A **bottom-up** approach assumes that the community determines the appropriate goals and objectives for itself. Indeed, there are many definitions of this perspective. The goals of development differ, depending on the community. However, they often revolve around people coming together to "gain some control over . . . a frustrating and changing world" (Biddle & Biddle, 1965, p. 78). The need to gain control over externally imposed conditions is important for any local community development work (Bhattacharyya, 1995). Bottom-up community development may begin in response to a local issue, such as local substance use problems, or in response to an externally imposed condition. One example of an imposed external condition would be the arrival of the logging industry to a small, remote community, without the community's consent and involvement. This would have multiple impacts, some of which, if not managed appropriately, would be negative. For example, the arrival of the logging industry could diminish the quality of life in the community (e.g., new bars will open, housing will be less available); create inequities within the community (e.g., some community members might get new jobs while others will not); compromise democratic functioning (e.g., the industry executives could become significant influences); restrict community members' potential (e.g., logging might become the main industry in the community); and strip away a sense of community while reinforcing the myth of individualism (Rubin & Rubin, 2001). In response to this externally imposed condition (i.e., the arrival of the logging industry), the goals of bottom-up community development may be to restore quality of life, diminish inequities, reinstate democratic functioning, enhance members' potential, and restore a sense of community among members.

Community development is, fundamentally, a democratic and social process (Minkler, 1990). It is "a process that increases the assets and attributes which a community is able to draw upon in order to improve their lives" (Gibbon, Labonte, & Laverack, 2002, p. 485). As well, community development is "people acting collectively with others who share some common concern" (Checkoway, 1997, p. 13). It is "the capacity of local populations to respond collectively to events and issues that affect them" (Gilchrist, 2003, p. 16). Finally, community development is "working with people at a local level to promote active participation in identifying local needs and organizing to meet those needs" (Wright, 2004, p. 386). The success of community development work depends on "collective problem-solving, self-help, and empowerment" (Schiele, Jackson & Fairfax, 2005, p. 22).

The sustainability of community development efforts is important, and ways to ensure longevity can be informal or formalized. For example, informally identifying issues and problems and then generating and applying plans for change can enhance strength and self-sufficiency, and aid in maintaining strong interpersonal relationships (Williams, Labonte, & O'Brien, 2003). Others suggest that the sustainability of community development efforts requires local people to "form their own organizations to provide a long-term capacity for problem-solving" (Rubin & Rubin, 2001, p. 3).

Another way to describe community development is to distinguish it from other forms of community work (Popple, 1995). **Community development** emphasizes self-help and mutual support, and it also enhances local capacity for problem solving, and promotes collective action to bring matters to political decision makers. **Community action,** on the other hand, focuses on direct action against public or nonpublic bodies that perpetuate structural divisions in society. **Community organization** is about collaborating with community agencies to promote joint initiatives, while **social planning** is concerned with assessing needs and capacities for the purpose of program planning and evaluation. And **service extension** seeks to expand the services of local agencies to meet the needs of underserved members of the community.

NURTURING COMMUNITY

Community development takes different forms and paths depending on local needs and assets. However, there are some general factors that have an impact on a community's strength. We have identified 13 factors that have either negative or positive impacts on communities. Every community has its own unique blend of needs and challenges, and different factors may be more or less of a priority than others. The list that follows is not exhaustive, but offers a starting point for discussions about purposes and approaches for local community development.

Factors That Weaken Communities

Factors that weaken communities include lack of a sense of history, stigma, transience, fragmentation, and a lack of services, of local decision making, and of boundaries.

Lack of a Sense of Collective History A lack of a shared understanding about our history can make us feel disconnected from present realities and destined to repeat the mistakes of the past. This can be true at both local and national levels. The starting point for building a sense of community is often interviewing older residents, reviewing records, and gathering artifacts that tell us something about our collective past and allow us to celebrate our culture.

Stigma No one wants to live in a community that the outside world perceives as second-rate or dangerous. In such places, people may feel ashamed, fearful of their neighbourhoods, unwilling to make a long-term commitment to the area, and anxious to move on as quickly as possible. Rates of illness, crime, addictions, and other social problems may be high in such communities.

High Mobility All neighbourhoods go through natural evolutionary cycles as families age, children move away, and the elderly relocate. This movement poses problems for planners, who periodically have to contend with underutilized schools, churches, and other facilities in aging communities.

A certain amount of transience is to be expected in any community. When the rate of movement, however, becomes unacceptably high, it can affect the quality of life for all residents. Often, safety is a concern when people don't know their neighbourhoods and when they are reluctant to invest the time in getting to know them.

Fragmentation Another factor that can weaken a neighbourhood is the existence of people from different social classes and ethnic backgrounds who do not work together. Planners have sometimes attempted to avoid the creation of stigmatized communities by, for example, dispersing social housing across a range of different communities. However, this strategy has not always been successful. Unless deliberate effort is made to view diversity as community strength, people will interact with those from their own social class and ethnic group exclusively, and ignore or label others. When communities are fractured, it is difficult to work toward common goals, and blaming can become widespread.

In some communities, the tensions arising from perceived social and ethnic differences are often felt most acutely by children in schools, and take the form of bullying, name-calling, racism, and the formation of gangs. It is difficult to build a sense of identity when such behaviours are allowed to continue unchecked.

Lack of Services If you've ever watched the British soap opera *Coronation Street*, you were likely struck by the amount of commercial activity taking place in that relatively small geographic area. There is the pub—the Rover's Return—a school, a sweet shop, a grocery store, a garage, a small factory, a café, a taxi company, a hairdresser, and, not too far away, a supermarket. A senior's residence is close by, and apparently there is enough work in the area to support several self-employed people, including a window cleaner and a builder. This is, of course, a TV show. The chances of finding such a self-contained community in Britain are almost as remote as finding one here in Canada, although such communities were widespread 50 years ago.

Today, one issue facing urban and rural communities alike has been the loss of such locally owned businesses. Go into any urban community and the chances of finding a neighbourhood corner store, bank, post office, drugstore, hardware store, or other owner-operated business are increasingly unlikely. Similarly, in many rural communities, small local businesses have closed their doors as their former clients have deserted them in favour of stores located in distant urban centres. Governments and other large organizations, including banks, grain elevators, companies, and railroads, have often compounded this problem: many have closed local operations in the name of greater economic efficiency. As local services begin to disappear, so too do residents, which causes an overall deterioration in the quality of life for those who remain behind.

Lack of Local Decision-Making Authority A strong community is one where residents feel they have some control over the decisions that affect them. The quickest way to encourage apathy and learned helplessness is to remove people's ability to have real input into decision-making processes at the local level. Too often, community consultation simply never takes place at all. If it does, it is interpreted as merely informing residents about decisions that have already been made, rather than engaging in constructive and open dialogue early in the decision-making processes.

When decisions are arrived at collectively, honestly, and respectfully, more people are likely to be committed to the project's eventual success. Conversely, when individuals feel that no one is really interested in listening to them, or that they have been manipulated, they become demoralized and apathetic. They are also less willing to become energetic and collaborative members of the community. For example, some years ago in a large Canadian city, parks planners became frustrated when their attempts to beautify a neighbourhood by planting trees always ended in failure because local youths repeatedly vandalized the saplings. In dismay, they were ready to give up until one person had the bright idea of consulting the community, which, in turn, suggested that the youths themselves should be involved in this process. The result was that the young people decided that they would like to plant their own trees in their community. The parks department provided the trees and technical support, the trees were planted, and the vandalism came to an end.

Lack of Boundaries People can be somewhat territorial. In our communities we often identify with geographic areas that are surrounded by natural barriers, such as arterial roads, railroad tracks, rivers, and so forth. In the early 1970s, Oscar Newman (1973), an innovative architect and urban planner in the U.S., coined the phrase *defensible space* to describe this phenomenon.

Oscar Newman's thesis was that at the neighbourhood level, we can design communities in a way that can encourage (or discourage) interaction between neighbours, and, by giving residents some sense of psychological control over public areas, vandalism and crime rates can be reduced. Thus, in some areas, residents of public housing high-rises have been given the right to paint the common areas on the floors outside their apartments a colour of their choice and even hold block parties there, which has promoted a stronger sense of community.

Factors That Strengthen Communities

Factors that strengthen communities include the presence of a wide range of organizations, a sense of identity, a gathering place, a common need, good transportation, and participation in decisions about land use.

Active Voluntary Organizations John McKnight, a community organizer from the U.S., mentioned that one of the first things he does when he visits a new community is to look in the yellow pages under the heading **Voluntary Organizations** to get a sense of how healthy that community is (McKnight & Kretzmann, 1994). Many communities have multiple listings under Associations, Societies, and Foundations, and there are probably countless more. In addition, many have an extensive network of community leagues, and social, recreational, and sometimes political events in neighbourhoods. While these non-profit organizations are often struggling to fulfill their mandates and raise funds, their existence suggests that not all communities have surrendered all of their functions to distant bureaucracies. McKnight has argued that the more functions the community provides, the stronger our democracy, and that, conversely, without vibrant communities our democracy is dead (McKnight, 1995).

Identity One of the first tasks a community worker often has when entering a community is to recognize evidence of collective pride through recorded history, or a logo for a community organization or sports team. Fun-filled events, such as carnivals and street dances, can bring a community together. Local newspapers, newsletters, and skills-exchange opportunities also play a useful role in promoting a sense of community identity.

Community Centre A focal point where residents can meet together informally is important for the creation of a vibrant community.

Common Need or Enemy People are often much more willing to be collaborative when they are confronting a common issue. Senior citizens in Britain, for instance, are often heard talking about the wonderful community spirit that existed during World War II. And the loss of commitment to mutuality and co-operation, which once existed among the settlers on the Prairies, is an often-voiced concern among older Canadians.

Good Transportation Systems One challenge facing urban planners is how to move traffic from the ever-expanding suburbs to the downtown core without eroding the quality of life in some of the older, more centrally located neighbourhoods. Good transportation systems outside neighbourhoods, including roads, public transit, sidewalks, and bike paths, and well-designed safe roads within communities, have a major impact on those communities.

Balanced Land-Use Plans Strong communities have adequate parklands, accessible services, a good supply of well-maintained housing, a strong economic base, and well-developed land-use plans to manage population density and design and promote sustainable development.

SOME MYTHS ABOUT COMMUNITY DEVELOPMENT WORK

Community development work is still not well understood, as the following example from one of the authors' work experiences illustrates:

> Several years ago I resigned my position as the director of a small community development team in a municipal social services department in England and was on my way to Canada. As I said my farewells to some of the other workers in this rather conservative organization, I vividly recall Alice's effusive handshake as she wished me well. "Goodbye," she declared. "I still don't know what you do, but you seem to be a good guy." This apparent ignorance from someone I had spent many hours trying to educate about my role was disappointing, but not entirely unexpected. This was not to be the first time I would come across such a lack of understanding about the nature of community work from people in the human services field. Professionals who schedule their time tightly and well and see most of their clients in their offices can't always fathom what community workers do during their frequent absences from the office. Yet the fact that the "burnout" rate is relatively high among neighbourhood workers suggests that their task might actually be more demanding than it at first appears. (David Hannis, personal recollection)

Part of the challenge of doing community development work is dealing with how it is perceived by other professionals in the human services field. Indeed, from our experience, there are several beliefs about community work that we have heard from colleagues that do not necessarily fit with our experiences of the job.

Myth 1: Community Work Is Easy

Professional community work practitioners sometimes have difficulty justifying what they do to their busy office-based colleagues, to administrators, and to their employers. To outsiders, community workers can seem to be fairly disorganized and unaccountable. They come in late in the morning (because they go to a lot of meetings at night), produce few immediate and tangible results from their work (because good process takes time), their activities sometimes encourage community members to make waves and upset politicians (that is what participatory democracy is all about), and they are sometimes seen as being too critical of conventional ways of addressing social need (i.e., having philosophical and practical differences). Community work is never easy. It is difficult to maintain a normal family/social life when so much of your time is spent working at night (often immersed in emotionally draining activities) for employers who may be indifferent, or even hostile, toward the activities being pursued. To minimize some of these tensions, it is important that clear job descriptions exist, and that workers know their boundaries.

Myth 2: Anyone with a Professional Credential or a Big Heart Can Be Effective

Many excellent community workers lack formal qualifications, yet seem to have an instinct for this type of work. Conversely, some well-credentialed professionals have difficulty grasping the egalitarian nature of this type of practice. Part of the problem is the lack of opportunities over the past couple of decades for people to access good community work training.

Myth 3: Community Services Are Well Funded

Historically, many social services were delivered by non-government agencies. Later, these agencies were gradually taken over by bureaucratized organizations. For the past few years, in the wake of downsizing, a rediscovery of community has been accompanied by attempts to return services to the community. In some cases, this represents the dumping of complex tasks onto communities that are not appropriately funded to deal with them.

Myth 4: All Communities Are Democratic

Sometimes policy-makers assume that the person speaking on behalf of a community is well informed, accountable, and elected. This is not always true. People purporting to represent a community may, in fact, be speaking for themselves or only for a particular interest group. Community organizations often have difficulty filling elected positions, and acclamation is an all-too-frequent occurrence. Under such conditions, the ablest citizens may not be invited to represent the community.

Myth 5: All Communities Speak with One Voice

Communities are diverse and multi-faceted. Too often, however, policy-makers hear only the loudest voice. It is important that organizations committed to listening to the community ensure that they use effective processes for involving a broad range of opinions.

Myth 6: Outcomes Are Easy to Measure

Since the process of effective community work is often slow, preventive, and "transformative," it is difficult to provide administrators with the kind of hard evidence of effectiveness they favour. You can count volunteer hours, gather the socio-economic characteristics of the persons served, document the number of hours worked and tasks performed, and ask people to supply some subjective data. But these figures do not really capture the essence of community work. For this reason, it is often difficult to assess the effectiveness of interventions at the community level.

Myth 7: Solutions Are Easy to Find and Implement

The origins of many of the problems apparent at the community level are structural in nature. Examples include unemployment caused by the globalization of trade, poverty resulting from gender inequalities, and marginalization reflecting the pervasiveness of racism. Solutions to such difficulties are hard to find and implement at the local level— but finding them is certainly not impossible, as many strong community groups and organizations can attest to!

Myth 8: Community Development Is the Same in All Communities

Most community development textbooks are written by urban-based experts and founded on urban-based practice. Working in a rural setting, however, reflects different realities. The distribution of power is much more transparent in small communities, and the activities of community workers can be more visible. Small communities frequently have fewer financial resources, although the diversity of human skills is often great. Under such circumstances, attempting to organize local people to gain greater access to resources can be a particularly challenging undertaking.

EXAMPLES: MEETING BASIC NEEDS

Community development is not a universal solution for resolving all of the complex social issues of our time. But, as the following examples demonstrate, many communities have come together to effectively address some of their basic needs for food, shelter, employment, safety, and a sense of place.

Food

Increasing concerns about food additives, genetic modification, preservation of the environment, and the promotion of sustainable, small-scale farming practices, have led to many creative community responses toward producing food and beautifying the urban environment. Examples include community gardens, farmers' markets, community kitchens, co-operative greenhouses, and farmer-direct purchasing schemes. In Canada, some examples of these innovative community activities include Providence Farm on Vancouver Island, British Columbia, and Churchill Park Greenhouse Co-op Association in Moose Jaw, Saskatchewan. Both of these initiatives also provide employment opportunities for people born with developmental handicaps. The Raging Spoon, a restaurant on Toronto's trendy Queen St. West, hires survivors of mental illness. Field to Table, a non-profit Toronto-based organization, supplies "Good Food Boxes" to low-income families. Restaurants in Toronto (Rivers) and Edmonton (Kids in the Hall) provide training and work experience for at-risk youth. In Winnipeg's inner city, the Neechi Foods Co-operative Limited is an Aboriginal, worker-owned retail food co-operative store (Indian and Northern Affairs Canada, 2006b; Roberts, Macrae, & Stahlbrand, 1999).

Shelter

Intentional communities have a long history in Canada. They became popular in the 1960s. In many urban centres, for example, housing co-operatives, where people live together in stigma-free, affordable, diverse, supportive communities, have been around in Canada for several decades. Co-operative housing, where residents live in intentional communities but own, rather than rent, their units, is a more recent initiative. And an even more recent trend in Canada has been the development of land trusts, which attempt to provide affordable housing by creating non-profit trusts that own the lots on which the owner-occupied housing is built. In Canada, the first of these was in Quebec City, while the second was in Edmonton, Alberta. Such trusts provide affordable family housing and also rejuvenate some of the older inner-city neighbourhoods. In Winnipeg, Just Housing, a neighbourhood revitalization project, is purchasing and renovating older homes and hiring social assistance recipients to receive the training to carry out that work. The houses are made available on a rent-to-own or non-profit rental basis (McIntyre, 1998).

Employment

Many of the examples already mentioned have strengthened community while providing local employment. One consequence of globalization and the growth of big business has been **financial leakage**: profits earned locally have drained away to more distant places. Local economic development initiatives stem this flow of capital and recycle money through the community. Some communities have gone one step further and moved toward a barter system, much to the chagrin of Revenue Canada. Thus, in Calgary, members of the Arusha Centre can exchange hundreds of goods and services using a local scrip equal to $10 of Bank of Canada money (Roberts, Macrae, & Stahlbrand, 1999).

In addition, a steady and escalating interest in job creation at the local level has resulted in a number of creative economic development initiatives. In Toronto, survivors of mental illness have formed their own courier service, and in Edmonton, the Women's Economic and Business Solutions Society (WEBBS) has been established as a non-profit business incubator to provide employment for women. One of its first initiatives has been to facilitate the training of women as carpenters and, in the process, enhance the earning potential of some women.

Some of these micro-businesses have been funded by Community Loan Funds, which provide low-interest loans to individuals wanting to set up small businesses. In Edmonton, the Community Loan Fund was founded in 1995 and now has a capital base of over $1 million dollars. Many loans, ranging from $300 to $10 000, have been made with a default rate of about three percent on the total amount of funds loaned. This rate is much lower than that given by banks lending only to qualified recipients.

Safety

In recent years, some police departments have rediscovered the advantages of community policing. Beat cops have become a more regular feature of our communities. In addition, initiatives such as Block Parents and Neighborhood Watch encourage citizens to play a more vital role in crime prevention. In Edmonton, a Safer Cities initiative has nurtured closer ties between citizens and policy-makers around such issues as street prostitution. This initiative has also sponsored partnerships between police officers and social workers in tackling, for example, spousal violence and elder abuse.

Sense of Place

While policy-makers do not always instinctively listen to citizens, many progressive jurisdictions have established mechanisms to enhance citizen participation and promote a stronger sense of community identity. Again in Edmonton, efforts have been made to encourage more residential housing downtown, and community workers have been actively engaged in promoting vital neighbourhoods. In addition, a citizen action project in a central district has recently received funding to undertake some important community work, and another group of citizens has established a coalition of representatives from churches, trade unions, adult education institutions, and social service agencies to work toward greater structural change at the community level by using some of the organizing principles pioneered by the late Saul Alinsky, the "father of community organizing." We will discuss the contributions of Alinsky in Chapter 3.

SUMMARY

- Community development is defined as a community-led process.
- Community development can be distinguished from community action, community organization, social planning, and service extension.

- There are several factors that weaken communities, including a lack of collective history, stigma, high mobility, fragmentation, and a lack of services, of local decision-making authority, and of boundaries.

- There are several factors that strengthen communities, including active voluntary organizations, a community centre, a common need, good transportation, and balanced land-use plans.

- There are several myths about community development work, including the following: it is easy; any individual can be effective; services are well funded; all communities are democratic and speak with one voice; outcomes are easy to measure; solutions are easy to find; and community development is the same in every community.

- Community development has been effective at addressing basic local needs in different communities across Canada.

DISCUSSION QUESTIONS

1. How do you see community development? What parts of the definitions resonate with your experiences?

2. What are the pros and cons of top-down and bottom-up community work?

3. Are there factors missing from the list in this chapter that weaken or strengthen communities?

4. What rewards would you anticipate from doing community development work?

5. In your communities, what development initiatives could be used to address basic needs, such as food, shelter, employment, safety, and sense of place? What challenges would you anticipate?

WEBLINKS

www.well.com/~bbear/hc_articles.html The Change Project

http://comm-dev.org/ Community Development Society

www.sfu.ca/cscd/ Centre for Sustainable Community Development

www.hrsdc.gc.ca/en/gateways/topics/cyd-gxr.shtml Human Resources and Development Canada

www.newwestced.bc.ca/ New Westminister Community Development Society

www.enterweb.org/community.htm Community Development on ENTERWeb

www.manitobamarketplace.com/toolbox.html Manitoba Community Development Toolbox

KEY TERMS

chapter three

History of Community Development

LEARNING OBJECTIVES

After reading this chapter, you will be able to:

1. Describe historical events that illustrate community development.
2. Recognize the role of government and local communities in community development during Canada's post-war period.
3. Understand the roles played by international figures in contemporary community development.
4. Understand the part played by indigenous and Western figures in Canadian community development practice.
5. Compare and contrast the styles, circumstances, approaches, and effects of six key influences on Canadian community development.

Various influences have shaped contemporary community development. For example, some of the prominent figures in the field—through their own personal style and the circumstances in which they found themselves—have had a major impact on the evolution of community development in North America. Some influences can be traced back to Biblical times, and some indigenous influences can be traced to the time before Europeans landed in North America. (These influences are covered in detail in Chapter 9.) Community organizers who have made significant contributions to Canadian community development include three Americans. Two of these individuals—Jane Addams and Saul Alinsky—worked in Chicago's urban core neighbourhoods, and the other—Myles Horton—hailed from rural Tennessee. The Brazilian educator Paulo Freire has also had a significant impact on community development practice in Canada. Canadians Jimmy Tompkins and Moses Coady from Antigonish, Nova Scotia, as well as Georges Erasmus from the Dene community of Rae Edzo in the Northwest Territories, have made tremendous contributions in their own country. In this chapter, we briefly introduce some leaders who have shaped community development in

Canada, and then profile the seven leaders mentioned above, who are often referred to in contemporary community practice literature. The leaders' profiles include attention to their personal styles, settings they worked in, their approaches, as well as the impact of their efforts.

CHAPTER OUTLINE

Historical Overview
Community Development After World War II
Preventive Social Services Act
Local Community Service Centres

Key Figures
Jane Addams: Settlement Houses
Myles Horton: Highlander Folk School
Saul Alinsky: Industrial Areas Foundation
Paulo Freire: Education for Critical Consciousness
Jimmy Tompkins and Moses Coady: Economic Co-ops
Georges Erasmus: Aboriginal Self-Government

Summary

Discussion Questions

Weblinks

Key Terms

HISTORICAL OVERVIEW

It is difficult to determine exactly when community development as an intentional activity began. The Old Testament tells of how Moses and his brother Aaron organized one of the first recorded nonviolent revolutions in history when they encouraged the Israelites to band together and begin their great exodus to escape the oppression of the Egyptians. Centuries later, Saul of Tarsus (St. Paul) organized the first Christian communities into small, strong communities founded on principles of equality and sharing. Years later in medieval Italy, St. Francis of Assisi, in response to the poverty and corruption that existed around him, began to organize religious communities dedicated to the relief of suffering. His pioneering work provided the impetus for a movement of religious orders that swept through all of Europe. In North America in the 1700s, the brilliant Shawnee organizer Tecumseh formed a powerful confederacy of North American Aboriginal peoples to act as a defence against the advancing Euro-Americans.

In the nineteenth century, the European **New Towns Movement** began with the pioneering work of Ebenezer Howard. This movement involved the creation of several new towns. Residents of the older cities were encouraged to relocate as community workers. They were among the first employees to be hired in these new communities, designed to facilitate healthy social networks. In Canada, new towns were created or moved throughout the West by the Canadian Pacific Railway (CPR). The CPR, who held great power by virtue of the placement of train stations, was given title to the surrounding land by the federal government. In fact, the cities of Moose Jaw, Saskatchewan, and Medicine Hat, Alberta, were founded by the CPR (Berton, 2001).

The turn of the twentieth century witnessed the work of Jane Addams as the major founder of the Settlement House movement in the U.S.; the work of Sylvia Pankhurst in organizing the women's suffrage movement in the U.K.; and the work of Mohandas K. Gandhi in advocating for India's oppressed people. More recently, the work of Chicago-based Saul Alinsky, Canada's Moses Coady, Brazil's Paulo Freire, Tennessee-based Myles Horton, César Chávez (who organized the United Farm Workers of America), and Dorothy Day and the Catholic Workers Movement are all examples of successful community organizers at work (Lee, 1992).

Community Development After World War II

A particular push for community development strategies in Canada came after World War II. It became apparent during that time that the days of the British Empire were numbered. During the war, Britain had become so preoccupied with the hostilities that many of her colonies found themselves virtually abandoned. Consequently, these territories were forced to take more responsibility for running their own affairs. This development helped nurture a growing nationalism after the war. As the breakup of the British Empire became inevitable, the British authorities began to focus on helping their colonies prepare for independence. They did this by supporting community development and self-help initiatives aimed at building strong nations and maintaining loyalties to Britain.

In many of the colonies, the 1960s were seen as a "golden age" for community development. Economies were strong. Governments put a lot of money into social services. In Canada, the welfare state was growing. By the late sixties, medicare was born, the social safety net had been established, slums were being torn down, and more people than ever had access to an expanded post-secondary education system. Yet the perfect community was still a long way off. People continued to live in poverty, despite the significant expenditures on social programs (Ife, 2002). The government began to look for new ways to combat this problem. As a result, more money became available to support innovative community-based initiatives.

Against a background of growing hostility toward the Vietnam War and the accompanying groundswell of anti-establishment feeling, the Canadian government began to fund the **Company of Young Canadians** (CYC). In 1966, the CYC gave many youths a channel to funnel their energies into helping others; many were activists. However, the CYC ended in 1977; the fact that it was abolished so early is perhaps a testament to its success in bringing pressure to bear on the institutions of the time. (It also seems to support the adage that you should "never bite the hand that feeds you.") Many important leaders are among the alumni of this organization, including Georges Erasmus, whom we profile in this chapter.

During the 1960s, the efforts of many community workers were focused on organizing the poor to take direct social action to secure a bigger piece of the "economic pie." At the same time, many authorities stressed the need to reorganize the way social programs were delivered. During this time, for example, many multi-service, community-based centres were established. The federal government began appointing community developers to work in communities throughout the country, and some provincial departments for community development were created. Two examples of initiatives during this period are the Preventive Social Services Act in Alberta, and the creation of community-based neighbourhood centres in Quebec.

Preventive Social Services Act The 1966 **Preventive Social Services (PSS) Act** was introduced in Alberta during the last days of the Social Credit government and was a successful and relatively unusual community-based initiative (Bella, 1978). This unique legislation channelled federal and provincial funds toward both rural and urban municipalities, which were then required to determine their own priorities for preventive social programs. Local PSS boards were established, and PSS directors were hired to assist local people to address their own issues. Priority was given to programs designed to keep people off welfare, discourage dependency, promote family life, and encourage self-improvement (Bella, 1980). Local taxpayers bore 20 percent of the cost of these programs, with the remainder of the funds coming from the provincial government, which, in turn, could recoup some of its expenses from the federal government.

Local Community Service Centres The province of Quebec established the first of many neighbourhood-based health and social service centres (CLSCs or *centre local de services communautaires*) in 1970 with an emphasis on providing services responsive to local social and economic priorities. These centres continue to this day, with each centre serving populations of between 40 000 and 45 000 and employing community intervention practitioners to facilitate participation, consultation, democratization, and planning (CLSC, 2006). Recent research on this initiative indicates that the responsiveness of these centres to local residents is rated highly, and that the cost savings to the health care system, in particular, are substantial (Hagan & Garon, 1998).

KEY FIGURES

The major contributors to community development practice in Canada were both Canadian and non-Canadian, and the significance of their work continues to influence the approaches that Canadian activists take. Jane Addams, an American, borrowed from London, England, the notion of the **settlement home**—that is, a multi-service neighbourhood organization that worked to meet basic needs and take political action for those living in poverty. The Settlement House Movement swept central and western America. Several hundred settlement houses now exist. Myles Horton, another activist, was inspired during a trip to Denmark, where he observed training programs for grassroots activists interested in political change. The Highlander Folk School, which he founded, continues to be a leader in social change, led by grassroots groups in rural Tennessee. Saul Alinsky was arguably one of the most controversial organizers of his time, who saw and approached issues as political battles between the rich and the poor. He started the **Industrial Areas Foundation** (IAF), which was dedicated to building organizations for political power and social change. There are currently 56 IAF affiliate organizations throughout the world. Paulo Freire, the Brazilian educator, saw the power of adult education as a means of both oppression and liberation. Freire educated adults to develop a critical awareness of the structures that oppressed them, because he believed that groups with this **critical consciousness** could change their circumstances. Jimmy Tompkins and Moses Coady also realized the importance of education in community development. They used study groups to teach workers that they could create their own economic organizations, which would help them keep their own profits, locally. **Economic co-ops**, owned by the workers themselves, sprung up and provided a local alternative to the financial institutions owned and operated by those who lived far away from the communities they served. Today, the Aboriginal leader Georges Erasmus has been involved in local, territorial, and national political scenes for many years. He has skilfully bridged cultures and advocated for the integrity of treaties signed years ago. Moreover, he has kept Aboriginal rights issues in the political spotlight, and has advocated for Aboriginal self-government and restitution for survivors of the residential schools.

Jane Addams: Settlement Houses

Jane Addams (1860–1935) was born in the small community of Cedarville, Illinois. Her father was a member of the state legislature, director of a bank and a railroad, and close friends with Abraham Lincoln (Bettis, 2006). Addams attended college and was active in student affairs. After graduation, her attendance at medical school did not sit well with her stepmother or father, and, after the sudden death of her father a few years later, she decided to leave school. It was during this period in her life that her approach to community development started to take shape (Nobel Foundation, 2006). She became inspired during a vacation, where, after witnessing severe poverty while touring Europe, she encountered East London's **Toynbee Hall**, a settlement for university students from Oxford and Cambridge to work with people from the community. Addams's impression of the place was very positive.

> It is a community for University men who live there, have their recreation and clubs and society all among the poor people, yet in the same style they would live in their own circle. It is so free from "professional doing good", so unaffectedly sincere and so productive of good results in its classes and libraries so that it seems perfectly ideal. (Addams, 1930)

The first Settlement House in North America was based on Toynbee Hall and opened in 1889 (Barbuto, 1999). Addams and her friend Ellen Starr rented an abandoned mansion in an industrial neighbourhood in Chicago. Most of the people living in the area had recently immigrated from Italy and Germany. Addams and Starr invited local residents to the home for book readings and art displays, and soon found that the women needed a place for their children to go (Hull House, 2006). Driven by the needs of the community, a kindergarten was opened, a space for mothers to gather was created, a club for teens began, and cultural events were held. Hull House, as it was called, grew to include 13 buildings, with 70 residents (Addams, 1930). The purpose was to help local immigrants retain whatever they wanted from their history and culture, while giving them a hand adjusting to life in a new country. This involved not only providing support services, but political activism to improve living conditions in the local community and for the poor who lived outside of it (Lasch, 1966).

Addams was involved in multiple efforts at legal reform. She and others lobbied the state of Illinois on laws related to child labour, factory inspections, and juvenile justice. She worked tirelessly to protect immigrants from exploitation, limit working hours, make education compulsory, and recognize labour unions. She led the campaign for women's voting rights, and was a founder of the American Civil Liberties Union as well as the National Association for the Advancement of Colored People. In 1931, she was awarded the Nobel Peace Prize (Carson, 1990). The **Settlement House Movement**, as it became known, grew (Hutchinson-Crocker,

1992), and by 1910, the National Federation of Settlements listed over 400 settlement houses, primarily in Midwest and Eastern urban centres (Lasch-Quinn, 1993).

Myles Horton: Highlander Folk School

In 1932, Myles Horton (1905–1990) founded the **Highlander Folk School** in Tennessee. He received his early training at the Union Theological Seminary and modelled the Highlander Centre on the Danish folk schools he observed on a trip to Copenhagen. The school continues to be an important social change training institution for "grassroots" activists (Horton, 1990).

Essentially, Myles Horton believed that the solutions to community problems could be found at the local level rather than by relying on outside experts. Horton, therefore, tried to bring ordinary people together in discussion groups to share their experiences and, together, seek solutions. He believed in peer education; people should do their own research and become their own experts. Horton encouraged people to test out their ideas in practice, analyze their actions, and learn from this process.

Horton's early work was in Tennessee among his neighbouring farmers, miners, woodcutters, and mill hands, who had no access to formal educational institutions. The Highlander Folk School became an institution committed to social change and to workers' right to organize. As Horton's ideas developed, he became active in the Civil Rights Movement, and Highlander began to focus its resources and programs on school desegregation, voter education, citizenship schools, and other aspects of the Civil Rights Movement.

During the 1960s, the original Highlander Folk School was replaced by the Highlander Research and Education Centre, which continued to play a key role among the disenfranchised and extremely poor people in Tennessee as part of the Kennedy and Johnson administrations' "War on Poverty." In 1982, Highlander Centre was nominated for a Nobel Peace Prize, and in 1990, *Time* magazine called Highlander "one of the South's most influential institutions of social change" (McWhorter, 2001).

Saul Alinsky: Industrial Areas Foundation

Social workers come to the people of the slums under the aegis of benevolence and goodness, not to organize the people, not to help them rebel and fight their way out of the muck—NO! They come to get these people "adjusted"; adjusted so they will live in hell and like it too. (Alinsky, 1969, p. 82)

Saul David Alinsky (1909–1972) was one of the most controversial community organizers in North America. He was the only son of Jewish Russian immigrants; his mother was 17 when he was born. His father owned a tailor's shop located in the slums of Chicago's west side, and the family lived in the back of the store. Years later, Alinsky recalled that his idea of luxury had been "where I could use the bathroom without one of my parents banging on the door for me to get out because a customer wanted to get in" (Horwitt, 1992, p. 35).

In 1930, Alinsky graduated from the University of Chicago after studying archaeology and sociology. One of his first jobs was to study crime and the activities of the infamous gangster Al Capone, and by the time he was in his mid-twenties, Alinsky was beginning to be recognized as a notable criminologist. At a time when many experts agreed that the major causes of crime were poor housing, discrimination, economic insecurity, unemployment, and disease, Alinsky—in his abrasive and condescending speaking style—argued that supervised recreation, camping programs, and "character building" efforts did not address the real issues of power and powerlessness.

Alinsky's criticisms of hypercritical professionals, whether they were business people, social workers, church leaders, criminologists, academics, or anyone else, were relentless. While studying juvenile delinquency in a south-side Chicago slum, Alinsky observed the activities of the trade unions as they tried to organize the packinghouse workers in the abattoirs and learned that coalitions were the most effective way to achieve social change.

As Alinsky's career developed, he formed an organization through which he hired either himself or one of his 12 "apostles" to work with marginalized groups to achieve specific, concrete change (Finks, 1984). He befriended senior members of various religious denominations, film stars (including Humphrey Bogart), and other prominent groups in order to fund his activities. As a professional activist, he worked alongside the poor and helped them develop the confidence and practical skills to challenge established sources of power, from city hall to a large corporation.

Alinsky's model of social change was confrontational, and his planning was like that of a military strategist preparing for a major battle. Alinsky was bright, witty, abrasive, and caring and urged people to pick a target, freeze it, personalize and then polarize it (Alinsky, 1972). He would force mayors and corporate officials alike to respond to large groups of people, demanding more jobs or better pay, while the media eagerly captured their discomfort on film.

Alinsky sought allies in the Christian church and would often use biblical quotations to support his position, such as, "He that is not with me is against me" (Luke 11:25). Alinsky married three times and died of a heart attack in 1972. Since his death, his organizing principles have continued to find expression through the training activities of the U.S.-based **Industrial Areas Foundation**, which has been involved with more than 50 "people organizations," ranging from East Brooklyn to the east side of Los Angeles, as well as in other countries.

Alinsky (1972) had several rules for power tactics, which he listed in his book, *Rules for Radicals.* They are paraphrased here:

- Power isn't what you have, but what the other side thinks you have.
- Do not go outside of the expertise of your people.
- Go outside of the expertise of the target whenever possible.
- Force the targets to live by their own rules.
- Ridicule is potent.
- A good tactic is enjoyable, and one that drags on is not good.
- Keep applying pressure.
- A threat is worse than the actual experience.
- Use others' mistakes for your benefit.
- Have an alternative in mind in case the target comes to you.
- Pick a target, then freeze it; make it personal and polarized.

Paulo Freire: Education for Critical Consciousness

Paulo Freire (1921–1997) is one of the most interesting and controversial figures in adult education in the developing world. Born in Recife, Brazil, his ideas developed from his own childhood experiences of living among the poor and oppressed.

Freire made some observations about the characteristics of the oppressed. He noted that they frequently exhibited a kindly acceptance, sometimes supported by selected Biblical quotes, such as "Blessed are the poor." He also noted a self-deprecation among the oppressed, a devaluing of their knowledge, as well as learned helplessness, and a belief that they were sick, lazy, and unproductive. In addition to this lack of confidence, Freire noted that the oppressed had an almost magical belief in the invulnerability of the oppressor. When working with the oppressed, Freire recognized a culture of silence that characterized their behaviour (Freire, 1985). He saw the poor as submerged in their world, preoccupied with meeting basic needs, and consequently unable to develop a critical consciousness. His philosophy was similar to Myles Horton's. Although for most of their careers the two men did not know each other, they did eventually meet later in life. Their conversations have been captured in Brenda Bell's 1990 book, *We Make the Road by Walking.*

Freire noted that the relationship between the oppressed and the oppressor is characterized by dehumanization. The oppressed are dehumanized by their life situation, while the oppressors are dehumanized by their necessity to oppress. Freire advocated a new pedagogy (i.e., process of education). First, he aimed at **conscientization**—that is, helping people to recognize the social, political, and economic contradictions that surround them, and helping them to take action against these oppressive elements. He noted that the oppressed may themselves at first fear this new awareness along with the destabilization that can accompany challenges to the myths that support the existing social order.

For Freire, education was a liberating process, not one that perpetuated oppression. He argued that true learning does not take place when it is presented as a "narrative" between a teacher (the expert) and students (patient, listening objects). According to Freire, learning is not about the mere memorizing of facts, but is the integration of knowledge (Freire, 1973). Such knowledge must make sense to the students and the world they live in.

Effective education, according to Freire, has to be authentic and relevant, and has to take the form of a genuine dialogue between teachers and students. If students and educators are to be equally liberated, educators need to establish a climate for learning where learners do not become docile listeners, but rather partner with their teachers to become critical co-learners in search of answers. Traditional teaching serves to numb and hamper creative power. Problem-posing education, on the other hand, consists of authentic reflection and involves a constant unveiling of reality. Traditional teachers, according to Freire, are little more than "bankers," dispensing packages of knowledge with scant regard to its relevance.

Freire suggested that the role of a good teacher is not to dispense words of truth, but rather to listen and to pose questions that stimulate critical discussion and draw out creative ideas. According to Freire, education should not serve as a tool to fit people into their appropriate slots in an unjust society. Education should liberate people and allow them to achieve their full potential.

In his book *Pedagogy of the Oppressed* (1970), Freire outlined the elements of ineffective education:

- The teacher is always right.
- The teacher knows more than the students.
- The teacher must be listened to at all times.
- The teacher doles out consequences.
- The students comply.
- The teacher determines what is important.
- The teacher controls the learning process.

Jimmy Tompkins and Moses Coady: Economic Co-ops

Antigonish is a small Nova Scotia town that became the centre of a unique initiative in adult education and social change during the 1920s and 1930s. The **Antigonish Movement** has mostly been associated with a charismatic personality and Roman Catholic priest, Moses Coady, but of equal importance were his cousin Father Jimmy Tompkins and the organizational genius A.B. MacDonald (Lotz & Welton, 1987).

Jimmy Tompkins (1870–1953) arrived in Antigonish in 1902, at a time when the area was experiencing severe economic depression. Rugged Scots farmers whose farms were too small to support their large families had originally settled the region. At the same time, the middlemen—"Cod Lords"—dominated the fishing industry and controlled the local economies (Lotz & Welton, 1997). The poverty that pervaded the area at the turn of the century became even more severe with the collapse of fish prices after World War I. This not only caused more suffering, but quickened the pace of rural and regional depopulation.

Tompkins also believed that the key to social change was education. He envisioned a role for St. Francis Xavier University at Antigonish to provide the missing link between "knowledge and the little people" (Lotz & Welton, 1987). Tompkins was an abrasive and persistent advocate who antagonized the local bishop to the point where he banished Tompkins to the windswept, desolate, and impoverished fishing village of Canso (Mifflen, 1974). Tompkins was not silenced by that move, however, and through the media he was able to alert the Canadian public to the deplorable conditions that existed in such communities as Canso. His efforts eventually led to a Royal Commission that, in 1928, recommended the establishment of producer co-operatives to raise the incomes of fishermen in the area.

Tompkins did not introduce co-operative principles to Canada. These had arrived from Rochdale, England, in 1875, and had failed before in the Maritimes. Tompkins saw adult education as a way of ensuring the success of such ventures. The Workers' Educational Associations in the U.K., the Danish Folk School movement, and the Swedish Discussion Circles influenced his thinking. In 1921, the first **People's School**, a six-week residential course, took place at St. Francis Xavier University (Coady International Institute, 1986). As well, over the next few years, Tompkins played a key role in establishing libraries throughout the region. The U.S.-based Carnegie Foundation largely funded these latter efforts.

The Antigonish Movement gathered momentum after the report of the Royal Commission and the establishment of a department at St. Francis Xavier University dedicated to adult education. After this, Moses Coady (1882–1959) became a dominant figure. The Antigonish

Movement stressed the importance of self-help and mutual support, and linked adult education to social change (Coady, 1939). In this way, it offered an alternative to militant political
action.

Coady was an inspiring orator. His starting point for social change was to call a mass
meeting, which Coady would often address himself. From there, "study clubs" formed to discuss specific local problems and to explore solutions (Delaney, 1985). Field workers from the
university supported these efforts, and pamphlets were produced to help with discussions.
Later, these efforts were enhanced by the newly established local libraries and by the advent
of radio, which spawned "listening-in" groups. In addition to these activities, rural and industrial conferences were held to promote the principles of co-operation and self-help.

At its peak, at the outbreak of the World War II, the Antigonish Movement had initiated 2265 study clubs throughout the Maritimes, involving 19 600 people (MacLellan, 1985).
These clubs led to the formation of 451 credit unions and 210 co-operative retail stores
(MacLellan, 1985). Shortly after the death of Moses Coady in 1959, the **Coady International
Institute** was established at St. Francis Xavier University, and today this institute continues to attract community development students from around the world (MacDonald,
1987).

Georges Erasmus: Aboriginal Self-Government

Georges Erasmus was born in Fort Rae, Northwest Territories, in 1948. He and his 11
siblings moved with his family to Yellowknife when he was one year old. Georges later
graduated from a Catholic high school there. His career in politics was shaped by the
history of his Dene community's relationship to the federal government of Canada
(Barnsley, 2006).

The Dene peoples had lived for centuries in the Mackenzie Valley and Barren Grounds
of the Northwest Territories. In the eighteenth and nineteenth centuries they were involved
in the fur trade. However, awareness of the mineral-rich lands—first gold, then oil—
brought increasing numbers of Europeans into the region during the late nineteenth and
early twentieth centuries (University of British Columbia, 2006). Treaties were signed during this time. For the Dene peoples, the treaties were seen as peace and friendship agreements. For the Europeans, the treaties were seen as giving them title to the land. In
response to Dene concerns about how signed treaties where being honoured, local community residents formed the **Indian Brotherhood** of the Northwest Territories in the
1970s (Governor General of Canada, 2006).

Erasmus was heavily involved in the Indian Brotherhood from the beginning, seeking to protect Dene culture and ways of life, which included reclaiming sovereignty over
the northern lands. He started as director of community development and became president
of the organization and of its successor, the Dene Nation, at the age of 28. During his
presidency, he brought together 25 Dene communities to work out the details of a land
claim (Indian and Northern Affairs Canada, 2006a). In1983, he stepped down as president of the Dene Nation and two years later, became the vice-chief of the national
Assembly of First Nations (AFN) (Assembly of First Nations, 2006). In 1985, he was
elected as the National Chief of the AFN, and in that role he brought many Aboriginal
issues to the attention of the general public (Canadian Broadcasting Corporation, 2006b;
Dubuc, Erasmus, & Saul, 2002). He was heavily involved in discussions about the

Canadian constitution, for which he became known as the 11th premier (National Aboriginal Achievement Awards, 1998).

Georges Erasmus is likely best known as co-chair of the Royal Commission on Aboriginal Peoples (RCAP) (Indian and Northern Affairs Canada, 1996). The RCAP report led to an official apology from the federal government, in the 1987 document "Gathering Strength: Canada's Aboriginal Action Plan," for the abuses of the residential school system (Indian and Northern Affairs Canada, 1997). That same year, he was appointed to the Order of Canada, and has since received honorary doctorates from universities across Canada. Georges Erasmus is currently the chair of the **Aboriginal Healing Foundation**, whose "mission is to encourage and support Aboriginal people in building and reinforcing sustainable healing processes that address the legacy of Physical Abuse and Sexual Abuse in the Residential School system, including intergenerational impacts" (Erasmus, 2006).

SUMMARY

- It is difficult to determine exactly when community development as an intentional activity began.
- Community development in Canada began before the arrival of Europeans.
- After World War II ended, development became a more popular approach to working with disadvantaged communities.
- In 1889, Jane Addams opened the first Settlement House in North America, which provided for people's basic needs and advocated for legislative reform to address policies that contributed to social inequities.
- In the 1930s in rural Tennessee, Myles Horton opened a school for tradespeople who had limited exposure to public education, for the purpose of training to change unfair business practices.
- In 1941, Saul Alinsky started the Industrial Areas Foundation, based on the expertise of community organizing practitioners, to assist disadvantaged communities to form large organizations that could take on local political issues.
- In the 1960s, Paulo Freire emphasized techniques to effectively change adult education from a practice of oppression to a practice of liberation from poverty.
- In the 1930s, Jimmy Tompkins and Moses Coady assisted with the development of successful community-owned businesses in eastern Canada.
- From the 1970s to today, Georges Erasmus has kept Aboriginal issues in the Canadian political spotlight, and been an effective and tireless promoter of community healing and self-government initiatives.

DISCUSSION QUESTIONS

1. How did the early life experiences of Jane Addams contribute to her political efforts?
2. Why was the Highlander Folk School needed in southern Tennessee in the 1930s?
3. What kinds of communities are most likely to accept Alinsky's tactics? Which are least likely? Why?

4. Think about your own experience as an adult student. Do your instructors teach for critical consciousness? Why or why not?

5. Why did economic co-ops take off in rural Nova Scotia during the 1930s? Can this model be successful in contemporary urban settings?

6. What is Canada's record of treatment of indigenous peoples? How much progress has been made?

WEBLINKS

http://faculty.uccb.ns.ca/ tompkins/ The Tompkins Institute for Human Values and Technology

www.uccb.ca/CED/ced/main.html The Third Option: Community Economic Development

www.hullhouse.org/index.asp Jane Addams Hull House

www.stfx.ca/institutes/coady/text/index.html Coady International Institute

www.highlandercenter.org/ Highlander Research and Education Centre

http://marxists.anu.edu.au/subject/education/freire/pedagogy/index.htm Pedagogy of the Oppressed

www.industrialareasfoundation.org/ Industrial Areas Foundation

www.ainc-inac.gc.ca/ch/rcap/index_e.html Royal Commission on Aboriginal Peoples

www.ahf.ca/ Aboriginal Healing Foundation

KEY TERMS

Aboriginal Healing Foundation, p. 31

Antigonish Movement, p. 29

Assembly of First Nations, p. 30

Coady International Institute, p. 30

Company of Young Canadians, p. 23

Conscientization, p. 28

Critical consciousness, p. 24

Economic co-ops, p. 24

Highlander Folk School, p. 26

Indian Brotherhood, p. 30

Industrial Areas Foundation, p. 24

New Towns Movement, p. 22

People's School, p. 29

Preventive Social Services Act, p. 24

Settlement Home, p. 24

Settlement House Movement, p. 25

Toynbee Hall, p. 25

chapter four

Perspectives on
Community Development

LEARNING OBJECTIVES

After reading this chapter, you will be able to:

1. Describe and distinguish between socialist, anarchist, liberal, conservative, feminist, and environmentalist ideologies and explain how they relate to community development.

2. Describe an indigenous perspective and recognize some implications of this perspective for community development practice.

3. Distinguish between symbolic-interactionism, structural-functional, and conflict theories and theorists, and describe their relation to community development initiatives.

4. Recognize similarities and differences by regions in Canadian community development practice, including community economic development, social animation, participatory research, rural social work, and social support.

5. Describe the three different categories of community intervention, including locality development, social planning, and social action, as well as major advantages and disadvantages of each.

6. Describe three perspectives on community organizations, including policy and administration, community development, and types of community organizations.

Community development includes a range of organized change efforts taking place within a variety of contexts. The term also has a variety of meanings and uses, as we discussed in earlier chapters, as well as myriad purposes and practices, as we now turn our attention to in this chapter. Support for community development is found within different perspectives across the political spectrum for different reasons. In addition, theoretical perspectives from sociology help us to understand fundamental differences in outcomes from community development practice. Across Canada, community development has evolved in different ways in different regions. As well, research on community development practice across North America has led to different approaches to professional community work, and models that describe different types of organizations in the field.

CHAPTER OUTLINE

Community Development Across the Political Spectrum
  Feminist, Ecological, and Indigenous Perspectives
  Politics and Community Development

Theoretical Perspectives and Community Development
  Macro Theories
  Micro Theories
  Theory and Community Development

Regional Perspectives on Community Development
  Community Economic Development
  Social Animation
  Participatory Research
  Rural Community Work
  Social Support

Power and Program Approaches to Community Development
  Program-Based Community Development
  Power-Based Community Development
  Complementary Approaches to Community Development

Models of Community Practice
  Locality Development
    The Process of Locality Development
    Some Criticisms of Locality Development
  Social Planning
    The Social Planning Process
    Some Criticisms of Social Planning
  Social Action
    The Social Action Process
    Some Criticisms of Social Action

Models of Community Organizations
  Policy and Administration
  Community Development
  Types of Community Organizations

Summary

Discussion Questions

Weblinks

Key Terms

COMMUNITY DEVELOPMENT ACROSS THE POLITICAL SPECTRUM

The Western political spectrum includes a range of ideologies, from the left to the right. And the origins of the terms *left* and *right* can be traced back to eighteenth century France. In the legislative assembly, those seated on the left were, in general, opposed to the monarchy's interests, and those on the right were supportive of the monarchy's interests. As well, a major difference between these perspectives was related to their desire for change: those seated on the left supported reduced social and economic control by the monarchy, and those on the right supported a high level of control by the monarchy.

In the classic use of the terms, then, those on the left were liberal and those on the right, conservative.

In its classic sense, **conservatism** includes a commitment by a government to look after the social and economic well-being of its people. In eighteenth-century France, **conservatives** sought to "conserve" the monarchy, as well as its role in the market and social affairs. One of the earliest writers who represented this perspective was Plato. *The Republic* was written in Greek during the fourth century BC and has been translated many times since (e.g., 1992). The book represents some of Plato's thinking about politics. The ideal form of government, for Plato, was leadership by a ruling class of philosopher-kings. Plato thought that democracy was flawed because the intentions of those elected were not to serve the people but, rather, themselves. Like other classical conservatives, Plato believed that people were easily corrupted by power and unfit to govern themselves. He also thought that members of a ruling class were best able to control economic and social affairs because they had the best interests of all citizens in mind.

Liberalism, in its classical sense, endorses reduced government involvement in the economy or social affairs. In France in the eighteenth century, **liberals** wanted to "liberate" the market and the people from the monarchy's control. One early writer who represented this perspective was Adam Smith. In 1776, Smith originally wrote the *Wealth of Nations*, which has been published many times since (e.g., Smith & Krueger, 2003). In this book Smith saw people as motivated by self-interest and greed. And greed, Smith believed, fuelled competition. Competition then acted as an invisible hand to maintain order in the market. Classical liberals like Smith viewed economic and social competition as healthy; the strongest survive. In the market, the laws of supply and demand will keep order. There is little or no need for control by the government in social or economic matters.

Anarchism emphasizes the liberty of individuals and freedom in both social and economic terms. *Anarchy*, which comes from the Greek for "no ruler" (*anarkhia*), refers to the state of having no ruler, or *hierarkhes* (i.e., hierarchy). One writer associated with this perspective was William Godwin, who in 1783 wrote *Enquiry Concerning Political Justice and Its Influence on Modern Morals and Happiness,* which has been published many times since. In this book, Godwin was critical of the English monarchy. He saw the monarchy as corrupt and believed that there was no need for government, because each person would do what was best for him or her and others. Anarchists like Godwin saw government as the cause of social and economic problems.

Socialism in its classical sense suggests governance by citizens and a high level of involvement in economic and social affairs. Socialism is distinct from classical conservatism in that socialists believe that government ought to be run by regular citizens, not by a ruling class. An early writer who espoused this perspective was Karl Marx. In 1876, Marx wrote *Das Kapital*, which was critical of capitalism; Marx saw capitalism as leading to the emergence of two social classes: those who owned the means of production (bourgeoisie), and the working class (proletariat). He wanted government run by the working class. Only then, he argued, would the working class be protected from continued exploitation by the bourgeoisie. For socialists like Marx, government needed to be led by the working class to control economic and social matters so that the interests of the rich bourgeoisie did not dominate.

In modern use, however, the terms *conservative* and *liberal* have in many ways become the opposite of their classical meanings. For example, today we might define conservatives as those who support an economy based on a free market with no control by government. We might describe liberals, on the other hand, as those who believe that the government should look after its people. Modern conservatives, then, seek to "conserve" the market economy that is in place, while modern liberals support "liberation" from a free market system, through government control over the economic well-being of citizens.

And modern socialists want government to control the economy and regulate social affairs so that there is equitable access and distribution of resources (Cockshott & Cottrell, 1993). A modern socialist would view the role of government to be protecting the social and economic well-being of citizens (particularly the poor) and promoting change in laws that lead to economic and social inequities (e.g., tax breaks for the rich). Modern anarchists, such as Chomsky (1987), are similar to classical socialists in that they want workers to control production. Modern anarchists support any voluntary co-operative of individuals only when all members have equal decision-making power. Governments, anarchists argue, favour those who are rich and powerful (e.g., corporations) at the expense of those with less money and power (e.g., small business owners).

The four modern positions reviewed so far—liberalism, conservatism, socialism, and anarchism—would have very different positions on current political issues such as tax levels, support for a gun registry, and same-sex marriage legislation. Their positions are summarized in Table 4.1.

In addition to these major ideologies, other important perspectives provide a foundation for understanding modern community development, such as the Western women's movement, ecologism, and indigenous views.

TABLE 4.1	Perspectives on Social and Economic Issues		
	Tax Levels	Gun Registry Support	Same-Sex Marriage Support
Conservatism	low	low	low
Liberalism	moderate	moderate	moderate
Socialism	high	high	high
Anarchism	variable	variable	variable

Feminist, Ecological, and Indigenous Perspectives

One valid criticism of the perspectives discussed so far is that they developed from the ideas of men. Indeed, it was not until 1918 (1940 in Quebec) when women gained the right to vote in Canadian elections, long after traditional political ideologies were developed. Of central importance to **feminism** is **patriarchy**, which is the social power exercised by men over women. Even today, patriarchy continues to oppress women in our society. For example, women still have lower participation rates in the highest occupation and pay level categories, and have higher rates of victimization by violence. While there are many types of feminism, with different goals and philosophies, the basic concept of feminism is the belief that men and women are equal. A major contribution of feminism to political thinking is the recognition of the personal as political; previously, women's input was considered less important because few women lived public lives. But now, women's disadvantages in many political and community contexts have become the basis for organizing (Adamson, Briskin & McPhail, 1989). For example, women's groups organize marches to show unity, draw attention to issues, and remember victims of violence.

Supporters of **ecologism**, who focus on environmental preservation, also have critiques of traditional political ideologies, which are not always concerned with preservation of the environment (Baxter, 2002). Sustainability is crucial to ecologists: they believe that we must not only meet the needs of the present, but take no action that will negatively affect the next generations and address those effects that human beings do have on the physical world (e.g., greenhouse gas emissions and the Kyoto Protocol).e.g., Ecologists warn of the limits to continued harvesting of natural resources and their replacement by pollutants; they argue that other political ideologies fail to adequately take these issues into account.

Indigenous perspectives are also crucial to recognizing diversity in community development movements. These views include those of Aboriginal peoples, including First Nations, Metis, and Inuit peoples of Canada. Indigenous cultures, values, and traditions vary considerably. However, as noted by Clarkson, Morrissette, and Régallet (1992, p. 14), all Aboriginal "ancestors organized themselves into communal groups that were egalitarian, self-sufficient and intimately connected to the land and its resources." This differs from Western values of diversity, competition, and taking from the land. All political ideologies presented up to this point have Western origins and are grounded in European belief systems based on colonial values and attitudes. **Colonization**, which is the settlement of a group of people in a new territory with ties to a mother country, also often resulted in the attempted replacement of an indigenous culture by newcomers. As a result, many people blame colonization for the oppression of Aboriginal peoples today. As well, residential schools and government-enforced relocation have contributed to the economic and social challenges faced by many Aboriginal peoples and communities. Understanding European–Aboriginal history is important to put into context present-day initiatives taken by Aboriginal peoples to enhance their well-being (e.g., urban reserves).

Politics and Community Development

Political ideologies are important to community development because they influence the decisions made by people in power. For example, a conservative decision maker, hoping ultimately to strengthen a disadvantaged community, may argue that program funding should come from a community source (e.g., charitable foundation), rather than a government source. In trying to ensure certain standards are met, a conservative decision maker may also advocate for laws and policies that restrict how community funds are spent. In contrast, a liberal decision maker may believe that the community that will benefit from the program should join forces with the government and share the costs of the program. A liberal decision maker may also believe that the community and government share to decide how the dollars are spent. A socialist decision maker, on the other hand, may feel that the government should pay the costs of the program but should let the community decide how those funds are spent.

Within feminist, ecologist, and indigenous perspectives there is a range of views. Some, for example, would support a government or private sector partnership. Some may support increased or decreased government control of the economy. Others favour public or private, centralized, or localized resource and income distribution systems. What makes feminist, ecologist, and indigenous perspectives different from each other are their focal points. The roots of social and economic problems are, for feminists, patriarchy; for ecologists, neglect of the physical environment; and for indigenous groups, colonization. What unites these groups is their emphasis on the structural determinants of problems. They also believe in the positive effect that a collective of supporters can have on the extent and duration of social and economic problems within communities.

THEORETICAL PERSPECTIVES AND COMMUNITY DEVELOPMENT

Major theoretical perspectives from sociology help us understand ways that community development is practised. These theoretical perspectives are divided between macro and micro theories. Macro theories focus on the social system that exists independently of the person who is born into it. They emphasize characteristics and features of a group of people and the roles that members play. Micro theories focus on the person, not the group, as a determinant of experience.

But does the individual influence the group, or does the group influence the individual? Usually both processes are at work, although theoretically, they are distinct. Macro theories are based on the belief that society influences individuals; micro theories, that individuals construct society. Macro theories focus on the structural or societal causes of community problems, while micro theories focus on personal causes. Macro theories focus on the impact of larger social institutions on personal welfare; micro theories focus on the creation of social institutions through the efforts of individuals.

Macro Theories

Two well-known macro theories are functionalism and conflict theory. **Functionalists**, such as the French sociologist Emile Durkheim (1858–1917), view society as a group of individuals who share a common value base and work together for the benefit of all. From this perspective, societies have certain basic needs, such as food, clothing, and shelter. And in order for society to function, these needs must be met. Each person who lives in the society contributes by doing her or his part (e.g., providing a needed service, such as building construction). The goal of society is stability. When a role is not fulfilled (e.g., builders stop building homes), there are problems, such as poor housing and overcrowded living conditions. From this perspective, social problems are created when needed roles are not filled. A solution is to fill the role so that full function is regained (e.g., train new builders to build homes). Social change happens gradually, and it is predictable because the goal of social change is to fill a gap in service, and social change is reinforcing because the missing role gets restored.

Conflict theorists—such as the socialist Karl Marx—see society as competitive. Resources are limited, and there are different interests among classes or groups. Basic needs, such as food, shelter, and clothing, are either met or not, depending on a group's control over production. The means of production is the equipment needed to produce material goods (e.g., building materials), and the relations of production are the social relationships people enter into to produce material goods (e.g., knowledge of building practices). Problems such as poor housing and overcrowded living conditions are caused by those who have money and knowledge to build (producers), and by those producers working for those who can pay the most (i.e., other producers). The resulting shortage of housing forces those who have the least money to live in the poorest and most overcrowded homes. A solution requires a reversal of power (e.g., starting a labour union for workers). In other words, social change is needed because society is unstable. Society is unstable because there is continuous tension between the classes.

Micro Theories

Symbolic interactionists, such as the German sociologist Max Weber (1864–1920), have a different approach to understanding social behaviour. As micro theorists, they focus not on how society influences individuals, but on how individuals influence society. Individuals act of their own free will, are not determined by prescribed roles, and together, in groups, individuals determine the nature of community life through interaction. In this theory, community problems do not exist until a critical mass of individuals agrees that they do. For example, a housing shortage and overcrowded living conditions do not become problems until a group of residents decide that it is a problem and that something should be done about it. Change can only begin after there is consensus about shared experiences, and once there is a common ground from which the problems and resources can be identified. Those in positions of authority (e.g., local leaders) can and do exercise influence as members of a group.

Theory and Community Development

These theoretical perspectives contribute to the practice base of community development by identifying basic assumptions about the causes of and solutions to community problems. Community development from a symbolic interactionist perspective requires consensus among those involved on the problems and on strategies to address them. Change is positive, slow, and deliberate. From a functionalist perspective, community-wide consensus is also necessary. Problems result from imbalance when a function is not being fulfilled. Action is needed only to restore balance and make changes to correct problems that have been caused by forces outside of the community. Change is reactive, slow, and helps to restore functions to the pre-problem state. From a conflict perspective, community development is about getting a fair share of resources for the community from the larger society. Social change is ongoing, necessary, and often radical in nature. Actions necessary to force change of a broader society are extreme.

REGIONAL PERSPECTIVES ON COMMUNITY DEVELOPMENT

Community development initiatives across Canada are identified from the regions where they originated. Ken Banks (2002) describes types of community development practice based on the location of its earliest development, including community economic development in the Maritimes, social animation in Quebec, participatory research in Ontario and Manitoba, rural community work in Saskatchewan and Alberta, and social support in British Columbia. In this section, we define these regional perspectives and provide a context for their historical development before we describe the major tactics.

Community Economic Development

Community economic development (CED) looks at economic systems and their role in community life, and works to enhance the participation of residents in the local economy:

> CED is a process or strategy that is used to analyze economic systems and their impact on a community. CED looks at how money moves through a neighborhood or a community and what impact that movement of money has on the people within the community. It also looks at what is needed within the community. The key concept of CED is using local resources to meet local needs while at the same time creating healthy and economically viable communities. CED is about working with communities to develop positive and sustainable processes, not imposing a system from outside the community. CED looks at all aspects of the economy, not just commercial, and is a powerful tool in working towards happy, healthy communities. (United Nations Platform for Action Committee, 2005)

The development of economic co-operatives in Canada began with the **Antigonish Movement** in Nova Scotia during the Great Depression of the 1930s. Economic activities during the 1700s and 1800s centred on agriculture, fishing, and mining. With the Industrial Revolution of the eighteenth and nineteenth centuries, however, came the rise of corporations that effectively separated the local producers of these activities from the local consumers, and created companies that were in charge of distribution. Farmers, fishers, and miners were then forced to pay huge portions of their wages to the companies, which held tight grips on their workers because they were also major holders of local properties, credit, and supplies.

The church played a major role in community life at the time. As described in Chapter 3, the Reverend Jimmy Tompkins and Dr. Moses Coady saw education as a key to social change. Through **consciousness-raising** (Freire, 1993), Coady was able to spark interest, collective discontent, and organization, often with local leadership, in many affected communities. He achieved this through group meetings, first large ones, and then smaller ones called study clubs, which brought people together to talk about their challenges and how they could, through co-operation, work for themselves and eliminate the role of private corporations in order to keep profits in their communities (Alexander, 1997). Several farming, fishing, and financial co-operatives developed; all were owned and operated by community members.

Social Animation

Social animation emphasizes the role of a leader, who can bring community members together to discuss local issues and solutions that the community can implement.

> Social Animation *(promoting community participation and self help)* mobilizes and organizes a community. This means that the social organization of the community is changed, however slightly. The animator, therefore, is a social change agent, or catalyst. (Bartle, 2006)

Social animation in Canada is associated with the writings of Michel Blondin (1969), who prepared a document for the *Conseil des Oeuvres* (Council of Agencies) in Montreal. In the sixties, the CoA explored community-based approaches to change, in neighbourhoods with the highest levels of poverty. The CoA wanted a lot of resident involvement and autonomy because the group had seen many problems that came with high agency involvement, such as a disconnection between the services and the residents' needs. According to

Blondin (1969), self-determined communities were free to act of their own volition, and accept the consequences of those actions.

In this approach, residents were involved in the analysis, solution generation, and the carrying out of the necessary tasks (Blondin, 1969). Central to this process was the role of animator, who trained the group on committee functioning, promoted cohesion among its members, brought the group needed information, and acted as a facilitator to engender genuine member participation. Improvements to recreational and educational facilities in Montreal's poorest neighbourhoods were attributed to the work of communities who, as a result of the animation process, were better able to negotiate with funders.

Participatory Research

Ken Banks is a social worker who has partnered with several groups in Toronto and south-western Ontario on participatory research projects (Banks, 2002). He has this to say about participatory research:

> **Participatory research** starts from the premise that the community worker probably doesn't know what is most needed in the community that has been selected for community development. A research process that will draw out the local perceptions of needs gives one confidence that community members will become engaged in a local improvement process. When you listen to their solutions and support implementing some of them, enthusiasm reigns! (Banks, 2002, p. 309)

In 1975, Budd Hall co-ordinated the first edition of an academic journal on the topic of participatory research, which was followed, two years later, by the first international conference on the subject. The conference brought together community developers and adult educators from around the world who were interested in the subject. At a conference in Aurora, Ontario, soon after, participants produced the following definition:

1. Participatory research involves a whole range of groups of people.
2. It involves the full and active participation of the community in the process.
3. The problem is defined, analyzed and solved by the community.
4. The goal is the transformation of social reality and the improvement of the lives of the people.
5. Participatory research can create a greater awareness of people's own resources and mobilize them.
6. The participation of the community in the research facilitates a more accurate and authentic analysis of social reality.
7. The researcher is a committed participant and learner in the process of research. (Hall & Kidd, 1978, p. 5)

One example of a participatory research approach is in the work of professors and students in community studies at the University of Manitoba. The professors and students have partnered with local agencies and residents on several community development projects in Winnipeg's inner city. Project ideas have come from community residents directly, through informal conversations with students or professors who were holding classes in the agency, or through residents' connections to agency staff or other local groups. Crucial to the participatory approach of these initiatives was a commitment to work collaboratively, share expertise, and take action based on results (Petras & Porpora, 1993). Community residents played many different roles in the projects, from steering committee members, to interviewers, authors, and presenters of results to a variety of audiences, including the local community, academics, and funders. Their purposes were varied and included program development, policy change, and advocacy (Brown, Higgitt, Wingert, Miller, & Morrissette, 2004).

Rural Community Work

According to Banks (2002), rural community work "focuses on practice in rural conditions that disadvantage women and First Nations people in particular" (p. 309). Rural approaches to community development on the Prairies have developed in concert with local communities, each with its own particular mix of cultures and traditions.

Rural community work includes restorative approaches to community problems. **Restorative approaches** are based on principles of restorative justice, and as such they focus not on problems, but on solutions. Solutions are based on relationships between those who have caused harm and those who have been harmed; the emphasis is on interpersonal accountability, not punishment. These initiatives have grown, particularly in areas where external systems of service delivery (e.g., justice and child protection) have not addressed the unique blend of challenges found in each community. Instead of casting blame and removing residents from the community, restorative approaches require collective responsibility for problems and solutions, based on truth and honesty, by those directly involved and affected *within* the community (Ross, 1996). Safety is heavily weighted in these processes.

In Aboriginal communities, there are a range of relationships between residents, leaders, and external authorities in the governance of locally delivered services and programs, which may fall under federal, provincial, or band jurisdiction. Local communities, for example, have identified restorative approaches as necessary to address problems in justice and child welfare systems in the Prairie provinces. Examples of restorative approaches include Manitoba's Aboriginal Justice Inquiry (McKay, Young, Chartrand, & Whitecloud, 2001), Saskatchewan's Commission on First Nations and Metis Peoples and Justice Reform (Baldhead, Campbell, & members, 2004), and Alberta's Cawsey Report (Cawsey et al., 1991).

Social Support

Social support is an approach that first emerged in British Columbia with women's groups. The approach draws from the work of Madeline Novell and Jennifer Newman, who wanted to provide women with opportunities for positive social interaction to combat isolation and loneliness (Banks, 2002). In their counselling work with at-risk families, Novell and Newman saw a need for women's support groups to focus not on psychological problems, but on common issues in parenting. They soon found, however, that group members preferred to interact with the professionals, and not the other participants. Therefore, they saw a need to pay particular attention to relationship building among participants, many of whom had limited skills for developing and maintaining friendships.

The purpose of "Friendship Group" was to build community by starting with the smallest building blocks: friendships (Lovell, 1991). It was a directive and skills-based approach, with formalized practice sessions, assuming that people needed to learn specific ways to give and receive compliments, take turns listening and talking, and safely disclose meaningful things over time as trust developed. The goal of these approaches was to teach the basics of being a community member, so that individuals were more comfortable and more likely to participate in activities with others. The potential for developing a group identity separate from the training group was encouraged. Once members felt connected to those with similar interests, they had the foundation for organizing.

POWER AND PROGRAM APPROACHES TO COMMUNITY DEVELOPMENT

Stoecker (2001) characterizes community development efforts as falling within one of two approaches: power-based and program-based. The power-based community development approach "emphasizes poor communities organizing themselves and using confrontational strategies to demand the removal of barriers and biases so they can receive the same opportunities as more affluent communities" (Stoecker, 2001, p.1). The programs-based community development approach "emphasizes poor communities cooperating with resource providers such as government or corporations to develop programs focused on helping individuals in poor communities" (Stoecker, 2001, p.1). The following sections outline the history and assumptions of each approach, as well as the different contributions each makes to community development practice.

Historically, power-based community development is more common in the United States than in Canada, due, in part, to lower U.S. public investment in social programming. Program-based community development is more common in Canada because there has been greater use of public funds for social programs and, therefore, less need by poor communities to demand economic and political power (Stoecker, 2001). In the future, while Canadian public investment in social programs declines, the depth of poverty may increase and organizing could become more common.

Program-Based Community Development

Program-based community development is based on an assumption of mutual interest. There are basic common needs in society that are accepted by all, and each person has a role in ensuring that those needs are met. Program-based community development promotes stability in the current economic and political system. It relies on financial resources transferred from those who have money and political power to those who have less. Community development that relies on this money is accountable to those who provide it, and must therefore meet the requirements of that funding. Funding of an initiative that the public might view as controversial (e.g., the anti-poverty protest staged by the Ontario Coalition Against Poverty at the 2006 Stratford Festival) is unlikely to be granted by particular groups who are then seen as responsible for the disruption.

Power-Based Community Development

Power-based community development is based on the assumption that in a society there are those who have political and economic power and those who do not. The "haves" and the "have-nots" are in competition for scarce resources, and only by moving someone out of a powerful position can someone else enter a powerful position. The inherent instability and tension within this arrangement provides the opportunity for the "have-nots" to achieve some change through action and conflict. This approach has not been at all attractive to major funders, for the very reason that success, or an empowered community, may be seen as a threat. For example, the issue of urban reserves has been hotly contested by some who see tax advantages for businesses on the reserve as unfair to other business owners who are not on the reserve.

Complementary Approaches to Community Development

Each approach to community development has strengths and weaknesses, and Stoecker (2001) suggests that the two approaches are complementary. Program-based approaches are good at maintaining change, and power-based approaches at promoting it. Program-based approaches are known for their technical skills (e.g., acquiring funds, managing funds), while power-based approaches, on the other hand, are known for their grassroots leadership. Program-based approaches focus on training and education to participate in politics and the economy, and power-based approaches focus on confrontation and negotiation to participate in politics and the economy. In short, power-based developers are probably best at starting change and gaining power, and program-based developers are better at maintaining change and keeping power.

MODELS OF COMMUNITY PRACTICE

A dramatic increase in community initiatives that took place in the 1960s and early 1970s led to a great deal of diversity of activities at the local level. As well, a wide range of some-times-contradictory definitions of community organization emerged. Jack Rothman (1995) discovered over 100 definitions of the term *community organization* in the literature. From his research, Rothman was able to categorize community interventions into basic types, including *locality development*, *social planning*, and *social action*.

Locality Development

Locality development requires citizens from all walks of life to learn new skills and engage in a co-operative self-help process to achieve a wide variety of community improvements. It implies a condition of limited resources and an effort to increase and expand such resources for mutual benefit (Rothman, 1995).

Locality development stresses co-operation, self-help, development of local leadership, education, and the encouragement of civic consciousness. Locality development is frequently practised in disadvantaged communities with such negative social indicators as high crime rates, unemployment, poor housing, low standards of health, and above-average rates of physical and mental illness. The concept of locality development rests on the idea that people can and want to work together and that when they do, certain tangible advantages can occur. Locality development involves incremental change with communities working relatively harmoniously with governments and bureaucracies. This model stresses consensus rather than conflict with those in power, and although it has been responsible for more modest reforms than some social activists would like, agencies founded on the locality development philosophy are more enduring than more militant organizations.

There are three operational assumptions that typically underlie locality development efforts (Biddle & Biddle, 1979):

1. Each person is valuable, unique, and capable of growth toward greater social sensitivity and responsibility.
2. Human beings have both good and bad impulses.
3. Satisfaction and self-confidence gained from small accomplishments can lead to the commitment to address more and more difficult problems, in a process of continuing growth.

In this model the role of community developer may vary, depending on the community's needs. Possible roles include encourager, friend, and source of inspiration; objective observer, analyst, truth seeker, and kindly commentator; discussion participant, clarifier of alternatives and the values these serve; participant in some actions, but not all; and, adviser, conciliator, and expediter of ongoing development. The importance of the locality developer is usually greatest in the early stages and may then taper off toward a termination date, but involvement may increase temporarily at any time.

Advantages of locality development strategies include a reduction in individual feelings of worthlessness, dependency, alienation, apathy, cynicism, and unresponsive bureaucracies. In many countries in the developing world, emphasis placed on locality development is said to have assisted in building a sense of national identity and common purpose, promoted pride in emerging nations, and encouraged mechanisms for two-way flows of communication between decision makers and local groups.

Locality development rests on four underlying propositions (Roberts, 1979):

1. People are capable of perceiving and judging the condition of their lives.
2. People have the will and capacity to plan together in accordance with these judgments to change those conditions for the better.
3. People can act together in accordance with these plans.
4. Such a process can be seen in terms of certain values.

According to Khinduka (1979), locality development will do practically everything to improve the psychological lives of the poor, such as create among them a sense of self-respect and confidence, or civic pride, and identification with their locality—which may be an uninhabitable slum; encourage them to provide recreational programs; and even lead them to organize courses and learn handicrafts to increase their earning capacity. But Khinduka also explained that locality development will not usually question the economic system that permits the co-existence of poverty and plenty. While this is generally true, one of the most recent and exciting developments has been the expansion of local (micro-) economic initiatives as spinoffs of community-organizing initiatives. For example, the development of business co-operatives, such as community-owned grocery stores, that are successful at creating local jobs and providing goods and services to the local community, contradicts Khinduka's claim. The process of locality development is described in the following section.

The Process of Locality Development The role of the community worker in locality development is to establish relationships, communicate effectively, provide support, and assist groups to clarify issues/strategies, develop group and individual competence, and nurture leadership. Locality development involves the ability to inspire, guide, persuade, and teach, and particularly to act on one's own intuition. Community workers have very limited formal authority to assist with their tasks. For example, locality development workers enjoy no reward power (the power to reward members of the group), no coercive power (the perceived power to force group members, by sanctions, to act in certain ways), and no legitimate power (power bestowed on them because of their position in the organizational structure of the group). Community workers' influence derives, in fact, from whatever expert power they have (the way they show that they have some useful expertise to offer), and possibly from referent power (the extent to which they are people whom the members of the group aspire to be) (Roberts, 1979).

All locality developers should realize that they have one dilemma: what right do we have to interfere in others' lives? An important task for any community worker approaching a neighbourhood with low levels of participation is to encourage citizen involvement. According to Rothman (1987), people become active in community affairs when they perceive that certain personal advantages will accrue when they do. These benefits may be divided into two major categories: instrumental and expressive. Instrumental benefits include immediate material benefits, such as new playground equipment or a new community centre, and anticipatory benefits, which are those material benefits that are likely to accrue in the longer term. Expressive benefits include interpersonal benefits—such as the prospect of making new friends and having enjoyable social experiences—and symbolic benefits, such as receiving an award or being mentioned in a newspaper article. As well, the degree of community engagement tends to reflect an individual's life cycle, with levels likely to be highest during the child-raising years and during the period of early retirement (Putnam, 2000).

Some Criticisms of Locality Development   Described as "a soft strategy for social change" (Khinduka, 1979), locality development can be successful at the local level but have little impact on broader, more far-reaching issues, such as the distribution of wealth, unemployment, housing supply, racial discrimination, and other forms of structural oppression. Even though residents may feel greater self-confidence as a result of local successes, there are disadvantages that come from a more collaborative approach to community problem solving (Khinduka, 1979). For example, an experience of working with a bureaucracy may promote a mistrust of it, rather than a desire to work more closely with it in the future. In addition, by focusing on people's psychological capacity to make decisions rather than on their economic power to do so, locality development may indeed promote self-respect and community identity, but do little to bring about fundamental change in an unfair situation. Workers may, in fact, be merely acting as agents of social control, making the disadvantaged content with being at the bottom of the heap, rather than giving them the tools to ensure a more equitable distribution of wealth.

There is also a "dark side of social capital" (Putnam, 2000), which includes the tendency for the most vocal members of a community to get their needs met at the expense of other less outspoken citizens, and a tendency for a dominant community view to develop, which may reinforce intolerance toward certain marginalized persons, such as gays and lesbians, and members of minority ethnic groups. In other words, the price paid for achieving a sense of belonging and community solidarity may be the avoidance of healthy dialogue and the perpetration of "suffocating narrow views" (Putnam, 2000).

Social Planning

Social planning is the second of Rothman's three categories of community work. Social planning emphasizes a technical process of problem solving by experts on substantive social problems, such as delinquency, housing, and mental health (Rothman, 1995). The approach presupposes that change in a complex industrial environment requires expert planners who, through the exercise of technical abilities—including the ability to manipulate large bureaucratic organizations—can skilfully guide complex change processes. Rational, deliberately planned, and controlled change has a central place in this model. Community participation may vary from much to little, depending on how the problem presents itself and what organizational variables are present. Designing social plans and policies is of central importance to this approach, as is their implementation in effective and cost-efficient ways. By and large, the concern here is with establishing, arranging, and delivering goods and services to people who need them. Building community capacity or fostering radical or fundamental social change does not play a central part.

Social planning takes place in a number of different contexts, including using services from within an existing social services agency; co-ordinating the delivery of social programs at the community level; incorporating social concerns into other planning endeavours (e.g., land-use plans, economic development strategies, fiscal policies); planning to solve a particular social concern or issue (e.g., poverty, after-school care); and identifying the social impacts of another policy (e.g., a land-use plan, development of oil/gas reserves). There are several Social Planning Councils across Canada that have been involved in social change.

As applied social scientists, social planners are involved in fact finding and problem definition (Lauffer, 1979). At a basic level, they have to be able to collect and analyze data, build credibility and trust, and communicate effectively. At the government level, social planners need to cut across bureaucratic territorial defenses and convince others of their expertise. This is not always easy. Tasks of the social planner include identifying major social problems, translating social goals into effective programs, introducing social considerations into other planning initiatives, as well as responding to gaps, fragmentation, and other social program failures (Kahn, 1969). Social planners also redesign services to meet the needs of the intended target population, review other nonsocial programs and policies to determine if, in fact, they have human implications, and respond to inconsistencies in services. They may also allocate scarce resources, such as professional expertise and financial support. Finally, social planners encourage creativity by transforming concepts and techniques from other fields.

The Social Planning Process In the past, a number of towns and cities have attempted to develop plans that address social and health concerns as well as economic ones. For example, in 1979 the League of California Cities outlined six basic stages of a comprehensive social planning process: (1) preparation, (2) needs assessment, (3) policy development, (4) program development, (5) implementation, and (6) monitoring and evaluation.

Preparation involves establishing co-operative relationships with other organizations and departments. Needs assessment involves identifying problem areas where needs are not currently being met. For example, this stage might lead to the creation of a social profile, a services inventory, and a basic statement of social concerns, prepared for and by a given community. Policy development involves the articulation of the policies and goals developed to address the previously identified unmet needs. Program development involves the development of particular techniques, strategies, and approaches. Implementation is putting those programs into place. And monitoring and evaluation involves the continuous collection of program and activity data and the periodic checking to see if the program is meeting its objectives. Evaluation involves a more thorough, less frequent examination of the relationship between program efforts and ultimate goals. This stage also marks the first step of a new needs-assessment stage, thereby emphasizing the cyclical nature of the social planning process.

With such social planning initiatives, the goal is always to encourage as much input from citizens and organizations as possible. While the emphasis in social planning is on addressing needs in rational ways, such initiatives are often conducted within a highly politicized context when businesses, land-use developers, competing government departments, and citizens all attempt to influence the decision-making process. Social planning initiatives are often brought in by government departments and, sometimes, social agencies for a particular purpose, such as creating a land use plan for a neighbourhood.

Some Criticisms of Social Planning Social planning is a technical research endeavour that can become disconnected from the needs of the community. In general, applied social research has its own vocabulary, education, and training, which are not commonly shared within many grassroots organizations. For example, research procedures, such as identifying a question, using an appropriate theoretical framework, selecting qualitative, quantitative or mixed methods, sampling, and data analysis, may be highly technical. Hiring a researcher to identify and represent a community's interests is a bit like hiring a lawyer to represent your interests, because you do not understand the ins and outs of their rules or procedures. Many of us have also had the unfortunate experience of taking a car in for repairs, and paying the bill without fully understanding what was done and why. The same can be said for social research.

Research can be used for a variety of purposes. In some cases, the results are determined before the study is even done. The financial backer of a study has a purpose for funding it, and selects a researcher who can deliver. Results that are inconsistent with the funder's interests may be unacceptable, and, in some instances, not ever released. In this way, social planning is far from an objective or selfless process and is likely to reinforce the perspectives of those involved. These are valid reasons why communities are skeptical of research and planning, particularly if they are not in control of the development of each phase of the project.

Social Action

The third and final category of community work identified by Rothman (1995) is the most exciting of the three models. Social action is "the organization and the use of pressure tactics by a group of people on their own behalf" (Cameron & Kerans, 1985). Saul Alinsky was probably the best-known proponent of this style of community practice. Writing about his particular approach to social change in *Rules for Radicals*, which was published shortly before he died in 1972, Alinsky suggested that the job is getting the people to move, to act, to participate; in short, to develop and harness the necessary power to effectively conflict with the prevailing patterns and change them. When those in power label social action organizers as "agitators" they are correct. The purpose of social action is to agitate the community or power structure to the point of conflict and to be a catalyst for change.

Alinsky developed his approach to community change based on his observations during the 1930s of a slum in Chicago known as Back of the Yards. He was studying crime issues in the neighbourhood for a university professor, and, by talking to the residents, became convinced that crime there was due to poverty and powerlessness. He envisioned an "organization of organizations," including labour unions, small businesses, youth groups, and the church, who, together, could advocate for change (Horwitt, 1992). The Back of the Yards Neighborhood Council held its first meeting in 1939, and forced several changes to the local meatpacking industry, which provided jobs in the area. In 1940, Alinsky formed the **Industrial Areas Foundation** (IAF), a national network of community organizations.

Several features characterize IAF organizations (Chambers & Cowan, 2003). They are known for having a problem orientation; focusing on specific, immediate, and realizable goals; having individual members, as well as representatives of smaller, more localized groups with a specific interest; primarily utilizing tactics of confrontation and conflict; and attempting to disrupt social stability and then renegotiate a compromise more favourable to the organization. In addition, IAF organizations tend to rely on a broad base of funding, rather than on one or two main sources, and focus on multiple issues, so that as one issue is resolved, the organizations move on to other ones. Alinsky organizations also make use of community organizers from outside the locality, while placing great emphasis on training local leaders. There are IAF organizations around the world, including one in Canada, based in Edmonton, Alberta, called the Greater Edmonton Alliance (Industrial Areas Foundation, 2005).

Since the 1980s, the IAFs have refocused their work toward achieving economic change at the local level. An IAF community organizer engages with a community with the primary focus of recruiting and training volunteer leaders, and teaching basic principles of organization. Before an IAF organizer is hired, local people are expected to establish their own sponsoring committee. This committee is then expected to raise enough seed money to finance at least a two-year organizing effort, including money to pay a full-time organizer, cover office and clerical expenses, and contract with the IAF to set up leader training programs. Often the critical issues faced by communities connected to IAFs have been housing, education, and employment.

Social action is not always a short-term model; therefore, essential characteristics for groups are perseverance and careful selection of issues (Hessel, 1972). As a result, an important skill for social action organizers is to ensure that high levels of group morale and commitment are maintained during times when few successes are being recorded. Social action continues over time, represents a deliberate action on the part of a group of people, remains a group effort that concentrates on changing structures, both local as well as at a broader societal level, and involves commonly held goals (Hessel, 1972).

Social action is, moreover, about politics, which functions at both formal and informal levels. Formal politics involves the methods used to select leaders to represent the electorate at the municipal, provincial, and federal levels. Informal political processes, on the other hand, are less obvious and may be reflected in the ways that organizations select priorities and develop policies. Examples of such informal politics might be the hiring/firing practices of a local employer, the decisions made about the products it produces, and the impact of the activity on the environment and on local communities.

The major goal of social action is to challenge the current situation in order to improve the quality of life for certain groups. The effectiveness of the approach depends on creative planning and patient organization with relatively little emphasis on spectacular deeds or rhetoric. Social action, to be effective, must be directed toward a common task, which is the seeking of radical ends by realistic means. While some social action strategies will be directed toward achieving relatively modest reforms in public policy or institutional practice while respecting the rule of law, the most radical end of the continuum finds expression through violent revolution.

And finally, successful social action organizers possess a particular set of characteristics (Cameron & Kerans, 1985). They believe they can create change but do not think that they must conform to existing norms and procedures. Organizers have the confidence to look at an unorganized community and believe they can bring about change, are willing to take personal risks, and relish challenge as well as their freedom. Organizers are entrepreneurs.

The Social Action Process   There is a five-step social action process: (1) defining, (2) researching, (3) formulating an action goal, (4) developing a method, and (5) evaluating the action (Cameron & Kerans, 1985). First, activists define the social problem by asking victims of the policy, leaders of action groups, policy-makers and administrators, experts on the problem, and others to identify what needs to change. They then research the problem/issue/policy that exists by seeking historical information from both allies and opponents. Activists then formulate the action goal by including specifications on who will do what, to whom, by when, all of which can be modified in light of changed circumstances and new information. Developing a methodology for achieving that goal is crucial, and activists do so by selecting specific activities and techniques appropriate to the situation—e.g., through awareness building, lobbying, demonstrations, boycotts, petitions, and lawsuits. The tactics that activists choose should be flexible and agreed to by action groups. The final step is evaluation: to what extent has the goal been achieved? How has the target group been influenced and/or changed? To what degree have related or adjacent structures been affected? How have popular value systems been altered? How congruent have the process and goals been? Where is the action system developing or terminating? Assessment and evaluation of strategies are always easier when clear goals have been established at the outset.

Some Criticisms of Social Action   Upon Saul Alinsky's death, several of his key organizers began to reflect on the effectiveness of many of the citizens' organizations that followed his organizing principles. They discovered certain dysfunctional patterns that tended to create instability, ineffectiveness, and eventual dissolution (Rogers, 1990). Organizations that depended on charismatic leaders, for example, fell apart in the absence of the leader. Those that were formed around a single issue died when the issue lost its potency. Groups that relied on public money, private grants, or the generosity of a few wealthy contributors never became truly independent. Organizations that became overly procedural lost the momentum and flexibility to act. Leaders who acted autonomously without a system of internal accountability became corrupt when no one monitored their actions. And organizations that played to the public spotlight confused their desire for media attention with their strategy for change, and those that scrambled continuously to respond to a crisis got caught up in a whirlwind of activity that soon exhausted their leaders.

However, several positive observations have been made about social action in Canada in particular (Drover & Kerans, 1993). Social action has overcome resistance and produced results in many situations where more passive methods have failed. Many of the successes of social action have involved improvements to local environments (e.g., transportation systems, parkland). In addition, social action has had a positive impact on the personal growth of previously disadvantaged people. Learning new skills and increasing self-confidence, which some community members have experienced, have helped those community members break out of the cycle of poverty and become outstanding citizens, contributing previously untapped talents to the benefit of society as a whole. Finally, social action has led to an increase in community pride and the growth of social support systems in previously stigmatized neighbourhoods. However, social action has had little impact on national trends and priorities, such as the distribution of wealth. In sum, social action has been most effective with immediate issues. Many organizations disintegrate after about five years as issues change and organizers burn out. This lack of ability to sustain initiative has been a major challenge for some social action initiatives in Canada.

While social action is immediate, high profile, and exciting, pressuring those in power may achieve certain short-term gains but comes with the price of alienating policy-makers in the future. Also, since many organizations are dependent on government funding, either directly or indirectly, social action can be perceived as biting the hand that feeds it, and at a personal level can have career-limiting implications. At an organizational level, social action might also jeopardize an agency's funding base.

MODELS OF COMMUNITY ORGANIZATIONS

Community development initiatives often lead to the creation of new community organizations. There was a great deal of attention paid in the 1980s to the kinds of community organizations that emerged from community development initiatives. Rothman & Tropman (1987) included policy and administrative practices as approaches to community practice. Kramer and Specht (1983) described activities that lead to the development of community organizations and their interconnections with other organizations, while Rubin & Rubin (1986) described different types of community organizations.

Policy and Administration

Rothman and Tropman (1987) described **policy and administrative practices** as community development activities. In community organizations, administrative practice could include many activities designed to build stronger connections with other grassroots groups (e.g., offering joint programs or complementary services). Administrative practice also involves a variety of internal activities to remain connected with the community (e.g., outreach), led by the community (e.g., board membership), and that recognize and promote community capacity (e.g., hiring from within the community). Policy work in a community organization practice includes advocating for the creation of, or change to, internal or external policies that are not in line with the community's needs.

Community Development

To Kramer and Specht (1983), community development is based on the needs of community members who are negatively affected by existing and often distant organizations. Mobilizing the community, then, leads to the development of new organizations that are responsive to those who are not well served by existing organizations (e.g., organizing a residents' group in a private rental property). In this model, the product of community development is a community organization: action in the form of community development is needed to get a new organization off the ground and to co-ordinate services among organizations. In the community development model, organization staff members represent their agencies *and* their community because they are members of the local community.

Types of Community Organizations

Organizations can be geography- or issue-based. That is, membership can be drawn from within a building, neighbourhood, or town that has physical boundaries; or, membership can be drawn from those who have an affiliation by virtue of a physical, social, or spiritual situation or interest (e.g., disability, poverty, religion). From there, Rubin and Rubin (1986) describe five types of community organizations: self-help, partnership, co-production, pressure, or protest. Self-help organizations focus on the issues of their membership, working internally without the help of external organizations (e.g., babysitting exchange among neighbours). Partnership organizations are also based on the needs of community members, but do rely on some external assistance, often with funding or technical matters (e.g., research). Co-production organizations take over functions previously served by government agencies (e.g., some child protection services are delivered by non-government organizations). Pressure organizations lobby for change to government policy or procedures by working in partnership with elected representatives and others in positions of influence (e.g., petition for changes to lighting in a neighbourhood). And finally, protest organizations also pressure for change, but use unconventional tactics (e.g., forming a human fence in front of a pesticide-spraying truck entering a neighbourhood).

SUMMARY

- Support for community development can be found across the political spectrum, including among those from conservative, liberal, socialist, and anarchist backgrounds.
- Feminist and environmentalist ideologies also have a significant impact on the practice of community development in Canada today.
- Symbolic-interactionism, structural-functional, and conflict sociological theories are based on distinct models of society, and indicate different causes and solutions to social and community problems.
- Across Canada, community development practice has different characteristics, including community economic development (Maritimes), social animation (Quebec), participatory research (Central), rural social work (Prairies), and social support (West).
- There are three major categories of community intervention, including locality development, social planning, and social action. Each approach has advantages and disadvantages.

DISCUSSION QUESTIONS

1. How do cuts to social welfare spending across Canada affect community development initiatives?

2. What is colonization, and how does it affect development in Aboriginal communities?

3. Which regional approach to community development resonates most strongly with you, and why? What are the advantages and disadvantages of that approach?

4. Select an issue that your community is facing. Discuss the three major approaches to intervention, and how each might be applied in this case, and select one to make a case for its use in this issue.

5. Are there organizations that fulfill more than one of the functions in the Rubin & Rubin model? Have those organizations changed over time? Why?

WEBLINKS

www.digitalronin.f2s.com/politicalcompass/ The Political Compass

www2.fmg.uva.nl/sociosite/topics/theory.html Sociological Theories and Perspectives

www.seascape.ns.ca/~twocats/AMWEB.html The Antigonish Movement: Web Resources

http://comm-org.wisc.edu/ Comm-Org

www.indiana.edu/~ythvoice/socialtools.html Social Action Tools

KEY TERMS

Anarchism, p. 35

Antigonish Movement, p. 40

Colonization, p. 37

Community economic development, p. 40

Conflict theorists, p. 38

Consciousness-raising, p. 40

Conservatism, p. 35

Conservative, p. 35

Ecologism, p. 37

Feminism, p. 36

Functionalists, p.38

Indigenous, p. 37

Industrial Areas Foundation, p. 49

Liberal, p. 35

Liberalism, p. 35

Participatory research, p. 41

Patriarchy, p. 36

Policy and administrative practices, p. 51

Restorative approaches, p. 42

Social animation, p. 40

Socialism, p. 35

Symbolic interactionists, p. 39

chapter five

Building Relationships
with the Community

LEARNING OBJECTIVES

After reading this chapter you will be able to:

1. Describe general systems theory and the implications of this perspective for building relationships in community practice.

2. Recognize how different motives, values, and styles influence relationship development in community practice.

3. Define *power* and *authority*, distinguish between different types of each, and recognize their place in relationships.

4. Understand professional, organizational, and community contexts of relationships.

5. Distinguish between four types of relationships in community practice, as well as the uses, benefits, and drawbacks of each.

6. Understand different ways to get involved in the community.

Relationships are crucial to effective community work. Many of the strategies and techniques community workers use are based on strong relationships. In a review of the most successful approaches to community development, O'Grady (2000) concluded that "the one absolutely clear commonality . . . is that high-trust relationships and high-investment relationship building are the most fundamental elements in creating lasting community change" (p. 249). In this chapter, we describe the person-in-environment perspective, general systems theory, and the ecological perspective to show principles of relationships between people and groups in communities. We also discuss motives, values, and styles of working in the community. Power and authority also play a major role in relationships. Moreover, relationship development is affected by a community worker's professional, organizational, and community responsibilities. In this chapter, we also look at types of relationships in community development, including collaboration, confrontation, negotiation, and co-optation. And, finally, we present some different ways workers can get involved.

CHAPTER OUTLINE

PERSPECTIVES ON RELATIONSHIP DEVELOPMENT

There are many ways to describe relationships. One perspective that has been applied often in the human services is a **person-in-environment** perspective (Walsh, Craik, & Price, 2000). According to this perspective, people have biological, psychological, social, and spiritual dimensions (Wapner & Demick, 2000), and the environment includes physical, interpersonal, and socio-cultural components (Demick & Wapner, 1988). Socio-cultural components include the number and quality of relationships, including immediate and extended family, as well as social networks of friends. As well, the quality of the work or school environment, neighbourhood or community, and the broader governmental and social forces influencing a person are also part of the socio-cultural environment (Jordan & Franklin, 1995). And all of these components interact. The person-in-environment perspective provides a background for looking at relationships between individuals and groups, groups and organizations, and organizations in the broader environment (Mayo, Pastor & Wapner, 1995).

As you can imagine, the number and complexity of connections each of us has to our environments is massive. One technique that community development workers use to sort out all of these connections is a **genogram** (Maluccio, Pine, & Tracy, 2002), which is a chart that shows individuals and their relationships to one another in a family. Community workers may also use a **social network map** (Tracy & Whittaker, 1990), which is a type of genogram that includes all relationships within as well as outside of a family. At the community level, a development worker might use a **community asset map** (McKnight & Kretzmann, 1990), which is made up of three components: resources located in the neighbourhood and under the neighbourhood's control; resources located within the neighbourhood but controlled by outsiders; and resources originating outside of the neighbourhood and controlled by outsiders.

The person-in-environment perspective provides a conceptual reference point for many community workers. It gives rationale for working with individuals and groups. For example, some individuals who do community development work start from an assumption that personal healing and healthy social relationships for individuals are necessary for healthy community change to occur. Others community development workers start from an assumption that healthy community change is necessary for personal healing and the development of healthy social relationships.

In the next section we provide an overview of key terms in general systems theory and a human ecological perspective. These perspectives provide a framework for understanding the nature of relationships between people and groups in communities and societies.

General Systems Theory

General systems theory is an interdisciplinary perspective that emphasizes interactions and interdependence. A system is a group of interrelated parts that together perform some function. In 1934, Ludwig von Bertalanffy, an Austrian biologist, was the first to write about general systems, while Gordon Hearn (1969), a social worker, used the perspective to describe helping individuals, families, and communities:

> The general systems approach . . . is based upon the assumption that matter, in all its forms, living and nonliving, can be regarded as systems . . . . If nothing else, this should provide education with a means of organizing the human behaviour and social environment aspects of the curriculum. (Hearn, p. 2.)

The systems theory perspective has also been applied in other human services fields, including psychology, education, nursing, communication, and medicine (Anderson, Carter, & Lowe, 1999).The general systems perspective focuses on the contributions of different components that work together and serve to maintain system survival or that strive to attain some goal. For example, a community's well-being may depend on the contributions of spiritual leaders, business people, and educators. If one of those functions is missing, such as educators who teach the children to read and write in their language, or spiritual leaders who provide direction to the community, the health of all members will suffer. Systems also need to be adaptable. People can change their environments, and they do just that in creative ways (e.g., by moving to a new neighbourhood). Individuals have unique perspectives on their realities (e.g., having a totally different reaction than your partner to a news story you watched on television together). Therefore, there are no universal truths—each person's reality is made up of personal and environmental factors, and together these realities make up the foundation of a human system. But the system is more than the sum of its parts. It includes not only people, but also relationships between them (Greene, 1999). Human systems, therefore, cannot be described using simplistic or linear models. They are too complex and dynamic (Anderson, Carter, & Lowe, 1999).

In community development, there are multiple systems with which members of a community interact. People are, in fact, in constant interaction with various systems, both within and outside the community. These systems include family, friends, work, social services, education, justice, health, employment, and culture, as well as goods and services. As a result, it is important for community development workers to understand some principles of systems. Key terms in general systems theory include *focal system, subsystem, suprasystem, boundaries, roles, relationships, interface, synergy, permeability, goal orientation, input, output, feedback, differentiation, entropy,* and *equifinality.*

Each system has connections to other systems. The **focal system**, first of all, is the system of interest. In community development, for example, the focal system may be a neighbourhood. And this system is connected to other, larger systems (e.g., the city or town), known as **suprasystems**, or smaller systems (e.g., a street or building), known as **subsystems**. Systems also have **boundaries**, which are patterns of behaviour that characterize the relationships within a system and give that system an identity (e.g., my "family" includes both immediate family and extended members who live far away from one another). Boundaries can be more or less **permeable** (e.g., my "family" has welcomed new members—my children have godparents). Some systems have a lot of movement from the inside out, or outside in. Some systems do not. Some system boundaries are closed and, therefore, resistant to outside influence, while others are open, and amenable to influence from outside the system.

A **role**, according to systems theory, is "a culturally determined pattern of behaviour expected of an individual in a specified social relationship" (Norlin & Chess, 1997, p.16). For a particular person, under particular conditions, consistency with previous behaviours is predicted (e.g., I usually start arguments at "family" gatherings). And **relationships**, according to this theory, are the "mutual exchange; dynamic interaction; and affective, cognitive and behavioural connection" between two or more persons or systems (Barker, 1999, p. 407). There is reciprocity, or equal give and take in relationships. Relationships also change over time, from more to less intense, stressful, positive, or healthy. Relationships are also influenced by a complex combination of thoughts, feelings, and behaviours. Other important terms in general systems theory are **interface**, which is the point of contact between two systems (e.g., my "family" and your "family" get together), and **synergy**, which is what happens when two systems combine efforts (e.g., we have a joint family reunion) (Norlin, Chess, Dale & Smith, 2003). The point of contact is where communication takes place, information is exchanged, and energy is transferred. When two systems combine resources, they have more to work with, but the coming together may affect their separate purposes.

There are three main functions of systems: goal-direction, input, and output (Huitt, 2003). Systems are purposive. They have goals. They direct energy in line with those goals. **Input** is information or energy that comes into the system from other systems. **Output** is what happens after the input has been processed by some system. For example, a goal may be to maintain equilibrium, which is to ensure that inputs and outputs are equal. Or the goal may be to change, which requires a temporary imbalance between inputs and outputs. The very presence of a worker who may be new to a community or a position of employment can represent change to a system. Effort is required, therefore, to build relationships with existing systems. For some time, inputs may be more heavily weighted than outputs. **Feedback** is a type of input, where the system gets information, positive or negative, about its performance; the system learns about what it is doing well and what it could do better.

Differentiation, another general systems theory term, is the tendency of systems to become more complex over time (Norlin, Chess, Dale & Smith, 2003). New relationships develop, and interactions multiply. Differentiation can lead to entropy or negative entropy. **Entropy** is progress toward disorganization; **negative entropy** is progress toward higher levels of organization. And, finally, **equifinality** is recognition that there are many ways to achieve the same goal—that is, there are many means to the same end.

Implications of Systems Theory for Relationship Building What does systems theory have to do with relationship building? In a word, lots. It is important for community workers to recognize the various systems in place. A community may be made up of many systems, such as residents' groups, cultural organizations, and block-watch groups, all of which comprise people who live in the community. In addition, residents interact with other systems outside the community, such as child protection, income support, health, and justice. There are also systems in the community that may include members from both inside and outside the community, such as local businesses, schools, and helping agencies.

It is useful to think about community work within an **arena of action** (Homan, 2003). The arena of action is the context for community development. It includes all of those systems that contribute to or detract from a goal of the community. The arena of action contains several systems, including the benefit system, action system, and the target system (Kettner, Daley, & Nichols, 1985). For any community change to take place, these systems will intersect. Members of the **benefit system** are the beneficiaries of community change. The **action system** refers to the members who do something to disrupt the situation, and cause a change. And the **target system** is the affected system. For example, if a residents' group wanted to pressure a local property manager to improve service to tenants through legal means, three systems would be involved. The action system could include lawyers and the courts. The beneficiary system could be the resident group. The target system could be the property management company.

It is also important for workers seeking to build relationships to recognize the boundaries of systems in operation. As mentioned, some systems are closed, while others are open. If you are a community member inside the system—that is, a member of a resident's group as in the previous example—you will have the benefit of access to that system. But you may well perceive the property management system as closed. Working within a community requires strategic relationship building, and recognition that membership in one system can influence your relationships to other systems. Community workers are involved in multiple systems within and outside a community.

The roles you play as a community worker will depend on the circumstances you find yourself in. In some situations, active leadership is appropriate, and in others, a more supportive role may be appropriate. There are also situations in which a passive role is called for. For example, in systems where there is strong local leadership in place, a worker seeking to build relationships will probably find it counterproductive to assert herself as a leader. But in systems where no leadership has emerged, a stronger leadership or co-ordination role may be appropriate.

As mentioned, relationships require give and take. In communities where there are rich and strong networks in place, workers may have to put in a great deal of time and effort before community members accept them as members. In communities where there are fewer networks in place, community workers may gain membership more quickly in response to their time and effort. It is crucial to recognize different realities, as well as perceptions of effort and time. For example, a single parent who relies on public transportation is making a huge effort to attend an evening meeting, let alone participate in it or take homework from it.

It is also useful for community workers to have a clear sense of the goals of the systems in which they and community members are interacting. These systems may have different purposes and rules, which can conflict in significant ways. For example, the goal of income support may actually be to get people off income support. The goal of a family system may be to have enough income to meet a family's needs. The goal of a local business, on the other hand, may be to make a profit. Within these systems, a family receiving income assistance may live separate lives so that one parent can collect assistance, and another can be employed.

Human Ecological Perspective

In the 1920s, Robert E. Park and Ernest Burgess were the forerunners of a new urban sociology program at the University of Chicago. They developed a theory of urban ecology in which they proposed that cities developed in the same way as ecosystems because of competition for scarce resources (Brown, 2005). Much has been written more recently about the "goodness-of-fit" between individuals and their environments (Germain & Gitterman, 1995; Gitterman, 1994), where the relationships between people and their environments are of central importance. When the fit between person and environment is not good, stress results. The human ecological perspective views people as actively creating or gravitating to environments where they fit.

According to this perspective, people interact within multiple environments that include all circumstances and interactions between human beings. *Environment* also refers to the actual physical setting that a culture or society provides. **Transactions** are the interactions that people have with their environments, and the purpose of transactions is to adapt (e.g., get involved in the neighbourhood watch program because others on your block are doing it). Failure to adapt leads to stress, which invokes coping responses (e.g., you're unhappy, because you were not invited to a BBQ put on by the neighbourhood watch members).

As well, interactions between people are embedded within a series of larger environments: the micro, meso, exo, and macro levels refer to layers of the environment (Egan & Cowan, 1979). The **micro level** refers to individuals and their families, as well as other immediate social settings, such as a workplace, classroom, and friendship group. The family includes parents, siblings, as well as extended members, such as aunts, uncles, cousins, and grandparents. The **meso level** represents the interactions between the individual and the immediate environment (e.g., what you do with your friends when you get together). The **exo level** includes institutions, which influence relationships in the more immediate environment (e.g., when you are drinking with your underage friends in a park and the police stop by, and you quickly disperse). Finally, the **macro level** refers to societal expectations, culture, and common beliefs (e.g., drinking is not condoned in this community).

Implications of the Ecological Perspective for Relationship Building The ecological perspective is based on an intimate connection between the physical and social environments people live in. Attention to both physical and social dimensions is crucial for understanding relationship dynamics in communities. Communities can be rich with physical resources but impoverished in terms of social networks. Or, conversely, members may be well connected socially but have few physical resources. These two communities have different strengths and, perhaps, different goals and directions.

This perspective also recognizes power differences between levels of environment. In relationships, this may mean that one partner has more influence than the other. Institutions often have considerable influence, particularly if they hold access to physical resources, such as money or services. Those in the community, therefore, may view community workers affiliated with institutions as wielding a great deal of influence. The institutional affiliation of community workers affects both the formation and maintenance of their relationships in the community. This can work in their favour or against them. If the relationship between the institution and community has been positive in the past, then access may be relatively easy to gain. If, however, the relationship between the institution and the community has never been initiated, or has been negative, then workers will need to build or repair the relationship.

The influence of each level of environment on those within it requires sensitivity on the part of the community worker, who must recognize the multiple effects of larger environments, while attending to the individual's desire to fit into her or his most immediate environments. The influence of friends and family should not be overstated. Community workers should be aware of the most immediate supports and take great care not to disrupt existing relationships that may well be imperfect, but functional. Typically, such relationships are longer lasting than any a worker may be able to provide.

COMMUNITY WORKER SELF-AWARENESS

The success of relationships is influenced in large part by a worker's approach. In fact, workers' motives and style of interacting are as important as their interpersonal skills. As a result, self-awareness can be a great ally in developing relationships. At a basic level, the assumptions workers make about basic human nature influence how they perceive a situation and what they do based on that appraisal (Ewen, 1998). For example, are people's innate predispositions good or bad, or both? Are they driven by a desire to help themselves or others? Are they more motivated to avoid pain or obtain pleasure? Is behaviour caused by previous experience or future goals? Can people even be consciously aware of all of their motives?

What are your motives for doing this work? What are the motives of those you are working with? One way to think about this is by ranking needs. A **hierarchy of needs** describes a set of universal wants that people must satisfy in sequence to advance to the highest levels of satisfaction (Maslow, 1968). The most basic human needs are physiological and include the basic needs for physical survival, such as food, clothing, and shelter (healthy food, appropriate clothing, and a place to live). Also included in the most basic of human needs is the need for exercise. Second stage needs are for safety and security. These apply to employment, income, family, and health as well as to physical safety areas of one's life (e.g., having enough money, a dependable job, and family stability). In the third stage, the needs centre on love and belonging, and the need for relationships with others emerges. These needs are emotionally based. People want to be part of a collective, affiliate with a group, and be a member of a community (e.g., gang membership, clubs). The fourth stage revolves around esteem needs. In this stage, people seek to have their need for self-esteem met by being held highly in the esteem of others, as well as believing it themselves (e.g., by having a profession, or a hobby). Finally, the fifth stage is self-actualization, the epitome of health and happiness.

What are the motives of those who reach the top of this hierarchy? According to Maslow (1971), they include the following:

* truth, rather than dishonesty
* goodness, rather than evil
* beauty, not ugliness or vulgarity
* unity, wholeness, and transcendence of opposites, not arbitrariness or forced choices
* aliveness, not deadness or the mechanization of life
* uniqueness, not bland uniformity
* perfection and necessity, not sloppiness, inconsistency, or accident
* completion, rather than incompleteness
* justice and order, not injustice and lawlessness
* simplicity, not unnecessary complexity
* richness, not environmental impoverishment
* effortlessness, not strain
* playfulness, not grim, humourless drudgery
* self-sufficiency, not dependency
* meaningfulness, rather than senselessness

You may easily recognize the values you agree with and are motivated by from this list. However, the vast majority of people are not motivated by self-actualization needs. Many people have far more basic needs, such as finding a meal or a place to sleep, which is the focus of their energies. Workers must recognize their own motives as well as those of others they are working with.

Cultural differences also affect how relationships develop. Specialist cultures and generalist cultures, for example, emphasize different values (Armour, 1998). Table 5.1 on page 62 summarizes nine dimensions that workers can use to identify some cultural differences. Relationship development will be different when working with members of a different culture. For example, in a culture that is highly hierarchical, one member may make decisions on behalf of a group. In an egalitarian culture, meetings with all members for decision-making purposes may be the norm. There may also be norms and customs that are different than one's own. Following traditional protocol is crucial for the development of a cross-cultural relationship based on respect.

Styles of working also affect the development of relationships. Recognizing your own style of working, including preferences and difficulties, can be helpful when developing relationships with others who have different strengths. One tool community-based organizations use as part of cultural sensitivity training is a temperament sorter (Kruger, 2005). Many versions of this test exist on the Internet, and generally follow a model of personality described by Briggs-Myers and Myers (1980). The basic dimensions where people differ are their source and direction of energy, how they prefer to take in information, make decisions, and relate to the outer world.

TABLE 5.1	Differences Between Specialist and Generalist Culture
Specialist	**Generalist**
Emphasis on the Individual	Emphasis on the Group
Compartmentalized	Holistic
Secular	Religious
Egalitarian	Hierarchical
Gender Integrated	Gender Separated
Independence	Interdependence
Beliefs Questioned	Traditional Beliefs
Isolation	Connection
Need for Space	Little Need for Space

Source: N. Armour (1998). *Specialist and Generalist Cultures* (Adapted from *Social Work 555* course handout). Calgary, AB: University of Calgary.

According to Myers (1995; Consulting Psychologists' Press, 2000), people fall somewhere between extroversion and introversion. Those who are more extroverted tend to focus on the outer world of people and things. Those with a more introverted preference tend to focus on the inner world of thoughts and impressions. Extroverts get their energy from being around other people, while introverts get it from their own ideas. Extroverts like to be around people, are comfortable in social situations, and get their best ideas working in a group. Introverts may think most clearly in a quiet space and on their own. Do you like small group or solitary activities, or do you prefer large group gatherings?

Preferred ways of taking in information also differ for different people. According to Briggs-Myers and Myers (1980), people fall along a continuum between sensing and intuitive preferences. Sensing is a preference for concrete information in the here and now. Information comes from the senses, including sight, touch, smell, taste, and hearing. Intuition is focused on the abstract and has an orientation to the future. Do you prefer to learn by a hands-on approach, or by talking about ideas and concepts?

The way people make decisions also varies (Briggs-Myers & Myers, 1980; Pittenger, 1993). People who prefer thinking tend to base their decisions on logic and objective analysis of cause and effect. Those who prefer feeling tend to base decisions on their own subjective evaluation of person-centred concerns. The difference lies in the way decisions are made. Do you make more decisions based on logic or on how you feel?

Relating to the outer world also varies on a continuum from judging to perceiving (Lim, 1994). This dimension is about organization and structure. People who prefer a judging approach like to have a plan and have things settled. Those who prefer a perceptive approach like a spontaneous and flexible approach to life, and want to keep their options open. Do you like things organized and clear, or do you prefer to go with the flow and keep your options open?

Implications of Self-Awareness for Relationship Development It is helpful to be aware of differences between people's motives, values, and ways of working. The benefits of valuing diversity can be far-reaching, as noted by a former Canadian federal minister of multiculturalism:

> Valuing diversity must be a priority in the formulation of new policy, laws and programs. Diversity must be viewed as strength in providing Canada with competitive advantages as well as a rich new source of innovation and creativity. Forward-looking, action-oriented strategies to deal with the challenges of the past, present and future will promote full citizenship, inclusion and social participation for all of Canada's population. (Canadian Heritage, 2005, p.1)

There are both benefits and challenges associated with group diversity (Nijstad & Paulus, 2003). In community work, some benefits of diversity are inclusiveness, complementariness, and creativity. Inclusive relationships bring different people together, resulting in a combination of abilities that no one person has. Moreoover, complementing one another can result in relationships that lead to creative approaches. However, a major challenge of developing relationships among people from diverse backgrounds is effective communication (Nijstad and Paulus, 2003).

There are several issues that community workers should address in order to develop effective communication between people from different cultural backgrounds (Coady, 2002). First, workers need to be aware of their own values and beliefs, including those that cause them discomfort when interacting with people from an experiential background that differs from their own. These biases could prevent them from seeing others as individuals. Second, community workers should learn about the culture of those they are preparing to work with, including their customs, beliefs, traditions, as well as their experience of oppression. Third, those who are preparing to work with others from a different cultural background than their own should also recognize the diversity within the culture they are learning about. Indeed, "it is as bad to overestimate the effect of difference as it is to underestimate it" (Coady, 2002, p.124). The key is to become sensitive to the possible impact of differences between cultures, and then, to open up to understanding each person's unique experience (Coady, 2002).

Power and Authority

One dynamic that is present in all relationships is power, although it has been defined in different ways. Rubin and Rubin (2001) define power as "the ability to affect decisions that shape social outcomes" (p. 6). It is the capacity to move people in a desired direction to accomplish some end (Homan, 2003). Power is also the ability to realize one's value in the world (Robinson & Hanna, 1994). The term also refers to the capacity of some people to produce intended and foreseen effects on others (Wrong, 1995). Also, power is the ability to prevent someone from doing something they want to do (Kirst-Ashman & Hull, 2001).

But essentially power is the ability to influence others, and the amount of influence a person has depends on whom he or she is trying to persuade. Power is reciprocal. All parties in a relationship have power, but not necessarily the same amount. And, while power is often described in negative terms, it is, in fact, neutral. It is the use of power, and its source, type, and intensity that affect whether people see it positively or negatively. There are different types of power (French & Raven, 1959), including coercive, reward, expert, referent, information, and legitimate power.

Coercive power is based on fear and influences through the threat of punishment (e.g., concern about being fired by an employer). **Reward power**, on the other hand, is based on an expectation of positive benefits and influences through the offer of a reward (e.g., being given a compliment by your teacher). **Expert power** is based on expertise and a particular set of skills or specialized knowledge (e.g., seeing a traditional healer to treat an infection). **Referent power** is associated with a person who possesses desirable resources or special traits. Its influence is the result of a desire by others to model or emulate the source (e.g., a role model in the community). **Information power** is based on persuasiveness or content of communication (e.g., a person giving a very passionate and moving speech). And **legitimate power** is associated with the position held within an organization or group, not the individual holding the position. Constituents of the organization or group need to accept the authority of this position for power to be legitimate (e.g., voting for the mayor of a city).

Authority, on the other hand, may be described as influence that is assigned to a person or position. It differs from power in that it implies a voluntary agreement on the part of others to recognize the right of this person or position to give orders. There are three types of authority (Weber, 1968): traditional, legal-rational, and charismatic. **Traditional authority** is based on the person, on history, and on following customs that have been set before (e.g., an Aboriginal elder). **Rational-legal authority** is based on the position, rules, and procedures that have been written down (e.g., the executive director of an agency). **Charismatic authority** is based on the person, but not on customs or rules. It is often associated with a revolution against customs or rules. Charismatic authority is religious or political influence that thrives on the short-term enthusiasm that accompanies social change (e.g., the leader of a group demonstrating in support of changes to low welfare rates at a provincial legislature).

Implications of Power Types for Relationship Building As mentioned, power exists in all relationships, and the degree of influence you have depends on the position or qualifications you hold. Major power bases in a community include both positions and people. It is important for community workers to recognize the positions of power, and those people who occupy them. For example, power resides in the positions held by public officials, such as federal, provincial, civic, and band leaders. It also resides in laws and regulations. Funders, in public or private organizations, also hold power. Professionals, such as nurses, social workers, physicians, teachers, and police, by virtue of their positions, can be influential. As well, the families of well-connected people, as well as particular grassroots organizations, local leaders, business owners, and human service providers may exert influence.

Recognition of local authority is important. Authority is built upon reputation, and reputation matters. Communities can be small places where everyone knows one another. Positions of authority can be easily identified, but until you spend time in a community, it is difficult to identify the people who have the support of others. As a worker in the community, you will want to pay attention to how you are received and regarded. Your credibility with that community depends on how you fit in.

THE CONTEXT OF THE RELATIONSHIP

There are several levels to the context of a relationship between workers, their professions, employers, and the community. Community workers have several responsibilities, which can conflict. The professional context includes codes of ethics and standards for practice, which are different for each profession and jurisdiction. Also, the organization or agency paying a worker's salary is part of the context in which a worker develops and maintains relationships. Finally, the community is a crucial context with which to be familiar, since it has a significant impact on a worker's role and work. In this section, we discuss each of these topics.

Professional Context

Professionals in the field of community development have been trained in several disciplines. Some are members of professional organizations, which itself comes with responsibilities. For example, registered nurses, registered social workers, and chartered psychologists make a commitment to abide by codes of ethics and practice standards. In addition, there may be standards that regulate practice in certain areas. All Canadian provinces, for example, have child protection legislation, which specifies the circumstances under which a child is deemed to be in need of protection.

There is not, however, a professional organization for community development professionals in Canada, nor are there standards governing qualifications or practice. The title of "community developer" is not protected by legislation. Therefore, anyone can call herself a community developer. However, if you are a professional involved in community development practice, you are accountable to your professional organization.

Codes of ethics for social workers, nurses, and psychologists in Canada describe values that professionals in those fields should use to guide practice. Codes of ethics are general principles, however; they do not dictate a particular course of action for each situation. Practice standards, where available, provide more direction about procedures for handling particular situations and ethical dilemmas. Copies of ethical codes can be found on Web sites for the Canadian Association of Social Workers (**www.casw-acts.ca**), the Canadian Nurses Association (**www.cna-aiic.ca**), and the Canadian Psychologists' Association (**www. cpa.ca**). Following, we briefly present the principles and values that guide decision making in these professions.

The Canadian Social Work Code of Ethics begins with the following:

> The social work profession is dedicated to the welfare and self-realization of all people; the development and disciplined use of scientific and professional knowledge; the development of resources and skills to meet individual, group, national and international changing needs and aspirations; and the achievement of social justice for all. (CASW, 2005, p. 2–3)

Core values described in the Code include the following:

- Respect for Inherent Dignity and Worth of Persons (Value 1)
- Pursuit of Social Justice (Value 2)
- Service to Humanity (Value 3)
- Integrity of Professional Practice (Value 4)
- Confidentiality in Professional Practice (Value 5)
- Competence in Professional Practice (Value 6) (CASW, 2005)

The Canadian Nurses Association has a code of ethics that includes eight values that guide practice:

- Safe, Competent, and Ethical Care (Value 1)
- Health and Well-Being (Value 2)

- Choice (Value 3)
- Dignity (Value 4)
- Confidentiality (Value 5)
- Justice (Value 6)
- Accountability (Value 7)
- Quality Practice Environments (Value 8) (2002, p. 8)

Psychologists in Canada also have a code of ethics (Canadian Psychological Association, 1995) that identifies four principles: respect for the dignity of persons, responsible caring, integrity in relationships, and responsibility to society. Respect for the dignity of persons refers to moral rights of individuals who are the most vulnerable. Responsible caring refers to the competence of the provider of a service. Integrity in relationships includes accurate and honest conduct, straightforwardness and openness. In their responsibility to society, psychologists are to:

> . . . respect social structures that have emerged over time, [and unless] structures or policies seriously ignore or oppose the principles of respect for the dignity of persons, responsible caring, integrity in relationships, or responsibility to society, psychologists involved have a responsibility to speak out in a manner consistent with the principles of this Code, and advocate for appropriate change to occur as quickly as possible. (CPA, 1995, p. 27)

Membership in these professions does not just mean working with individuals and small groups. In fact, these professions sanction working with large groups, organizations, and entire communities on broader social change. However, these codes tend to emphasize clinical practice, not community practice. According to Hardina (2004), ethics for community practice differ from ethics for clinical practice in several ways: (1) the goal is social change, not personal wellness (e.g., better parent-child relationships); (2) those who are affected by the change may not be in direct contact with the worker (e.g., all low-income parents in a particular neighbourhood); (3) ethics in community practice requires critical examination of social and economic forces that create individual problems (e.g., how day-care policies discourage women from entering the workforce); (4) workers may be part of the group (e.g., neighbourhood residents) they are representing; and (5) the decision about how to proceed is situational (e.g., depending on who the players are, the nature and resistance of the target system to change).

According to Reich and Lowe (2000), several principles should be used to guide ethical decisions in community practice, including the following: (1) identification of the ethical principles at hand, (2) collection of additional information to answer the dilemma in question, (3) identification of relevant ethical values that apply, (4) recognition of potential conflicts of interest and beneficiaries, (5) application of ethical rules and ranking in terms of importance, and (6) determination of the consequences of applying different rules.

For example, let's say you, as a community worker, develop a friendship with an older adult resident of a housing block where there are multiple well-known problems with the maintenance of rental units by the landlord. This person is also a member of a residents' group that is developing an action plan, and you are assisting them with a process. You have been invited to a birthday party for this resident's grandchild. Do you accept or decline the invitation? Codes of ethics comment on the nature of appropriate relationships, including dual relationships, where there is a power differential. As well, there are potential consequences to yourself, to other members of the residents' group, and to those residents who are not participating in the action planning. What do you do, and why? How does the code of ethics for your profession guide the decision?

Organizational Context

Organizations—whether government (at federal, provincial, civic, or band levels) or non-government—have their own history, identity, and plan. The mission, service area, population served, programs, staffing, and funding sources are all important (Timmreck, 2003). Organizations, furthermore, operate within a context. Each organization has contacts and connections with larger and smaller organizations. Some organizations are explicitly community development organizations, while others are not. The structure of the organization determines whether community development work is done as well as how it is done. For example, some organizations do community development through outreach. For some organizations, community development is an integral part of the work they do (e.g., all staff are from the local community).

A **mission statement** gives overall direction to an organization's activities as well as a purpose, a reason for existing. A good mission statement should answer three questions (Radtke, 1998): (1) What are the opportunities or needs that we exist to address? (2) What are we doing to address those needs? and (3) What principles or beliefs guide our work? For example, the International Institute for Sustainable Development has the following mission:

> Opportunities or needs: For development to be sustainable it must integrate environmental stewardship, economic development and the well-being of all people—not just for today but for countless generations to come. (IISD, 2005)

Activities to address those needs include "advancing policy recommendations" on several issues, such as climate change, for example. Guiding principles or beliefs are to "engage decision-makers in government" in a variety of settings, such as business and government, for example. (IISD, 2005)

Organizations also define the group or groups they work with. The **service area** is the physical or geographic community served, and the **population served** describes the demographics of those the organization works with in the community. These may overlap. For example, Organization A provides services to families across the city when a child is in need of protection. Organization B provides services to families in a particular neighbourhood who have children that want to go to day camps during the summer. These two organizations have overlapping service areas (both to same geographical area), and, in some cases, populations (both deal with families who have children). If you are a staff member of Organization A, your job is to protect children. If you are a staff member of Organization B, your job is to provide recreation opportunities to children. These different purposes will affect the relationships you develop with people in the organization's service area.

Programs, funding, and staffing are all integral to an organization. Programs are the services provided (e.g., parenting skills workshops, clothing exchanges). They may change in response to funding, staffing competencies, and community need. As well, funding source, type, and purpose affect the programs offered. Different funding sources have different rules about how the money is to be spent. Project funding or start-up funding, for example, is not continuous, while core funding may be renewed annually for several years. Funding may be for a particular issue (e.g., crime prevention) that the organization is working on, but not its sole purpose. **Staffing** includes the number of staff as well as their qualifications (e.g., a counsellor should have training or experience in counselling).

The organization you work for plays a large role in the relationships you form in the community. It can be helpful to have documents (e.g., annual reports, organizational charts, and job descriptions) from the organization to assist you in determining the following: 1) who you are supposed to be working with, 2) what you are supposed to be doing, and 3) for what purpose. It is also important to know how the organization functions, including whom you should approach for advice and approval (e.g., how far up the organization ladder to go) when you are unsure. When you approach superiors for permission to be involved in a particular community activity on behalf of your organization, you should be well prepared. Knowing the history, mission, structure, and function of the organization employing you helps you to put the most appropriate context on the proposed activity.

Community Context

Every community is unique; each has its own strengths and challenges. It is crucial, therefore, to understand the structure and function of community groups you are working with. What are the local issues? Who is already involved, and how? Who are the local leaders and the bases of power? How do residents view local leadership and community change? Ungar and colleagues (Ungar, Manuel, Mealy, Thomas & Campbell, 2004), in their study of community guides—voluntary, local, informal helpers—and the principles that direct their practice, described several qualities of community workers. They found five principles: visibility, relationships with community, self-definitions, contextual sensitivity, and intervention processes. Local guides describe themselves as invisible and self-effacing. They describe their relationships with the community as nonformal, with permeable boundaries. They are immersed in community life. Their roles often have no title. They use local experience and expertise to make decisions about ways to proceed. Community change is built on networks of concern within the community. Local guides' roles are to assist in making connections, bridging individual and group interests together.

Community workers can benefit from understanding the norms and practices of community development from the perspectives of those involved in grassroots community change. Ungar and colleagues conclude by stating that local "guides are exemplars of how to be community minded in our work as professional(s) . . . the work of the helper needs to be more invisible, immersed, and fluid . . . they work with and in communities, integrated into the seamless associational life of the community (Ungar, et al., 2004, p. 559–560).

TYPES OF RELATIONSHIPS

There are four major types of relationships in community practice (Homan, 2003): confrontation, negotiation, collaboration, and co-optation. Each type of relationship occurs under particular circumstances, and each is associated with particular activities to create community change, which have both benefits and drawbacks. Each of these relationships characterizes the connection between those who benefit from the change and those who are the target for change. Targets may be primary or secondary. **Primary targets** are those who can give you what you want, while **secondary targets** are those who have influence over the primary target.

Confrontation

Confrontation, the first type of relationship in community practice, is based on opposition, disagreement, or incompatibility between groups. Conflicts can exist at multiple levels, including intrapersonal, interpersonal, groups, organizations, communities, between jurisdictions within a country, and internationally. In community practice, **confrontation** is energy applied to change a target to respond to the needs of a benefit group. It is useful when the target is unmotivated, unresponsive, unprepared, or wants to keep a low profile.

Some confrontational activities include making the issue personal (e.g., attacking an opponent's character), lawsuits (e.g., taking a matter to court), cutting off support (e.g., media campaign about harm caused by a local business), and civil disobedience (e.g., traffic blockade) (Marshall, 1995). Some benefits of confrontation include strengthening the benefit group who is fighting a common enemy, feeling and appearing stronger, intimidating an opponent, and catching the other side off guard (Chalmers & Bramadat, 1996). Some limitations of confrontation include the need for a strong commitment from members, heavy emotional costs to the group if it loses, reluctance of the other side to work together in the future, and members who fight for the sake of fighting (Rubin & Rubin, 2001).

Negotiation

Negotiation, the second type of relationship in community practice, describes a relationship where there is potential for give and take. Negotiations are apparent in relationships at many levels, from parent-child interactions, to committee meetings, within a variety of organizations and in international politics. In community practice, **negotiation** is energy applied to obtain something from the target, which may come at the expense of the benefit or target group. Negotiation is useful when the target has given some legitimacy to your group's interests, you want to work together with them in the future, or there is something that they want from you, too (Tesoriero, 1999).

There is a difference between positional and principled negotiation. **Positional negotiation** is a win-lose situation. The target group gives up something, and the benefit group gains something. **Principled negotiation**, on the other hand, is a win-win situation (Thompson, 2000). The target and benefit group each give up something and gain something. Examples of negotiation activities are presenting demands (e.g., the membership will not accept anything less than a 5 percent raise); setting deadlines (e.g., an agreement must be reached by Monday); using good guy/bad guy scenarios (e.g., a new negotiator with softer stance is brought in); or walking out (e.g., leaving the negotiations before agreement is reached) (Nierenberg, 1995). Some benefits of negotiation include having a good chance of getting something you want, setting a precedent that disagreements can be worked out, willingness to see both sides gain, and setting the stage for getting together to discuss other issues (Thompson, 2000). Some limitations of negotiation include the following: losing some non-negotiable items; distracting from more important issues; settling for too little and weakening your position and handling the process poorly, resulting in little chance for effective negotiation to take place in the future (Bouwen & Taillieu, 2003).

Collaboration

Collaboration is the third type of relationship in community practice and describes a relationship where there are shared interests and efforts between groups. Collaborations occur at many levels: within families, neighbourhoods, communities, and groups within broad boundaries (e.g., a city). In community practice, **collaboration** means working together, sharing resources and ownership. Collaboration is useful when your group has resources to offer, wants to enter into a working relationship with another group, would like to teach the other group about your work, or increase the other group's dependence on you (Homan, 2003).

Some collaborative activities include open communication (e.g., informal information sharing), clear agreements (e.g., visioning documents), shared decisions (e.g., formal meetings with minutes taken), trust and respect, as well as mutual goal-setting and progress evaluation (Medved, Morrison, et al., 2001). Benefits of collaboration include the following: increased resources on an issue, increased influence, mutual support, complementing of one another, and increasing dependence on each other (McKnight, 1994). Some disadvantages of collaboration are nonresolvable problems, fear of talking about problems because of progress made, unequal share of responsibilities or credit, and energy needed to maintain the relationship (Mulroy & Shay, 1997).

Co-optation

The purpose of co-optation, the fourth and final type of relationship is community practice, is to convert targets into supporters. In community practice, **co-optation** is the deliberate intent to influence an external critic by bringing that critic into the group. Co-optation is useful when the target is not a good candidate for confrontation, there are members of the target group who may be amenable to affiliation, or there is a particular critic you would like to silence.

Some co-optation activities include inviting the person to sit on an important committee, giving the message that the target is a team player, and asking the person to assist in solving real problems with your group (O'Toole & Meier, 2003). The benefits of co-optation include silencing a critic, gaining some information about the competition, gaining access to a community that has not been open to you, and possibly forming an alliance with little investment. Some limitations include the potential of giving too much information about your own organization away, being influenced by the person brought in, and being seen as manipulative (Homan, 2003).

GETTING INVOLVED

Relationships are the basis for community development, and it is, therefore, important to practise their development. Many post-secondary students have experience forming and maintaining relationships with family, friends, and organizations. Putting this new knowledge into professional practice, however, may be a new experience. You can get involved in numerous ways—by contacting local grassroots neighbourhood organizations, or civic, provincial, or national groups. For example, many cities have directories of community services, which list the service providers in your local area, the location, and a contact person. Some organizations accept volunteers, or are looking for students who are available on a part-time or seasonal basis for work. Getting involved by working with an organization provides hands-on learning about local issues, people, and resources that will help you in your professional career.

Another way to get involved is through community-based learning opportunities that are part of programs in community development, social work, nursing, psychology, education, child and youth care departments, and many others. **Community-based learning** includes learning activities that bring together theory and practice (Kenny, 2001). Students in community-based settings learn about textbook concepts and how they apply to the real issues in communities. There is also a great deal of wisdom and expertise that cannot be found in a textbook. By interacting with community residents, students learn first-hand about the realities of community development.

SUMMARY

- General systems theory includes a set of principles about how relationships form and are maintained, between individuals and groups.
- There is a range of motives, values, and styles that affect the success of relationships.
- Power is part of all relationships. There are different forms of power and authority, which are present in all communities.
- Professional, organizational, and community contexts influence relationships in community development practice.
- There are four types of relationships, including confrontation, negotiation, collaboration, and co-optation, which have different benefits and drawbacks in community development practice.
- Community-based service learning provides an opportunity to get involved in the community, learn outside of the classroom, and make a contribution.

DISCUSSION QUESTIONS

1. Think about your own community. Where you live? Whom do you associate with? What are the micro, meso, exo, and macro systems that you interact with?

2. What motivates you to be involved in the community? What strengths do you possess that can help out? What do you need to learn more about?

3. What are the benefits and drawbacks of each type of power for professionals involved in community development practice?

4. You are employed as a counsellor. Lately, several clients have told you they are worried about getting to evening appointments safely because of their fear of being hassled by youth in the community. How would you propose changing this situation? Why?

5. Imagine a scenario with you as the community worker with a group of inner-city neighbourhood residents who are concerned about a crack house on their block. How would you help, by using what you know about different types of relationships?

WEBLINKS

www.ccednet-rcdec.ca/en/pages/learningnetwork.asp The Canadian Community Economic Development Network

www.cedworks.com/index.html Centre for Community Enterprise

http://communityaction.ca/ Community Action

www.canadiansocialresearch.net/ Canadian Social Research

KEY TERMS

Action system, p. 58

Arena of action, p. 58

Benefit system, p. 58

Boundaries, p. 57

Charismatic authority, p. 64

Codes of ethics, p. 65

Coercive power, p. 64

Collaboration, p. 70

Community asset
   map, p. 56

Community-based
   learning, p. 71

Confrontation, p. 69

Co-optation, p. 70

Differentiation, p. 58

Entropy, p. 58

Equifinality, p. 58

Exo level, p. 59

Expert power, p. 64

Feedback, p. 57

Focal system, p. 57

Genogram, p. 55

Hierarchy of needs, p. 60

Information power, p. 64

Input, p. 57

Interface, p. 57

Legitimate power, p. 64

Macro level, p. 59

Meso level, p. 59

Micro level, p. 59

Mission statement, p. 67

Negative entropy, p. 58

Negotiation, p. 69

Output, p. 57

Permeable, p. 57

Person-in-environment,
   p. 55

Population served, p. 67

Positional negotiation,
   p. 69

Primary targets, p. 69

Principled negotiation,
   p. 69

Rational-legal authority,
   p. 64

Referent power, p. 64

Relationships, p. 57

Reward power, p. 64

Role, p. 57

Secondary targets, p. 69

Service area, p. 67

Social network map, p. 55

Staffing, p. 68

Subsystems, p. 57

Suprasystem, p. 57

Synergy, p. 57

Target system, p. 58

Traditional authority, p. 64

Transactions, p. 59

chapter six

Process of Community Development

LEARNING OBJECTIVES

After reading this chapter you will be able to:

1. Describe community development as a process of 10 steps.
2. Understand and apply principles of applied research for community development practice.
3. Recognize the different roles that community workers play in community development initiatives.
4. Describe how principles of adult education apply to community development.
5 Understand basic steps in organization building.
6. Understand different ways to prepare for taking action.
7. Describe how evaluation can have a positive impact.

Effective community work is a process of engagement at a local level. In this chapter, we describe community development as a process that includes several steps. The 10 steps in this chapter refer to activities that community workers may be involved in. They are not universal or sequential, but they are interrelated and often overlap. A process of community development includes the following: (1) defining the professional's role, (2) learning about the community, (3) entering the community, (4) consciousness-raising, (5) assessing needs and assets, (6) setting goals, (7) organization building, (8) strategizing, (9) taking action, and (10) evaluation.

CHAPTER OUTLINE

COMMUNITY DEVELOPMENT AS A PROCESS

A process is a sequence of operations or events that takes up time, expertise, and other resources in order to produce some outcome. Community development "takes charge of the conditions and factors that influence a community and changes the quality of life of its members" (Frank & Smith, 1999, p. 7). The process of community development, therefore, involves changing conditions and factors that influence a community. The **outcome** is the product of community development: that is, some change to the quality of life among members of a community.

Community development is, moreover, a process of engagement to facilitate change in a broad range of settings. In some settings, the impetus for change comes from within the community itself. In such settings, community workers have an instinctive "feel" for how to bring about change without ever having read a book or registered in a course on the subject. In other settings, workers come from outside the community and often bring a good understanding of the change process. But they may have no history and, initially, no credibility with the local population.

Regardless of the setting, several matters need to be considered part of a community development process. In this chapter, we describe them as a sequence of steps. The process begins with a clear description of the community worker's role and ends with an evaluation of the outcome. The model we present in this chapter was developed by David Hannis, and is summarized in Figure 6.1.

Each step in this model is closely connected to the one before it, as well as the one after it. Good working relationships are necessary to take next steps. For example, a community worker needs to know about the community in order to develop any credibility. Information from a newspaper or community newsletter can provide some background. But developing relationships with those who are actively involved in the community can teach the worker a great deal more about local realities, including concerns, capacities, and approaches taken. As a community worker, it helps not only to be to be prepared, but modest, respectful, and curious.

FIGURE 6.1	A Community Development Process

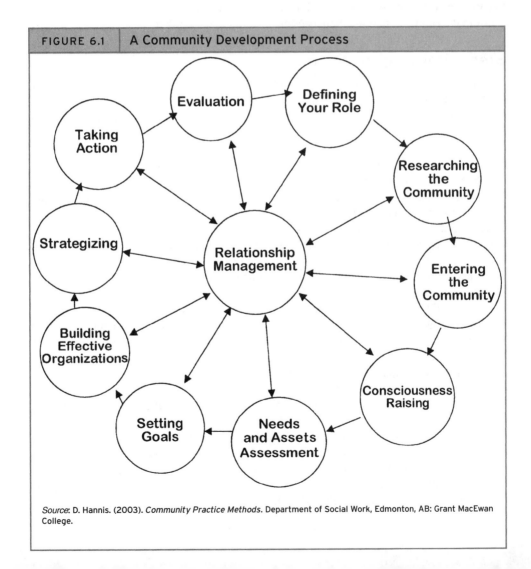

Source: D. Hannis. (2003). *Community Practice Methods*. Department of Social Work, Edmonton, AB: Grant MacEwan College.

Community development takes place in a sequence. Theoretically, each step is as important as the others, and the same sequence applies in all communities. In practice, however, these steps usually overlap. For example, informal evaluation will occur right from the beginning of community development efforts and influence the likelihood of advancement to the next step. And some steps are more important than others. For example, a worker who is new to a well-organized community will have to attend very carefully to the third step (entering the community). Only after trust begins to develop can the other work begin. Sometimes a worker's role is limited to particular steps. For example, a worker may enter into a community after a needs assessment has been done. As well, community leaders may need additional resources to take next steps. The issue is not to determine what is needed and who should be involved; instead, it may be to assist with proposal development and fundraising.

Effective community work requires awareness of all the steps in this model and recognition of the importance of relationships at each point. Relationships hold communities together and drive community development, so we cannot overstate the importance of relationship development and maintenance for the community worker.

Step 1: Defining the Professional's Role

Community workers engage in a variety of activities. The demands of the situation often influence the particular responsibilities a worker carries. Employers also influence the types of activities engaged in as well as practical matters like hours of work and timelines for results.

Roles of Community Workers Community workers may fill roles of *organizer*, *teacher*, *coach*, *facilitator*, *advocate*, *negotiator*, *broker*, *manager*, *researcher*, and *communicator* (Well & Gamble, 1995). In community development, *organizers* work with people to arrange harmonious or united action (Gonzalez & Norwine, 2004). In community practice, the role of effective teaching includes rituals of engagement; sharing of power; a culture of participation based on safety, respect, and high expectations; and skilful and humble facilitation to create solidarity and equality within the group (Zachary, 2000). The role of *coaching* is about assisting a team. In community development, a coach progresses through different stages, from initial suspicion and distrust to meaningful connection (Jarrett, Sullivan & Watkins, 2005). A *facilitator* helps a group reach agreement without personally taking any side of the argument. Skilled facilitators assist groups in several ways, including helping group members feel safe and understood, keeping them on track, managing time, enforcing ground rules, checking for clarification, and summarizing contributions (Schwarz, 2002). In community development, an effective facilitator is crucial for group cohesion and growth (Wiatrowski & Campoverde, 1996).

An *advocate* is one who speaks on behalf of someone who lacks knowledge, standing, or skills to speak for him or herself. In community practice, an advocate is often a member of an affected group that seeks social change (Abram & Hoge, 2003). Next, *negotiation* is a process of dispute resolution. In the role of negotiator, a community worker may work with other groups to agree on a course of action, bargain for advantage, or craft an agreement (Musil, Kubalcikova, Hubikova, & Necasova, 2004). A *broker* is a third party who brings different groups together (Hardcastle, Powers & Wenocur, 2004).

In the role of *manager,* a community worker directs, manages, or controls with success. In community work, it is important to follow the advice of Driscoll (1996): "a useful starting point is to consider that every individual—regardless of role or experience—is a continual learner and potential leader" (p. 95). The next community development role is one of a *researcher*, who plans, collects, and interprets data. In community development, researchers and community residents work together to define a research problem, take action, and evaluate their work (Kelly, 2005). Communication takes many forms, which community workers should be aware of and able to use where appropriate: in person, postal mail, express mail, e-mail, fax, telephone, hand delivery as well as Web sites (Oakley et al., 2004).

Context and Community Worker Roles It is important that community workers have the same interpretation of their role as their employers. There are several approaches to community work, and each is legitimate. However, some are more appropriate to certain situations than others. Most social action strategies, for example, are confrontational and transformational. They strike at the very heart of local power structures. A decision to support such activities should not be taken lightly, either by a career community worker who might have family to support and a mortgage to pay for, or by the employer, if the agency is in receipt of government funds. Community workers take a big risk when they are seen to bite the hands that feed them.

Community workers might see their role as mobilizing the "voiceless" in the name of social justice. Their employers, however, might see it as one of promoting services and setting up support groups. Community workers should, at the outset, clarify their own expectations as well as those of the employer. A clear job description that defines parameters helps. Good community work practice involves working with people, not doing things for them. However, not all employers appreciate this distinction.

Good community work takes time. Workers should not bow to pressure from employers and funders to impose "quick fix" programs onto communities. Finally, a related but no less important consideration when defining a worker's role are the hours of work. Much of what community workers do occurs outside regular office hours. Attending public meetings, board meetings, and training sessions takes time. Usually, these meetings happen in the evening or on the weekend. Employers and workers (as well as their families) need to understand this.

Step 2: Researching the Community

A community can refer to a place or a group of people, or both. There are at least four good reasons to gather some preliminary information about communities: **responsibility** (need to have some context for what is going on), **credibility** (knowing some people and their histories gives credibility), **versatility** (knowing the key stakeholders and influences gives flexibility in who you approach, and how you work), and **accountability** (knowing what people want in the community makes you responsible to help make it happen) (Hardcastle, Powers & Wenocur, 2004). Community workers can learn about communities both indirectly and directly, from secondary and primary sources.

Secondary Sources Community workers can find information about communities in a variety of existing information, or from **secondary sources**. For example, many communities make available data on basic demographics, including number of people, sex, employment, and income. A community may also offer a directory that lists social agencies in the area. Using these sources, workers can learn about who lives there and what some of the local issues are. Secondary sources of information can be found in local libraries within community agencies, public libraries, schools, colleges and universities, as well as provincial and federal departments. Departments of health, education, justice, and social services keep statistics. Sometimes reports are easily available. National, provincial, local, and community newspapers may also be good sources of information. Some are searchable by keyword. Community workers may find many of those documents on the Internet, using a regular search engine. Some useful Canadian sites are listed at the end of this chapter.

Primary Sources Direct information is gained from spending time in a community and interacting with residents. This information comes from **primary sources**. Driving or walking through a community, shopping in local businesses, eating in restaurants, or attending a public gathering can provide a great deal of information about a community. As well, chatting with a shopkeeper or with other patrons can teach a great deal about important issues and social relationships. Students may have opportunities to learn in the field. Some courses may include opportunities for field experience. For some students, going to a place they haven't been before requires stepping outside of a comfort zone. But the learning students do in the field is important to understanding the life of a community, and will be of great benefit to students in their careers.

A Combination of Sources As mentioned, primary sources or secondary sources can be used to learn about community settings, structures, processes, and functions. For example, one key primary source approach is *fieldwork*. In **fieldwork**, you learn about the experiences of people who live in a community through direct observation and interaction. But you can also learn about a community through a combination of primary and secondary sources. For example, it is helpful to know the demographics of a community as well as who the service providers are, in order to know what to base questions on (e.g., how does a high family poverty rate affect people in this community?) and who to ask (e.g., the director of a family services agency that has been the community for several years).

There are a variety of pieces of information about a community that can be useful. Community workers are often concerned with the presence or absence of services for a particular group in a particular area. Information about demographics and local agencies are very useful for this purpose. However, other information, such as the local **power structure**—those who are seen to have influence (Hunter, 1969)—is also very useful when first learning about a community. Sources of this information may be indirect (e.g., contributors to community newspapers, agency board members, local politicians), or direct (e.g., asking who the influential people are in this community).

Step 3: Entering the Community

Once workers have some clarity about their roles, from their own perspectives and their employers', plus some background about the community, they are prepared to enter it. At this point, community workers should have a beginning sense of the social networks operating in a community. An important concept for community workers is social capital, which we discussed in Chapter 1. **Social capital** refers to social networks and ways of getting along that facilitate coordination and co-operation for mutual benefit (Putnam, 1995, p. 66). It has been argued that social problems, in general, stem from a decline in social capital (Putnam, 2000). However, a community strong in social capital (e.g., many gathering places, broad participation in communal activities) may still have more than its share of particular social problems (e.g., poverty, crime). The converse is also true: a community weak in social capital (e.g., social distance between neighbours, high security fences guarding properties) may not have its share of the same social problems.

Community workers seeking entrance into a community are aware of the "movers and shakers," their interconnections, as well as the strength of those connections. Communities with high social capital, then, have strong social networks and *external boundaries*. Communities with low social capital have strong *internal boundaries* between members. A community that is rich or poor in social capital presents different challenges for the community worker coming from the outside. For example, in communities where there are already strong connections between members, the boundaries may be very carefully protected. If community boundaries are protected by traditions, customs, or protocols, the worker needs to find out what these are and show respect for them. In communities where there are not strong relationships between members, the barriers to relationships must be considered (e.g., distance, mistrust, or lack of knowledge between members) and addressed.

Insiders and Outsiders Community workers may be new or may be experienced with the community they want to work with. They may or may not already have ties or membership to the community. Some workers live in the community, and others may live outside of it. In community work, those who reside inside a community of interest or are members of it are **insiders**. Those who reside outside the community of interest and are not members of it are **outsiders**.

For the community worker, there are benefits and drawbacks to both situations. It may take longer for an outsider to gain the trust and a thorough understanding of the community than someone who is well known to the community. On the other hand, outsiders may have the advantage of being seen as relatively neutral, with no links to a particular group or agenda. Outsiders may be able to view the community with a more objective eye. An insider, however, may already have an established status in the community and will understand more clearly the nature of local power structures and the appropriate techniques for harnessing the energies of the local players. But others may view the connections an insider has as biasing new discussions about change.

There are similar pros and cons related to a community worker's decision to live either within or outside the area of work. A community worker who resides outside the area may be able to find some balance between work and family life. But community members may view the worker as someone unable to fully understand the community's needs. On the other hand, a worker who lives inside the area may find it difficult to separate family and work, which can be a difficult balance to find and maintain. However, living inside the area does provide first-hand knowledge about the community, personal motivation to see things, and the benefit that others who live there will see the worker as one who understands.

This insider-outsider relationship is complex (Jewkes & Letherby, 2000). For one thing, *insider* and *outsider* are relative terms. A worker may be considered as an insider at times and an outsider at others. In some circumstances, outsiders can occupy roles of insiders (e.g., a member of a board of directors for an Aboriginal community development organization who is neither a member of the local community nor Aboriginal, but can offer legal advice). In other cases, insiders can occupy roles of outsiders (e.g., a resident who has developed a reputation for focusing on a single cause that affects him, but little else, and may be shunned at a community meeting).

Approaches For the worker who is just beginning to connect with a community it is vital to resist the temptation to impose programs that might not meet the real needs of residents, and instead take the time to get to know the area well. Community practice is a process that takes time and cannot be rushed. The most important initial task is to build trust, and this is best accomplished when there is a sincere intent to listen without judgment.

Many community workers find it helpful during these early stages of engagement to identify key meeting places and community leaders. Workers can offer practical services to residents, such as transportation, support, and information. At this point, the worker is primarily an active listener, who is interested in finding out how people view their community and what they think needs to be changed to make life better for them.

The worker can continue to collect information about history of the community, issues residents are facing, and organizations that serve the area. Community workers should attend to factors that strengthen and weaken the community and consider different ways that workers could help. Moreover, community workers will find it helpful to be aware of the existing formal and informal systems of power, and how workers may be perceived.

Reactions Community members may associate workers with the potential for change to the power structure within a community. Such changes are likely to draw different reactions. Community workers have to be able to recognize the potential effects of community work. Workers should take precautions to avoid problems that can accompany the community development process and resident *empowerment*. Power dynamics may change in several ways, and each type of power will draw different reactions: *power over*, *power with*, and *power from within* (Starhawk, 1990).

Power over is coercive. It requires submissiveness, dependency, fear, and obedience and is an unhealthy form of power that is oppressive and debilitating. People who have power over (e.g., police or slum landlords) may be threatened by a community worker bringing people together to talk about change. A community worker should expect reprisal from these players (e.g., selective law enforcement or evictions) if the proposed changes threaten their interests (e.g., making arrests or profits).

Power with is the type of power many community workers strive to achieve because it is collaborative power that comes from the right to speak and be listened to, and from not imposing ideas on others. This type of power depends on the strengths of individuals who combine their influence for change. It is a strong force. Some communities may have had very little experience with this kind of power. The worker needs to be sensitive to this, and recognize its expression while avoiding problems. People who have experienced power as force may perpetuate the same power when other alternatives are presented. For example, a worker who is assisting a community group with a proposal to bring in new co-operative housing units for older adults may find that the group is already making promises for the units to their friends, who live outside the community.

Power from within is personal power that comes from feeling safe enough to speak out, join with others, and withdraw consent from being subjected to someone else's power. Usually, it is this form of power that changes most dramatically at the community level. As individuals begin to sense through their collective activities that they can have more control over their lives, there is great potential for community change. The worker needs to be aware, however, that this can be difficult for some individuals. *Power from within* can also have some serious consequences (e.g., being cut off by family members after bringing charges for abuse). A sensitive worker will realize that this process is different for each person, occurs at a different rate for each, and the costs may sometimes outweigh the benefits of change.

Empowerment means finding both an individual and group voice. It is the result of experiencing power from within as well as collective power. Empowerment is often fraught with emotion, which, in a community, can be either energizing or disruptive. When people who have been silenced for the greater part of their lives begin to find their voice, that voice may, in fact, be an angry, confused, irrational, and frightening one. At such times, people feel vulnerable and exposed. Community workers must exercise great skill to ensure that groups do not get deflected from their central purpose by interpersonal misunderstandings. Also, workers should guard against the potential for people who have begun to experience their power to become disillusioned and retreat to the safety of silence or cynicism.

Step 4: Consciousness-raising

Consciousness-raising is "cognitive activity prompted by questioning, with the hoped for outcome of a new awareness of self in relation to all society" (Lee, 2001, p. 35). In community development, the purpose of consciousness-raising is to develop a **critical consciousness** among a group of people: that is, the ability to see social, economic, and political oppression, and to take action against oppressive elements of society (Freire, 1970; 1973). In the 1950s and 1960s, consciousness-raising groups were associated with students' and women's movements and involved small-group discussions about each attendee's personal experiences, which then evolved into political discussions.

Consciousness-raising is crucial to effective community development work. Using principles of adult education, a group can develop a critical consciousness on which to base action. Challenges for workers include staying aware of their own biases, attending to people's different ways of learning, as well as remaining sensitive to differing interests within the community. A visioning exercise, discussed below, can be helpful for building critical consciousness and confidence.

Adult Education What is adult education? According to the United Nations Educational, Scientific, and Cultural Organization, **adult education** is,

> . . . the entire body of organized educational processes, whatever the content, level, or method, whether formal or otherwise, whether they prolong or replace initial education in schools or colleges, and universities as well as in apprenticeship, whereby persons regarded as adult by the society to which they belong develop their abilities, enrich their knowledge, improve their technical

or professional qualifications, or turn them in a new direction and bring about changes in their attitudes or behavior in the two-fold perspective of full personal development and participation in balanced independent, social, economic, and cultural development; adult education, however, must not be considered as an entity in itself, it is a sub-division, and an integral part of, a global scheme for lifelong education and learning. (UNESCO, 1976, p. 2; Tuijnman, 1996, p.4)

Adult education is about teaching adults, which differs greatly from teaching children. Adult education is voluntary and is a lifelong process. Adults have accumulated experiences that influence new learning. Adult learning, furthermore, is practical, and motivation comes from the expectation that new knowledge will help achieve a goal. There is also a difference between "formal adult education" and "nonformal adult education" (Foley, 2004). Professional educators using a formal curriculum provide **formal adult education**, and completion usually leads to some qualification (e.g., a certificate, diploma, or degree). **Non-formal adult education**, on the other hand, refers to formal instruction, but in a non-continuous way (e.g., nonviolent crisis intervention training for staff).

Nonformal adult education was first practised in Canada when indigenous peoples taught the European settlers. They taught the colonists about local geography, climate, shelter, and survival methods (Draper & Carere, 1998). The colonists went on to form study groups during the seventeenth and eighteenth centuries that had a religious focus (Chapman, 2005). Then, during the nineteenth century, agricultural societies and mechanics institutes provided working people with opportunities for self-improvement through education (Radforth & Sangster, 1987). In the early twentieth century, connections to organized labour groups, such as the People's Forum in Winnipeg, included lectures and discussions on such issues as world war, language of education for children, and a need for increased political involvement by the working class (Welton, 2005). At about the same time, on the East and West Coasts, fishers and miners, living in poverty because they were getting so little for their product, organized to learn about the reasons why, and what they could do about it (Brown & Cook, 1974).

Two types of adult education are particularly relevant to community development: community education and radical adult education (Smith, 2005a; Smith 2005b). **Community education** is education for the community, within the community. Fostering community is of central importance; the purpose of community education is to bring people into a social network to encourage dialogue and learning. It has been defined as "a process designed to enrich the lives of individuals and groups by engaging with people living within a geographical area, or sharing a common interest, to develop voluntarily a range of learning, action and reflection opportunities, determined by their personal, social, economic and political needs" (Scottish Community Education Council, 1990, p. 2).

Radical adult education builds on the sense of community, and takes it a step further. The purpose of radical adult education is to understand and challenge oppression through collective action. The goal is critical consciousness.

Challenges in Consciousness-Raising All community workers have biases, because no one is totally value free. Each of us will view the communities we work with through our own lenses. These lenses are culturally based and have been shaped by such factors as our gender, our social class, our age, our ethnic background, and the level of education we have received. Community workers need to be aware of their biases if they are to avoid the tendency to impose their values and their solutions.

When consciousness-raising, the worker must consider how individuals learn, and promote opportunities for those with different styles. Visual learners, auditory learners, and tactile learners each learn differently. Visual learners learn primarily through seeing (e.g., diagrams, photos), auditory learners through listening (e.g., speakers, discussions), and tactile learners, through moving and doing (e.g., role-playing, learning activities).

Some community residents might be uneasy about their quality of life, but unable to express the causes of their discomfort or what should be done about it. In such cases, the worker may introduce the community to outside materials and knowledgeable resource people to stimulate learning and promote new insights.

Communities may not speak with one voice or have a clearly defined understanding of their needs. In fact, many communities that need the help of a community worker are fractured and divided. The challenge for the community worker is to determine who to listen to. Often the views of the formal power holders in a community will contradict those held by the less outspoken members. But, in order to help the latter group, a community worker will most likely require the support of the former.

Building Visions and Confidence Consciousness-raising can begin with telling our own stories and listening to others in a nonjudgmental way (Kuyek, 1992). Through this process, similar concerns begin to emerge and become the preliminary stages of empowerment. Empowerment, in turn, leads people to identify the changes they would like to make in their lives. Box 6.1 illustrates one method of beginning the process of consciousness-raising.

BOX 6.1	Building Visions

Exercise: If you were to improve your community, what would you change? Consider:

- Your relationship to the natural world.
- The food you eat: what, where, when, and how it is produced.
- The house you live in: How should it be designed? Where would it be situated?

- How you and your children are educated
- How and who makes decisions and how do we deal with dissidents?
- How people relate to each other: travel, share information, for example.
- How are we going to free our "inner child"?
- How are we going to let people know what we are doing?

Closely related to consciousness-raising is confidence-building. A community may have a very clear united vision of what needs to change, yet lack the confidence or knowledge to act upon it. At this point, the community worker functions as a trainer and self-esteem builder by introducing the community to relevant information and by making the commitment to support local people.

Step 5: Assessment of Needs and Assets

A **needs and assets assessment** is a set of procedures and tools for determining a community's needs and assets. *Needs* refer to the gap between what is and what should be. There are several reasons that a community may want needs studied and documented. One reason may be to determine whether there is any need for action. Another may be to help design or modify some contemplated action. Finally, the results of a needs assessment may be used to confirm the presence of a need that has already been identified and justify an already decided action. A balanced assessment also takes into account community assets. **Assets** are resources that help bridge the gap between what is and what should be. The community may want assets studied and documented in order to recognize, build on, or enhance the distribution of local capital.

The purpose for conducting a needs assessment influences the approach followed, procedures employed, and tools used. Once the purpose is clear, a plan can be developed. Implementing the plan includes collecting and analyzing data as well as preparing the results. The following sections describe steps in conducting a community assessment.

Developing a Plan There are several pieces of information that are useful for planning a community assessment. A solid plan should contain the following: (1) a definition of the community, (2) the intended audience for the results, (3) specific questions to be answered, (4) the approach to be followed, (5) resources available for the assessment, and (6) procedures to be employed.

The community of interest may be a geographic community, a social community, or a combination of the two. For example, a neighbourhood, small town, or reserve each has its own boundaries. However, the community could also be a particular group of people, such as youths, adults, or seniors. In other cases, the community may be a particular group of people within a particular area (e.g., youth in an inner-city neighbourhood, older adults living in a reserve community, or adults in a small town). There are no right or wrong answers. However, defining the community does influence the applicability of the results. For example, one cannot determine the needs and assets of adults in a small town by talking to older adults living on a reserve.

The audience for the needs assessment must be taken into consideration. As well, there are several layers of accountability, which must be clear to the planners (Heaven, 2005). Assessors are accountable to the people who are studied, those involved in the research process, the sponsoring organization, community stakeholders, and the community in general. There are other potential audiences, which may include others outside of the community, such as members of the media or the general public. If the audience is diverse, consideration may be given to providing results in alternate forms. For example, there could be a community meeting for participants, a presentation to project staff, a detailed written report to the sponsoring organization, a luncheon for local leaders and policy-makers, or a community feast for everyone. Additional audiences may include the media at a press conference or the public through an article submitted to the newspaper. Knowing ahead of time who you want to receive the results can save money and effort. For example, if the funder does not require a detailed report, it may be unnecessary to spend money on a professional-looking document.

Knowledge of the community of interest and the audience for the results help narrow the plan's focus. For example, if the community is interested in youth issues and the funder supports research on violence, the topic is further narrowed. Community assessments are often broad in scope. Having specific answerable questions helps to guide the process. For example, an organization wants to learn about responding to youth violence in your neighbourhood. Do the members want to look at all kinds of violence, or just gang violence? Do they want to focus on girls or boys, or both? Is there an age range to focus on? Do they want to find out what services are already available for youth in the community? What about the kinds of services that are needed? Do they want to find out what youth themselves think? What about the perspectives of their caregivers, service providers, or local leaders?

The types of questions also influence the approach. A distinction can be made between qualitative and quantitative research (Miles & Huberman, 1994). **Qualitative researchers** focus on words. They know, in advance, only roughly what they are looking for, and they become immersed in the subject matter. **Quantitative researchers** focus on numbers. They know in advance exactly what they are looking for. They remain objectively separated from the subject matter. The benefits of qualitative research are the richness of results and attention to the broader context. The benefits of quantitative research, on the other hand, are the specificity of results and precise measurements. For example, in an assessment of youth violence, a community may be interested in the crime rate for young offenders in a particular neighbourhood and whether the crime rate has gone up or down in recent years (quantitative). Or the community may be interested in the experiences of the youth who have been involved in crime to find out about their circumstances, concerns, and ideas for making things better (qualitative). Most assessments include both qualitative and quantitative data.

The time, cost, and technical assistance required to do a community assessment vary. In some cases, the community has several months to do an assessment. In other cases, there may only be a few weeks. What is achievable depends on the timing. If, in the youth violence example, you wanted to know if there was more violence in the warmer months, the timing would be a factor. Costs of needs assessments also affect what is achievable. Is there money to hire staff? For example, if there is funding to train and pay local youth to help out, they would benefit from the project in an immediate and tangible way. Individuals may handle certain aspects of needs assessment, such as questionnaire development or data analysis, more efficiently if they have done it before. If the community does not have these skills or the time to learn them, funds might be efficiently spent hiring out this work.

Data Collection and Analysis There are many ways to obtain information for a community assessment. A community may make use of existing data or collect their own. Although there are multiple organizations that collect data, they do so for their own purposes. Government data from federal, provincial, civic, or band levels and departments (e.g., for youth violence, possible sources include police reports and provincial court statistics) may be available at no cost. The data may not be specific to the local community or reflect issues the community is interested in, however. And in some cases, existing data is available at the community level, but at a cost (e.g., customized census data tables). In addition, local organizations or agencies may have data they are willing to share (e.g., youth-serving agencies and organizations where youth perform community service hours). Often, however, needs assessments require the collection of at least some original data.

Original data can be collected in several ways. **Public forums** and **listening sessions**, for example, are ways to gather general information about community members' perceptions of issues and options. Both are exploratory and open to attendees from a range of backgrounds (e.g., staff from youth justice, Elders, local business owners, victims of crime). However, a public forum is a much larger event and includes a broad range of issues

(Francisco & Schultz, 2005). Some suggestions for planning a public forum or a listening session include holding meetings at different sites that are both accessible and comfortable; holding meetings at times that avoid conflicts with other activities (e.g., work, school, holidays, community events); advertising deliberately (broadly for a public forum, and selectively for a listening session); personally recruiting key participants; providing transportation; serving refreshments; and providing time for mingling (Wolff & Kaye, 1994). The same authors offer suggestions for conducting a public forum or listening session, including designating a facilitator or discussion leader; introducing the purpose, agenda and people; selecting recorders to take notes; including time to discuss concerns, barriers, resources, and actions; and providing a written summary to all participants (Wolff & Kaye, 1994).

More formal methods of data collection that are used in community assessments are focus groups and surveys. A **focus group** is an in-depth, in-person qualitative interview with a group of people who have similar experiences. Usually groups are between 6 and 12 participants. A moderator guides a discussion using an outline of questions, and responses are recorded using video cameras, audiotapes, or written notes. Some advantages of focus groups include the following: a wide range of information can be collected in a short time; unanticipated topics that are related to the main topic can be explored; and complex sampling techniques are not required. But there are disadvantages: results cannot be compared or generalized; there are potentially high staff costs (facilitation and transcribing); and the quality of results depends a great deal on the skill of the facilitator.

A **survey** is a standard series of questions asked of a portion of a population. Surveys can be administered in person, by telephone, or by mail. However, efforts should be made to ensure that each member of the population has an equal chance of participating. In a survey, each person is asked the same questions in the same way. The number of responses required depends on the analysis that is planned and the size of the population. Some advantages of surveys are that specific questions can be answered, responses are standardized, and results can be said to represent a population. Disadvantages of surveys are that they require a population (accurate count of all possible participants), a complex sampling procedure, and potentially complex data analysis procedures.

Both focus groups and surveys are used in needs assessments. In general, surveys have written, close-ended, relatively narrow questions, which are quantitatively scored. In contrast, focus groups generally have spoken, open-ended, and relatively broad questions, which are qualitatively analyzed. The analysis of data—whether it is quantitative or qualitative—ranges from simple to complex. The amount of data and the sophistication of analysis affect the resources needed to work with it.

Once the analysis is complete, the results to the assessment questions should be apparent. The evidence is in, but a course of action is not always clear. Making a decision about next steps is where goal setting becomes very important.

Step 6: Setting Goals

Sometimes, the people that community workers spend time with have had limited experience articulating goals. This beginning stage of personal and collective empowerment can feel strange and frightening at first. As well, the process of community development will likely be accompanied by conflict as delicate egos get bruised, neighbours disagree, power bases get challenged, and old animosities surface. Workers must be skilled at implementing decision-making processes and handling conflict effectively as they move groups of people with common needs towards defining and prioritizing shared goals.

   Goals are brief statements about what a group wants to accomplish and should be based on reality. Goals are not broad, idealistic, and abstract like **visioning statements** (Kouzes & Posner, 1996). For example, a vision statement might be to have a healthy, vibrant community, in which the voices of youth are valued. A goal may be to form a neighbourhood youth council. Once decided, goals provide a way for a group to stay on track. For example, how will holding a community feast for families help us achieve this goal?

   A brainstorming session may be useful. **Brainstorming** is a group process that is focused, time-limited, and creative (Nijstad & Paulus, 2003). Those in attendance shout out solutions to a particular problem, or a focus for discussion, without any editing or criticism of ideas. Ideas are recorded for all to see. When the time is up, the group selects those they like the best. If further narrowing is needed, participants may generate criteria for the best idea, and perhaps apply a numerical ranking system to prioritize them (Parks & Sanna, 1999). As a general rule, workers should help define simple, realizable, specific, short-term goals, which people can have fun planning and implementing. As they begin to see results, experiences of working together will provide motivation to take on more challenging goals. For example, a group of neighbours who don't know each other very well might start the process of community building by planning a street dance or by inviting an elected representative to meet with them to hear their concerns. Later on, they might work on an area redevelopment plan, seek funding for a community centre, lobby against a pulp mill, or pressure the police department to assign more officers to their area.

Step 7: Organization Building

Change at the community level usually begins with a group of people who come together in an informal way to identify common needs and then develop collaborative strategies to meet those needs. It can be helpful to establish an organization, especially if the group is trying to raise funds. Many external funders will provide money only to incorporated non-profit organizations, and some, only to registered charities.

   Every organization needs a name and a mission statement. A **mission statement** briefly describes the purpose, business, and values of an organization (Radtke, 1998). Following are three questions that can help guide this process: (1) What are the needs we exist to address? (2) What are we doing to address these needs? (3) What beliefs guide this work? To continue with our earlier example, consider a residents' group coming together to address the issue of youth violence in its community. The problem may be a rise in gang activity. Contributors to this problem are the need for youth to belong, limited work experience, and a lack of viable local jobs. The residents' group may work from the following beliefs: each person has intrinsic value and self-worth, the culture of each youth needs to be respected, and family health is the overall goal. A mission statement for this organization, then, could be the following: "Our mission is to make a positive difference in the lives of youth, through group training, support, and encouragement of employment skills and real-life work experience based on individual strengths and cultural teachings, and to promote healthy family life within our local communities."

   An organization needs a board of directors, who may be the same people who crafted the mission statement. A **board of directors** is a body of people who have the responsibility to guide and oversee an organization (Watson, 2005). If there is a paid staff member, this person is usually the executive director, who is directly accountable to the board. However, some non-profit organizations have no paid staff and the work is spread out among the board members and others who help out.

Incorporation and Charitable Status Before going down this road, organizations considering incorporation should be sure that they can document the need for their organization, that they need incorporation to do what they want to do, and that they are interested in the long-term future of the organization (Ravensbergen, 2004). A non-profit organization can be incorporated federally or provincially (Corporation Centre, 2005). The process is straightforward, but can take time. Legal advice from someone who has gone through the process can be very helpful. As well, several Web sites deal with the specifics of non-profit incorporation, so we will not be describe the process here. Some of those Web sites, however, are listed at the end of this chapter. The benefits of incorporation include legal recognition of non-profit status and a guarantee that the name of the organization will be protected so that others cannot use it.

An incorporated non-profit organization can also apply for charitable status, which is handled through the Canada Revenue Agency. The process can, however, take a year or more, as there are numerous requirements to obtain and maintain charitable status. But it does give organizations the ability to issue receipts to donors for income tax purposes, and makes them eligible for certain tax exemptions.

External Funding The community worker may help to establish a board of directors, clarify responsibilities, develop bylaws, and set up accounting. However, a major challenge for new organizations is securing funding. An important first step is finding one, or ideally several, potential funders. There are many places to find this information. The Internet is an invaluable resource, as many funders have Web sites. Also, lists of Canadian funders can be found on portal sites such as **CharityVillage.ca**. Before putting a lot of work into a formal application for funding, however, it is important to make sure that your group is ready to put in that effort. Some funders make money available only to certain types of organizations, in particular places, for certain initiatives. Workers may find it useful to contact a representative from a potential funding agency to discuss mutual interests. It may be that you do not fit their mandate, or that there is going to be great competition for few dollars. Community workers could also get some helpful tips for preparing a successful application.

Funding rarely comes without strings. Because funders have priorities as to what they will and will not support, new organizations must not distort their aims merely to obtain grant money. Losing sight of its purpose in order to secure funding can cause the community to feel controlled by some outside bureaucracy, disempowered, and creatively stifled. When seeking funding, workers should also try to diversify the sources of income as much as possible to avoid becoming overly dependent on one single source. As well, workers must respect the funder's rules for accounting for expenditures.

Step 8: Strategizing

The process of strategizing involves determining the most effective ways of achieving goals, and requires the development of an action plan. There are many examples of community action plans that have been used in Canadian communities, including Red Deer, Alberta (McQuaig, 2005), Whitehorse, Yukon (City of Whitehorse, 2004), and Hamilton,

Ontario (Brown, Foye, Nawagesic, & Welch, 2000). These reports, and others, generally include common elements such as *objectives, strategies, changes expected, action steps,* and *implementation* of the plan.

Objectives are statements of what you want to accomplish by when. They are concrete and action-oriented. A common way to evaluate objectives is to apply the **SMART-C** approach: goals or objectives should be *Specific*, potentially *Measurable, Achievable, Relevant* to the change effort, be accomplished by a certain *Time*, and appropriately *Challenging* (Community Toolbox, 2005). For example, an objective for a youth violence initiative may be to increase the employment rate for youth in the community by 10 percent over three years.

Strategies, the second element of a community action plan, describe how the objectives will be accomplished. Strategies should identify the level that is targeted (e.g., individuals, families, organizations, institutions), and specify whether it is universal (e.g., all youth in the community) or selective (e.g., only those at high risk for gang involvement). Are the factors to be addressed personal (e.g., knowledge, skills, beliefs, education, training, experience, cultural norms, and social status) or environmental (e.g., social support, available resources, local services, and policies), or both? Strategies should also include the targets for change (e.g., youth who are gang-involved), the agents for change (e.g., local leaders, Elders, and youth-serving agencies), as well as ways they can be connected (e.g., through cultural gatherings, agency outreach). Approaches that workers may use include information and skills training (e.g., work experience), challenging key barriers (e.g., establishing relationships with prospective employers), enhancing supports (e.g., programs for youth who want to leave gang life), and changing incentives (e.g., alter requirements for social assistance among mothers with common-law partners).

Next, the **changes expected** are the responses of the target to the strategies. Workers need to be selective. For each strategy, they should identify the changes desired (e.g., regulations to hire from the community, cultural teachings in local schools, or new programs for youth in existing organizations), or the new programs to be created (e.g., integrated housing, education, and work experience). As well, workers must consider the impact of the change on different groups. For example, a protest outside of a local contractor's organization to make a statement about the lack of local people hired might lead to a backlash from employees and local customers. If community workers plan to approach funders that other groups in the community have either received funding from or are seeking funding from, they should consider collaboration as a way for both groups to get some funding.

The **action steps** specify who will do what by when. For each strategy, there must be agreement on the action to be taken, those who are responsible, and when the action is to be started or completed. Before taking action, workers need to consider who else might need to be involved or at least informed. For example, a group is planning to hold a block party, which would likely create some noise and traffic congestion. It would be wise to check with local authorities beforehand in order to avoid being shut down or fined, or getting bad press.

Implementation of the plan is actually performing the planned action. It is often helpful to prioritize or sequence activities. For example, do some actions need to be taken before others? Are some easier or quicker to complete than others? Are some more crucial to the initiative than others? Are some better for building motivation than others? Workers may be instrumental at this point. They can help by pacing a group that has become bored with planning and just wants to "get on with it" before thinking things through. Conversely, they may also assist with motivating a group that is comfortable planning, but reluctant to take action.

Step 9: Taking Action

Taking action can be frightening to someone who is not used to being assertive, and this is especially true if the action is confrontational. For example, a community worker might work with a group of people from a community to help them protest a new housing development. Such activities often meet with some resistance and verbal abuse. Because of this, community workers must prepare people ahead of time and make sure that such events are accompanied by some social activities to ensure that people do not become discouraged and feel isolated.

Practice can help reduce concerns and improve confidence. **Role-playing** is a useful way for people to explore a social situation, including their actions and the consequences. Community members might find it helpful to practise in advance of a particularly important meeting—for example, appearing before council to argue for funding for a project. Role-playing allows people to imagine themselves in certain roles (e.g., a bureaucrat, a politician, or a spokesperson for a community organization lobbying for funding) and practise acting as those people. Role-playing may also sharpen public speaking skills, help develop new insights, and strengthen advocacy skills.

After a group has appeared before a committee or taken some direct social action, time should be set aside to debrief feelings and plan further courses of action. Of course, such sessions should also be followed by some enjoyable social event to promote camaraderie, group membership, sense of purpose, and feelings of belonging. In this way, both the individual and the community begin to feel more powerful.

Step 10: Evaluation

Evaluation is often mentioned as the last step in the community development process when, in fact, it should be one of the first. Whenever a group is planning a particular course of action, time should always be set aside to consider the question of how the activities will be assessed in the long run. How will the group know if its goals have been achieved? What information should the group collect on an ongoing basis to strengthen any future applications for funding?

There are two types of evaluation: formative and summative (Klodawsky, 2002). An outsider, an insider, or both can conduct either type of evaluation. A **formative evaluation** is conducted at regular intervals as a project progresses. This type of evaluation groups information about how a group might change or fine-tune its operations as it goes along. A **summative evaluation**, on the other hand, is completed after the activity has been ongoing for some time, or at its completion.

Funding is usually conditional on some form of evaluation document being provided. So when preparing reports, community workers must understand the mandate of the funders and the reasons they provided financial support in the first place. Workers should use language that is familiar to funders. Evaluations are always easier to conduct when the project's mission, goals, and objectives are clearly defined. There are many ways for workers to document what they did and provide evidence about how well they did it. Thinking about these issues at the beginning, planning, and staying on track, can save trouble at the end (e.g., rather than trying to explain to a funder after the money is spent that the group diverted from the original plan).

A FINAL COMMENT

The real world is often quite different from the one that educators and textbook writers assume exists. This is certainly the case in the area of community development. While this chapter has outlined a logical process of activity, the situation may be much less orderly in practice. Employers may be impatient for results or funders may set impossible deadlines. As well, various events may occur that throw the community into crisis. There are also ever-present interpersonal conflicts that may drain energy and create major obstacles to change. Workers may simply burn out. When these events happen, community workers must recognize them as normal, practise some form of self-care, maintain a healthy perspective, and seek out support from professional colleagues. While their jobs may sometimes be difficult, workers should try to remain optimistic and, above all, retain a sense of humour.

SUMMARY

- Community development is a process that includes defining the professional's role, researching the community, entering the community, consciousness-raising, assessing needs and assets, setting goals, building organization, strategizing, taking action, and evaluating.
- Roles of the community worker vary significantly, depending on the community, employer, and personal style.
- There are many secondary and primary sources of information about a community.
- Adult education principles are very useful in community development for consciousness-raising.
- Needs assessments may include several types of data that are collected or organized for a particular purpose, and used to take action.
- New organizations may consider applying for incorporation and charitable status.
- Taking action requires careful consideration of the purpose for each action and the expected outcomes.

DISCUSSION QUESTIONS

1. What approaches would you take to learn about a community that you are not familiar with?
2. Which roles and steps of community development are you most comfortable with, and least comfortable with? Why?
3. Write a job description for a community worker position. Include tasks and responsibilities, personal attributes, hours of work, lines of accountability, and required credentials.
4. Draft an action plan for a community initiative. Use examples from this chapter or an example of your own choosing (real or imagined). Identify a goal, actions, and expected outcomes. Include alternatives considered, choices made, and a rationale.

WEBLINKS

www.aboriginalcanada.gc.ca/ Aboriginal Canada Portal

www.policyalternatives.ca/ Canadian Centre for Policy Alternatives

www.cprn.org/en/ Canadian Policy Research Network

www.canadiansocialresearch.net/ Canadian Social Research

www.socialjustice.org/ Centre for Social Justice

www.ncwcnbes.net/ National Council of Welfare

www.povnet.org/ PovNet News

www.statcan.ca/ Statistics Canada

www.oise.utoronto.ca/CASAE/maineng.html Canadian Association for the Study of Adult Education

www.charityvillage.com/cv/guides/guide4.asp#Incorporation Charity Village–Incorporation Links

www.charityvillage.com/cv/ires/fund.asp#can Charity Village–Sources of Funding

KEY TERMS

Accountability, p. 77

Action steps, p. 89

Adult education, p. 81

Assets, p. 84

Board of directors, p. 87

Brainstorming, p. 87

Changes expected, p. 89

Community education, p. 82

Consciousness-raising, p. 81

Credibility, p. 77

Critical consciousness, p. 81

Empowerment, p. 81

Fieldwork, p. 78

Focus group, p. 86

Formal adult education, p. 82

Formative evaluation, p. 90

Goals, p. 87

Implementation, p. 89

Insiders, p. 79

Listening sessions, p. 85

Mission statement, p. 87

Needs and assets assessment, p. 84

Non-formal adult education, p. 82

Objectives, p. 89

Outcome, p. 74

Outsiders, p. 79

Power from within, p. 81

Power over, p. 80

Power structure, p. 78

Power with, p. 80

Primary sources, p. 78

Public forums, p. 85

Qualitative researchers, p. 85

Quantitative researchers, p. 85

Radical adult education, p. 82

Responsibility, p. 77

Role-playing, p. 90

Secondary sources, p. 78

SMART-C, p. 89

Social capital, p. 79

Strategies, p. 89

Summative evaluation, p. 90

Survey, p. 86

Versatility, p. 77

Visioning statements, p. 87

chapter seven

Skills for Working
in Communities

LEARNING OBJECTIVES

After reading this chapter you will:

1. Recognize the characteristics of a bureaucracy, and understand the challenges as well as opportunities they present for community work.

2. Understand a process for planning, conducting, and evaluating an effective meeting.

3. Describe a variety of fundraising approaches and strategies, including qualities of a competitive grant proposal.

4. Form productive teams that manage their people resources well.

5. Recognize and address different types of conflict that arise in community work.

6. Understand different ways of advocating for yourself and community members from within and outside organizations.

7. Effectively utilize the media to communicate with others about your community.

8. Recognize different approaches to networking in community work.

In this chapter we address skills needed for community work, which community workers develop through a combination of education and experience. Specifically, workers should understand bureaucracies, group process, and fundraising. When it comes to bureaucracies, community workers should know what they are and how to navigate through them. Since community work can involve many types of group work, workers should also have skills in running meetings. Fundraising is crucial to community work, so workers will find that skills at obtaining funding very helpful. Additional skills for working in communities include team building, conflict management, advocacy, social marketing, and networking, all of which we will describe and discuss in this chapter. Not all community workers will have particular strength in all of these areas. Therefore, recognition of your own abilities as well as the abilities of those around you is important. Making use of different strengths among members of the group will help move the process more effectively toward its goal.

CHAPTER OUTLINE

NAVIGATING BUREAUCRACIES

Community workers should understand the nature and function of bureaucracies. **Bureaucracy** refers to the organizational structure of a government and its institutions, which are organized as a hierarchy, and within which multiple units with specific functions exist. Each unit acts according to a set of rules and procedures. Workers must be both knowledgeable and skilled to navigate within or through large, complex systems. In addition to government departments, such as health, social services, education, and justice, many corporations, hospitals, and schools may be organized in this way. Often, workers are employed by these systems. And sometimes, community residents are employed by the same systems, or otherwise involved with them (e.g., as clients). Effective community work may require collaborating with these systems (e.g., requesting funding or other resources from them), or seeking changes to the way they operate.

Characteristics of Bureaucracies

The word *bureaucracy* comes from the French word *bureau,* meaning "office," and from the Greek suffix *kratia,* meaning "power." The ideal bureaucracy was first described by a German political economist and sociologist named Max Weber (1864–1920). Weber described the ideal bureaucracy as a way to manage large and complex tasks. The fundamental structure was based on an elaborate and hierarchical division of labour (i.e., a complex model of accountability beginning with the immediate supervisor, and ending with the person at the top, such as the prime minister, premier, or chief executive officer). There were also explicit rules that applied to all (i.e., policies and procedures that must be applied to every occurrence without any bias). According to Weber, the staff members were full-time, lifetime professionals whose job defined them. However, the staff had no ownership in the means of administration, in their jobs, or in the sources of their funds (i.e., staff use the equipment of the organization to perform duties; and the person fits the job description—the job is not made to fit the person). Staff members were also expected to live off a salary, and their income was not related to job performance (i.e., they had no ownership of any part of the organization) (Turner, 1993). A bureaucratic official can exercise judgment and skills, but only for the impartial execution of assigned tasks. In this system, personal judgment must be sacrificed if it runs counter to official duties (Weber, 1968; 2003).

Even ideal bureaucracies can fall victim to their own success in several ways, such as *overspecialization, rigidity, groupthink*, and *Catch-22* (Farazmand, 2002). In **overspecialization**, the units or people in the organization become so specialized that they fail to recognize consequences or implications of their efforts for others. For example, the financial unit in a large organization may not see that making sudden changes to procedures for processing payments has detrimental effects on other units, staff, or the community residents (e.g., changes to income support payments). Another drawback of bureaucracies is that policies and procedures applied with great **rigidity** make simple matters complicated and time-consuming. For example, getting authorization and reimbursement for $20 to cover costs of coffee and juice for a meeting may be so complicated and time-consuming that the community worker simply pays it out of pocket. The system may also find it difficult to handle new situations (e.g., an urban hospital responding to an influx of new residents from northern communities who have different backgrounds, languages, and customs).

Groupthink is another drawback of bureaucracy that refers to conformity of opinions among members of a group. In bureaucracies, staff loyalty and assumptions of organizational virtue can contribute to problems. For example, beliefs that the government and church held about the need to colonize Aboriginal peoples in Canada led to the establishment of residential schools in the 1800s. The significance and impact of these efforts is very real for many Aboriginal peoples today:

> [W]hile it is not uncommon to hear some former students speak about the positive experience in these institutions, their stories are overshadowed by disclosures of abuse, criminal convictions of

perpetrators and the findings of various studies such as the Royal Commission on Aboriginal Peoples, which tell of the tragic legacy that the residential school system has left with many former students. (Indian Residential Schools Resolution Canada, 2006)

The last school did not close until 1996. In 1998, the federal government apologized for its role in the development and administration of the schools.

As bureaucracies grow in size and complexity they become less coordinated and experience a "Catch-22," where new rules are inconsistent with others, and functions are duplicated. **Catch-22** comes from the title of a satirical American novel about World War II, where an absurd rule, known as Catch-22, keeps a pilot from getting out of the military (Heller, 1961).

The term is commonly used now to refer to any type of double-bind, which is essentially a no-win situation (e.g., being given contradictory messages to "go get coffee" and "stay by the phone"). In large bureaucracies, staff doing essentially the same job, but in different units, may have widely discrepant procedures to follow (Clague, Dill, Seebaran, & Wharf, 1984).

Bureaucracies and Community Workers

Tension can exist between bureaucracies and community workers employed within them (Glassman, Swatos, & Rosen, 1987). They may have competing values related to decision-making, power sources and distribution, organizational change, communication, and the place of procedures (Zastrow, 2002). While community workers desire democratic systems for decision-making, bureaucracies tend to make decisions autocratically. Community workers favour distribution of power among employees, while bureaucracies generally distribute power vertically. A professional community worker values client influence on the system, while in a bureaucracy, those at the top exert the greatest influence. Community workers favour creativity and flexibility within a changing organization, while bureaucracies, due to size, can at times lean toward consistency and stability. Communication, for community workers, is personalized, bi-directional, and usually in-person, while in bureaucracies, communication is top-down. And while both community workers and bureaucracies espouse decision-making and responsibility, community workers favour shared leadership, but bureaucracies often have hierarchical leadership.

Workers employed in bureaucracies need to develop their own coping styles if they are to remain community-centred and avoid burnout (Hardina, 2002). There are many ways of coping. For community workers, it helps to have a support base both within and outside the organization. Workers need to be aware of their own style and way of working, and seek out other like-minded persons. Understanding the formal workings of the organization is also helpful; community workers should follow the appropriate documentation procedures and avoid power struggles and conflicts.

Understanding the structure and function of the organization can be a great asset (Heskin, 1991), which means recognizing both the formal structure (e.g., organizational chart) and the informal structure (e.g., the way things really happen). Community workers need to identify who holds the real power and influence in the organization; this may not be the same person as the boss. Workers should recognize the informal ways of getting things done, and use them (Milofsky, 1988), and they should be aware of the organization's behavioural norms and try to subscribe to them. For example, community workers can wear clothing, use language, and write in a style similar to that of the rest of the organization's members. Workers can also attend social functions and use them to strengthen their relationships with peers and supervisors.

The key word for working within a bureaucracy is *compromise*. Successful workers make efforts to fit in, be accountable, and do what the organization expects. However, at the same time, community workers must be aware that their primary focus is meeting the needs of the community. Sometimes this will bring workers into conflict with their employers. However, employees who have taken the time to build credibility within the organization may be more effective in implementing a strategy that will ensure that the community's needs are met (Selden, 1998).

Bureaucracies and Communities

Bureaucracies and communities are organized and function differently (Wilson, 2000). In many ways, the values that underlie successful community development efforts clash with the values of bureaucracies. In a discussion of the differences between community and bureaucracy in an educational context, Beairsto (1999) contrasts each perspective. Bureaucracies have specific goals, while communities have broad purposes. Bureaucracies function according to rules, and communities function according to rituals. The unit of interest in a bureaucracy is the role (i.e., what function the person serves), while in a community relationships are central (i.e., who you know and how you get along). The focus in a bureaucracy is on tasks, while in the community it is on people. Bureaucracies are interested in efficiency, and communities are interested in fecundity. Bureaucracies are held together by compliance, while communities are held together by commitment. Bureaucracies value predictability and control, while communities value responsiveness and creativity. Bureaucracies emphasize productivity and growth, while communities emphasize preservation and sustainability.

In their book *Bureaucracy and Community* (1990), Davies and Shragge suggest that administrators in bureaucracies often experience pressures to meet the conflicting needs of the system and those of the community. The bureaucracy expects them to practise good fiscal management, set clear goals, establish measurable outcomes, and be accountable to senior levels in the organization. Unfortunately, much of the work done at the community level is "fluid," seemingly chaotic, political, conflictual, difficult to measure, and sometimes conducted in an emotionally charged environment (MacNair, Gross, & Daniels, 1995), all of which bureaucratically organized systems dislike. Administrators who respond sympathetically to community pressures may risk the disapproval of their organizational superiors and be perceived as disloyal.

However, it is these very administrators whom community workers and residents may be interacting with, for the purposes of advocacy (a topic covered later in this chapter), or securing resources (in the fundraising section, also in this chapter) (Ramos, May, & Ramos, 2001). Administrators, who have people below them as well as people above them, can be powerful allies to the community worker. They give orders to those below, and have connections to those who make the big decisions (e.g., funding). To work effectively with administrators, community workers will find it helpful to know who those administrators are as well as their formal and informal connections. One good way to do this is to get involved. Workers can attend meetings where administrators are present or join the groups of which they are members. Workers can also develop relationships with them, and make sure that the administrators know what the community is doing and what it wants to do. Sometimes, administrators make quick decisions to disperse funds. Community workers will find it advantageous, therefore, to be known to those who fund what they are involved in. As well, when given any money, even a very small amount, workers need to demonstrate that they have used it for the purpose it was intended, in the time frame required, and that it had the desired impact. If workers can be trusted to spend a small amount well, they might get more in the future!

RUNNING MEETINGS

Meetings are integral to community work: they are the mechanisms through which decisions are made, actions are planned, and progress takes place (Jacks, 1986). Effective meetings have a purpose and help a group accomplish its goals (**task dimensions**). They also build and maintain relationships (**relationship dimensions**). Balancing task dimensions and relationship dimensions of a meeting is a challenge for even the most experienced facilitator or chair (Hawkins, 1997). However, both are necessary to encourage attendance and involvement of community members. Recognition and respect of the voices of members who may not have felt like valued members of a group is important for the development of trust, and some level of trust is necessary for group members to get work done together. A good facilitator or chair addresses both relationship and task needs of members.

A meeting has four phases: *planning, setup, running the meeting*, and *follow-up* (Kaye & Berkowitz, 2005). Effective planning involves working with others at the very beginning. A small group can identify a goal for the meeting, invite only those who need to be there, send out an agenda ahead of time, and if additional information is needed, prepare it. It also helps to think about the dynamics of this group (Hardcastle, Powers, & Wencur, 2004).

The second phase of a meeting is setting up, which is about logistics. Community workers should get in the habit of starting and ending on time. This may mean having a set time to end, or ending after members have had a chance to speak. It is a good idea to sign people in. A list of names of those attending, their affiliations, and contact information can come in handy. The meeting space should be accessible and comfortable. People should be able to see one another, so set-up in a circle is best, if possible. Refreshments are a nice addition. Coming early and staying late gives people a chance to chat informally, which is important. Also, a regular time (e.g., at 7:00 p.m., every second Wednesday of the month) can be helpful. But don't meet for the sake of meeting; always have a purpose.

Running the meeting is the third phase of the meeting and is the job of the chair. The chair asks members to introduce themselves, introduces special guests, and also gets agreement on the agenda. The chair is a busy job. The chair should stay neutral, keep the discussion on track, encourage people to participate, and be conscious of the time (Zepatos & Kaufman, 1995). The chair should also summarize decisions that have been made. It is important to remember that decision making does not require everyone to agree that the same thing is the best thing. A more reasonable standard is whether everyone can live with the decision (Payne, 2000).

Finally, follow-up is what comes after the meeting. Follow-up may involve getting some feedback about the meeting itself before people have actually left (Hawkins, 1997) and should also include telephone calls or follow-up correspondence. As well, a meeting summary is helpful. Some meetings have minutes, which is a formal record of the business covered (e.g., announcements, plans, decisions). If at all possible, the chair should not be responsible for the minutes. Taking and distributing minutes are important tasks that can be shared among members, with different people taking turns.

Chairing a Meeting

The chair should be aware of procedural as well as emotional issues. While much of what happens in a meeting is set up before the meeting takes place (Tropman, 1980), even the best plans can go awry. A major role of the chair is to support the group process so that it meets its goals. There are four main interventions that chairs can use to keep the discussion on track: *providing support*, *mediating conflict*, *probing and questioning*, and *reflecting feelings* (Hardcastle, Powers, & Wencur, 2004).

Providing support (e.g., "That's a really good point") helps to create a positive climate for the expression of ideas, especially ones that are unpopular or unconventional (Sampson & Marthas, 1981). **Mediating conflict** (e.g., "Lets get to the root of this difference of opinion, so that we can move on") helps members to be more open in their communication and address disagreements before they become entrenched (Sampson & Marthas, 1981). **Probing and questioning** (e.g., "Can you say some more about that?") helps to expand upon a point that might have been missed or left incomplete, while giving members permission to give more details. **Reflecting feelings** (e.g., "This decision is a very difficult one for the group") directs members to discuss the feelings behind their perspectives on an issue.

In reference to the conduct of members at meetings, Deep and Sussman (1998) describe three sets of behaviours they call "The Good," "The Bad," and "The Ugly." Under "The Good" behaviours are arriving on time; coming prepared (having read the agenda and done homework); listening to others (understanding what is said); speaking to contribute to the goals of the group (rather than speaking just to hear oneself talk or further a particular cause); building on the present discussion (not changing the focus to suit another purpose); maintaining a problem-solving focus (not a blame-placing attitude); staying upbeat (concentrating on what can be done, not what cannot be done); challenging bad ideas; helping the chair out (if she or he misses something); and staying dedicated to the goals. Under "The Bad" are missing meetings without notice; waiting until the meeting ends to share ideas in private with another member; ignoring the agenda and moving the discussion where you want it to go; monopolizing discussions; continuing to talk about the past (not focusing on the issues at hand); criticizing members instead of ideas; reacting defensively to well-intentioned criticisms of your ideas; doing other work or daydreaming during meetings; not returning on time after a break; and having your cell phone or beeper go off during a meeting. "The Ugly" behaviours include using the meeting as a place to deal with personal agendas; intentionally holding back needed information; breaking confidentiality (telling others about private matters discussed during the meeting); criticizing the group to outsiders; disrespecting another group member during a meeting (interruptions, name-calling); failing to support decisions made by the group (which all members helped pass); and speaking to the media without the group's approval.

Evaluating a Meeting

Reflecting on and evaluating a meeting are crucial for planning the next meeting. There are several pieces of information that should be taken into account when evaluating a meeting's effectiveness, including the people, the purpose, the atmosphere, the place and space, and closure (Kalbfleisch, 2004). The following questions provide some guidelines about how to analyze a meeting's effectiveness:

- *People.* Who was at the meeting? What points of view did they represent? How did they conduct themselves at the meeting?
- *Purpose.* Why was the meeting called? Were most of the people at the meeting there for the same reason? Meetings are called for a variety of reasons, including information giving and receiving. Were the people giving information also prepared to listen to others? Were important decisions being made? Were people clear about the options/choices (if any) being presented? Was everyone who had something to say, heard?
- *Atmosphere.* Were the people relaxed, angry, confused, supportive, or frustrated? Was the meeting well organized with the purpose of the meeting clearly outlined by the chair? Was there an agenda? Were the talkative and disruptive contributors managed well? Did people feel comfortable directing their comments toward the chair? Were most people attentive? Were there any disruptive latecomers?
- *Place and Space.* Was the meeting held in the right place? Was it wheelchair accessible? Was the room big enough and warm enough? Could people relax over a cup of coffee either before or after the meeting? Were the acoustics good? Was there enough parking?
- *Closure.* Did the meeting come to an orderly conclusion? Were most people clear on what had been achieved at the meeting? Were clear plans for future action developed? Were clear tasks assigned to individuals? Did others present share your perceptions of the effectiveness of the process applied at this meeting?

FUNDRAISING

Community development efforts require both financial and nonfinancial resources to do the work required. Although money is important, **in-kind** or nonmonetary assistance is of great benefit. Often, groups already have in-kind resources, such as the time and effort of members. However, a group may also have access to meeting space, photocopies, and basic office supplies (e.g., paper and pens). Groups may seek other in-kind contributions (e.g., an old computer and printer, telephone access) as part of their fundraising efforts, and leave this option open for those who do not have money to give. When approaching possible funders for money, it may be useful to document the in-kind contributions your group is already receiving. This shows that others have made a commitment to the work the group is doing.

Community workers need to be clear from the outset what the resources are for. There are right and wrong answers to the question, "What's the money for?" Wrong answers focus on things (e.g., salaries, telephone bills, rent, reaching a fundraising target, or paying overdue bills), while right answers focus on people (e.g., making a difference, helping others) (Brooks, 2004). Workers need to make clear the specific ways that their group will help people. Each group and issue will be different. For example, one request may be for funding to help adults learn to read or speak a language in their culture, while another community development initiative may need funds to train youth to be neighbourhood guides.

The impact of the first request could be to reduce family violence and bring families together, by helping parents in the community learn about their culture so they can teach it to their children. The impact of the second request could be to reduce crime in the community and promote positive school attendance by enlisting local youth to serve as neighbourhood helpers during evenings and weekends. In these examples, the money is needed to *help families and youth in the community*.

Community workers may consider different fundraising approaches. Grassroots groups use four major types of fundraising: *institutional grants*, *special events and product sales*, *direct marketing*, and major *individual donors* (Wyman, 1995). **Institutional grants** are available from multiple sources, such as governments, businesses, foundations, service clubs, the United Way, religious groups, unions, employee funds, professional groups, and other non-profits. **Special events and product sales** are similar in that the group gives the donors something in return for a donation (e.g., garage sales, socials, concerts, raffles). In **direct marketing,** workers approach donors directly for assistance (e.g., mail-outs, telephone calls, advertising, television, and going door-to-door). **Major individual donors** are carefully selected individuals or small groups who are approached for donations (e.g., one-on-one meetings with individuals, wills and bequests, and small groups).

Of these four types, individual donations from major contributors may be the most efficient and least utilized (Hanvey & Philpot, 1996). However, they are also the most intimidating and require careful preparation of those making a request. Direct marketing takes time and people to build a support base, but over several years, if maintained well (e.g., donor lists kept up to date, regular communication from the group to donors) can be a stable source of funding (Dyer, Buell, Harrison, & Weber, 2002). Special events have the highest risk for return on investment (Ott, 2001). The event or sale may or may not be a success. Special events also involve upfront supply costs and are rather labour intensive. Community groups often pursue grants (Marx, 2000), and the relative advantages are the low cost with the potential for a high return. But the downsides are the short-term nature of the funding from these sources, and the sometimes-technical aspects of grant writing. Over the longer term, a combination of approaches may be necessary for a community group to maintain operations.

Writing Proposals

A *grant* is a sum of money given to a group or agency to address a problem or need in the community. Grant recipients use funding for their purposes, as outlined in a *proposal*. This is different than a *contract*, which is a legally binding document that describes the work that a recipient will do for the issuing institution. Although the format and length vary from funder to funder, a proposal usually includes a cover page or letter followed by a brief summary, introduction, assessment of need, project objectives, activities, evaluation process, future funding plan, and budget with justification (Coley & Scheinberg, 2000).

Before submitting a proposal, community workers need to consider the project, the group's readiness to put forward a proposal, and potential funders. Is the group ready to take this step? Both the clarity of purpose and commitment of members will be evident in the process and product of proposal development. How ready is the group to share control with someone else? Funders also have rules about who can be funded to do what, and where. Sometimes the project the group envisions is not eligible for funding. Is the group willing to modify the project in order to get funding? Or do members want to keep searching for another funder who would consider it as is?

Locating an appropriate funder can take some effort. There are many resources on the Internet, such as Charity Village: "Canada's super site for the nonprofit sector, with 3,000 pages of news, jobs, information and resources for executives, staffers, donors, and volunteers" (2006). The number of options, however, can be overwhelming. Community workers might need to do their own research and also seek the advice of a trusted colleague who can give the group some leads. As well, workers should identify those who fund projects in their area of interest, geographical location, and target population. They should also pay attention to the amount and type of funding they provide (Ontario Healthy Communities Coalition, 2005). Once workers identify a potential funder, they need to research the organization (e.g., by reading annual reports or results of previous competitions) and nurture a contact within that organization. This contact can help with clarifying process, language, or deadlines and may also act as a useful advocate.

Community workers must do their homework in the community. By gathering support for the project, meeting with respected leaders, and contacting politicians, church officers, and business people. Workers can get letters of support and find credible spokespersons from within the group who can present the proposal.

When writing the proposal, workers must give all the information that is requested, and ensure that the proposal is easy to read, by avoiding jargon, using headings and point form where appropriate, being clear, concise, creative, and honest, and identifying clear outcomes. Ultimately, the proposal should show that the writer is well grounded in the issues and in the community and is the best candidate for the very important work that is needed. Workers can try to anticipate and address questions that the reviewers of the proposal may have, including the following:

- Are the people promoting this project credible?
- Does this proposal fit into our mandate?
- Which other funders are involved?
- What is the evidence of need?
- Is this project viable in the long run?
- Is the budget reasonable?
- How will this project be evaluated?
- Have similar projects been tried elsewhere, and, if so, how successful were they?
- What are the consequences of not finding funding for this project?
- Could funding this project cause problems for us?
- What is the priority of this project compared to others that have been received?

If successful, workers must remember to keep funders informed, by inviting them to annual meetings, fun events, and briefing sessions, and by acknowledging their support in any publicity materials that are prepared.

TEAM BUILDING

Effective teams are vital to community work. They promote a stronger sense of competence among group members while getting larger, complex jobs done. A *team* is a group of people with a common purpose (Dew, 1997). The many tasks involved in that purpose require members of a team to work together. The benefits of **team building**—the process of establishing groups for a particular purpose—have been observed in a variety of organizations. Organizations benefit from teams because they boost motivation and productivity. People like teams because they break down political and personal barriers, eliminate distractions, and give team members an opportunity to have fun as they work (Dyer, 1995). Indeed, many successful organizations have moved away from "top-down" management models toward more horizontal decision making by using self-directed teams. In teams, creativity and innovation can flourish (Benson, 2001).

Characteristics of Effective Teams

Effective teams are more than just workgroups. They are alliances in which members are mutually committed to the same goal and share leadership as they work towards attaining it. **Effective teams** foster a sense of community within a trusting and supportive environment where members feel safe expressing dilemmas and contradictions. Team leaders function more as coaches than as supervisors. By fostering a sense of community, teams reduce burnout by providing members with a sense of belonging, a feeling that they have some influence over decisions, some emotional connection with each other, and enhanced loyalty (Plas & Lewis, 2001).

The word *team* is also an acronym for "together everyone achieves more" (Temme, 1996). Effective teams have several qualities, including trust, empowerment, and authentic participation (e.g., members are involved because they want to be, not because they have to be). An effective team is one within which good communication and decision making are fostered, while integrating the personalities of members and managing conflict (Estlund, 2003; Fisher, 1998). A good team embraces innovation, creativity, and risk taking, and is flexible in how the work gets done. The roles and responsibilities of members are negotiated and clear, as well as consistent with the overall goals and objectives. As well, contributions of members are recognized (Robb, Barrett, Komaromy, & Rogers, 2003). Leaders give support, provide direction, and give assistance. They also delegate, to help others learn.

Team Development

Team development is a series of stages. In a classic model, Tuckman (1965) and Tuckman with Jensen (1977) proposed that teams need to pass through several stages in order to achieve maximum effectiveness. The stages include *forming, storming, norming, performing,* and *adjourning*. In the **forming stage**, members are just getting to know one another, so serious issues and feelings are avoided. The emphasis is on the overall purpose, setting initial goals, and establishing ground rules. In the **storming stage**, team members start to address important issues, differences of opinion emerge, and feelings come to the surface. The emphasis in this stage is on addressing the tension; in a well-directed, open, positive team, members' questions and constructive challenges of one another foster creative energy. In a hostile environment, however, this tension can cause a team to revert to the safety of the first stage, become disillusioned with the process, fragment, or break up. The **norming stage** is characterized by the passing of the storm. There is agreement about what is to be done and how it is to be done. In this stage, emphasis is placed on cooperation.

Once the team has a shared vision and is able to work together (conflicts still arise, but are managed well), they enter the **performing stage**, when the team is at full strength and can accomplish its goals. Once the goals have been reached, the team moves to the **adjournment stage**. Emphasis in the final stage is on recognition of accomplishments, evaluation of team performance, and healthy separation.

Key to the effectiveness of team development is the recognition of personalities and styles of members. In order to move teams through the stages of development, leaders should be aware of factors that influence how individuals work. There are at least five needs that should be considered (Payne, 2000): *security, affiliation, competence, achievement,* and *power.* Leaders should ask themselves about each of these. For example, do members feel emotionally and physically safe? Do they feel part of a team? Can they handle the work? Do they feel they are making progress? Do they feel in control of what is happening to them?

Trust is the emotional glue that binds a team. Leaders can contribute to the development of a safe social environment and trusting relationships through modelling (Hare, 1992). For example, leaders should describe the behaviours of others rather than evaluate them; present ideas and interpretations as tentative rather than certain; be spontaneous and open, not manipulative and perceived as having a "hidden agenda"; present issues as problems with several possible solutions, rather than "forcing" one solution; and communicate empathic, confirming messages, rather than distant, detached, neutral ones (Stern & Hicks, 2000). As well, leaders should communicate a sense of being equal to, rather than superior to, the other person.

In a team, members may take on different roles. Recognizing the contributions that each role makes to the team helps foster it in others (Miner, 2002). There are at least four complementary team player roles (Payne, 2000): *contributors, collaborators, communicators,* and *challengers.* **Contributors** are task focused and provide good information. They are hard-working team members and dependable. **Collaborators** focus on goals. They think about the big picture. They are flexible and open to new ideas. **Communicators** focus on team process. They are good listeners and are often willing to help resolve conflicts. **Challengers** focus on questions and issues. They force the team to evaluate itself, and push to move forward.

In any team, disagreements are inevitable (Sharan, 1999), but are healthy to the extent that their resolution moves the team forward (Sims, 2002). Disagreements are destructive, however, when they override team goals (Tilstone, Florian, & Rose, 1998). Confusion and emotional hurt can be minimized within team meetings when specific problem-solving steps are followed: (1) state the problem clearly; (2) gather all points of view on the problem; (3) make a list of alternative solutions; (4) discuss the pros and cons of each alternative; (5) reach a decision by consensus if possible; (6) agree to revisit the situation at a later date to see if the agreed-upon solution needs revision.

Team Functions and Responsibilities

There are several critical functions and responsibilities of teams (Garner, 1988):

- To meet often, keep accurate minutes of the team's discussions and decisions, and share these minutes with all team members as well as the team's administrators.
- To assess the needs of both the individuals and the group served by the team, and to set priorities for these needs in order to plan the team's program.

- To develop written plans that specify the needs, long-term goals, short-term objectives, and strategies to be used, both for individuals and for the group.
- To coordinate the implementation of the team's strategies, interventions, and activities, including their timing and sequence.
- To maintain regular communication with the community and to coordinate services with any other agencies and institutions working with the same community.
- To schedule the work of all team members, including time off and the arrangement of alternative supervision and services for the clients.
- To allocate the team's program budget.
- To solve specific problems faced, using group approaches to problem solving and decision making.
- To evaluate the effectiveness of the team's program and services and to modify these according to need.
- To provide support, encouragement, and guidance to the team's members.
- To provide regular feedback to team members regarding the effects of their behaviour on the team members.
- To participate in the periodic formal evaluation of each team member's performance.
- To participate in the evaluation and selection of new team members.
- To generate and discuss new ideas for improving the total program of the school, agency, institution, or hospital.
- To serve as a consultant to others evaluating proposals for change.

Teamwork is enhanced when all members attend regularly scheduled meetings and participate in all aspects of the process, including problem solving and decision making. An active team member does not sit in the corner with arms folded or write personal notes. Active participation involves initiating discussions; presenting the maximum amount of information known about an issue without blaming; sharing perceptions; sending clear, unambiguous messages; being alert to the body language of oneself and others; and communicating a willingness to collaborate with other team members.

CONFLICT

Conflict refers to opposition between people, interests, or ideas. It is a part of everyday life and can strengthen communities, or break them apart. For example, a sense of community can be considerably enhanced by the identification of a common enemy lying outside the area, such as an insensitive government or a dishonest multinational. On the other hand, unresolved conflicts within communities can tear groups apart, promote disharmony, and seriously undermine attempts to enhance personal and collective power.

Often conflict is not handled constructively. It is ignored, smoothed over, or crushed out (Aureli & Waal, 2000). Just as parents and teachers sometimes take little notice of children with unique perspectives, those who are the most powerful rarely hear dissenting voices. Many who challenge a dominant group will not be listened to. Those who are, may be humoured, co-opted, dismissed, or ridiculed. Non-mainstream opinion is likely to be silenced in western democratic societies by subtle and not-so-subtle means (Fry & Björkqvist, 1997). Indeed, conflict has come to be seen as a negative activity rather than one that, if handled effectively, can strengthen democracy, promote greater awareness, and enhance the quality of our lives (Rahim, 2001). A community worker needs to be able to recognize potential and real conflict at the local level and facilitate the process of drawing it out into the arena of individual and collective consciousness, where it can be addressed in respectful and effective ways.

Types of Conflict

There are different types of conflict. Conflict occurs within groups (*intra-group conflict*) as well as between groups (*inter-group conflict*). It occurs over tasks and procedures, as well as interpersonal relationships (Barker, Wahlers, Watson & Kibbler, 1987). There may be disagreement over the content of a discussion (*task conflict*) or the procedures involved in reaching a goal (*procedural conflict*). **Interpersonal conflicts** are the same as "personality clashes" and are inevitable. Conflict may be a dispute over territory (physical, social, or work boundaries), values, goals, policies, or behaviours (Coombs & Avrunin, 1988).

Effects of Conflict

The effects of conflict are many and varied (Smith, 2005). They are also unpredictable. Conflict may be harmful to individuals, families, or communities (Bar-Siman-Tov, 2004) by increasing bitterness, alienation, and divisiveness. In fact, conflict can increase tension within or between groups to the point where relationships are weakened or destroyed (Rabie, 1994). Conflict can, however, be positive. It can increase unity, cohesion, and solidarity within a group, and strengthen group boundaries. Conflict can help define and sharpen community issues to improve decisions. Conflict may result in the restructuring of a group, recognition for a group, alliances with other groups, or the formation of a new group (Cahn, 1994). Conflict may also be a strategy for social change, for example, to disrupt normal channels of co-operation. And finally, conflict may in some cases become violent.

Managing Conflict

Central to the whole process of community development is the necessity for relationships to be managed constructively so that disagreements are recognized and processed in ways that enhance collaborative initiatives (Rabie, 1994; Rahim, 1990). Some practical ways to maintain effective relationships within communities are by celebrating individual and collective achievements, validating individual and collective wisdom, celebrating differences, recognizing the existence of dissension as well as the causes of it, handling conflict constructively, listening to people, providing appropriate training, and having fun.

Celebrating Individual and Collective Achievements Volunteer appreciation nights, outstanding citizen awards, notes of thanks, acknowledging contributions in newsletters, posting photos and letters of praise from dignitaries on meeting room walls, and listing group achievements in annual reports are all ways of celebrating successes. They promote group harmony and minimize destructive disagreements. When people feel unheard or unappreciated there is a danger that they will withdraw from the group or remain in it but become obstructionist and subversive.

Validating Individual and Collective Wisdom Numerous writers on adult education theory have emphasized the importance of recognizing the knowledge and competence that adults bring to the classroom and their need for that wisdom to be validated (Burns, 2002; Calder, 1993; McCaleb, 1994). Community workers function as adult educators in many ways, but should never presume to know more than the people they work with or attempt to impose "disembodied" theories onto the citizens they are there to serve. Adults will be most receptive to new ideas if those ideas seem relevant to them and are introduced in respectful and egalitarian ways. Adults who feel valued and free to express ideas without being judged are more likely to become co-operative team players than people who feel unheard and marginalized.

Celebrating Differences Weak communities are ones that are divided and where obvious differences are misunderstood. Effective community organizations are built on the basis of identifying common goals and celebrating diversity rather than fearing it (Cross, 2000). *Stereotypes* are generalizations stemming from tiny grains of truth that, if allowed to go unchallenged, can develop into hardened forms of racism, sexism, ableism, or ageism. Such perspectives work against the nurturing of strong and healthy communities. Key to addressing this is greater understanding and tolerance. Community workers can create opportunities for people from diverse backgrounds and with different values to get to know each other better. One way to do this is to host cultural events and discussion groups. It is important to make efforts to include people from a wide diversity of backgrounds into community organizations.

Recognizing the Existence of Dissension as well as the Causes of It A first step toward maintaining harmonious relationships is to acknowledge disagreements when they exist and to take steps to address them. Long-standing feuds might exist in some communities, and it might be difficult to uncover their precise causes. In such circumstances, it would be challenging to address these tensions in constructive ways. Any attempt to address long-standing issues should, therefore, be undertaken by someone who is seen by both sides as skilled and impartial. Sometimes the roots of conflict lie in some long-forgotten perceived injustice or an unfairly stigmatizing event that is no longer relevant. By acknowledging and understanding the root causes of such interpersonal tensions, a community worker can begin to help people to identify common goals and establish collaborative intentions.

During the early days of a community worker's involvement, it often happens that residents, who do not know each other well, communicate mainly through the worker instead of with each other. An early indicator of success is when local people begin to put aside their differences and develop the confidence to talk to each other directly.

Handling Conflict Constructively The basic steps for the healthy resolution of conflict between individuals and between groups are essentially the same (Cox & Brooks-Gunn, 1999; Greene & Burleson, 2003; Harvey & Wenzel, 2002). Both parties have to want to resolve the conflict. The time and place for resolving the conflict must be appropriate. If a mediator is to be used, that person must be considered impartial and acceptable to both parties. Each party's description of the event causing the disagreement must be presented without blame or judgment and the description followed by a statement of the speaker's feelings. To avoid defensiveness and the inability to hear the other person, speakers should periodically reiterate how much they value their relationship with the other person and the strengths that person possesses. Some possible solutions to the difficulty should be offered and negotiated by both parties to work toward a "win-win" situation where both parties' needs are met equally. A commitment should be made to review the situation at some specific later date to see if the agreement is working effectively.

Listening to People People generally feel better about themselves and other people when they feel valued and heard. However, some people are better than others at expressing their needs and being heard. Community workers need to be aware when residents suddenly stop coming to meetings or uncharacteristically sit without saying anything. In these situations, it may be necessary to meet one-on-one to find out what is going on with them and if they have any suggestions for improving community activities.

Providing Appropriate Training The primary job of community workers is to work themselves out of a job. An important activity for workers, therefore, is to ensure they provide good training for residents in running effective meetings, successful conflict resolution, and improving interpersonal communication. Qualified people should provide the training. The intent is for community members to learn new skills that would help them to manage their own relationships more effectively.

Having Fun There is a great deal of literature on the benefits of humour to our well-being (Hafen, Karren, Frandsen, & Smith, 1996). Laughter, as we have always known, is good for the soul but is also good for our physical and mental health (Ryff & Singer, 2001). Moreover, a good belly laugh can stimulate creative thinking and improve the quality of our relationships with others.

People generally put more energy into the things they enjoy doing and tend to avoid the things they do not. This is very true in the area of voluntary activities. Community residents are most likely to be involved in activities that are fun, make them feel good about themselves, and have a definite start and end date (e.g., social events, eating, and dressing up). Long, drawn-out, task-focused meetings with little humour or time for socializing are likely to have a diminishing attractiveness for all but a few stalwarts who will, over time, find that the burden of running the community's affairs will increasingly fall on their shoulders.

A community that hopes to build a strong network of local organizations will need to do more than publish ever-desperate pleas for volunteers in newsletters. It will need to host some events where people can come and enjoy themselves but not be pressured to join any particular committee. The hope is that through such events, people will get to know each other better and will want to become more involved as volunteers. At these events, workers will also be able to get to know community members better and invite some of them to attend upcoming meetings.

Because conflict is inevitable and has the potential to derail group efforts, community workers should understand how to manage conflict effectively. Using the above strategies, workers can assist in the resolution of difficulties between others, while maintaining the integrity of the group's process.

ADVOCACY

Advocacy is a deliberate attempt to bring about some change on behalf of an individual or group of people. It is a crucial part of community work because, often, agencies and services are organized "so that they support and reinforce conformity, among both clients and workers, to the very institutions and values that generate the problems to which the services were addressed in the first place" (Galper, 1975, p. 46). Despite many improvements in the nature and delivery of human services, Galper's words are as true today as they were over 30 years ago.

Advocacy can take place within the worker's employing institution or outside of it, but is more likely to be successful within organizations when workers use moderate and non-confrontational strategies. It is easier to achieve from outside of an organization when a collaborative atmosphere exists.

A moderate approach toward advocacy is likely to be most successful when attempting to modify the organizational climate that you work in (Mullaly, 1977). For example, staff meetings provide important opportunities to raise questions, challenge assumptions, and encourage co-workers to be more open to new ideas. Timing is important, of course. But a process that encourages asking questions and seeking potential solutions through a redefinition of problems, conducted within an emotionally safe and respectful environment, is preferable to a more confrontational approach (Mullaly, 1977). To illustrate this concept, Mullaly presents a scenario from a child welfare unit meeting, in which a dominant assumption was that child abuse and neglect issues were family problems to be solved through family therapy. In this situation, the advocate asked the following:

> Why are we doing all this family therapy work when we know from our own experience that if most of the families we work with had a decent job with a decent income they wouldn't be having so many problems? Also, these articles I have here (and which are then distributed) clearly show that most child abuse and neglect situations are problems related to poverty and not to bad parents. (Mullaly, 1977, p. 183)

The focus of the discussion moved toward the consideration of advocacy, both within the employing organization and through community agencies and professional associations.

Several ingredients are necessary for successful advocacy from outside an organization (Jackson & Jackson, 2006). The advocating group's values, goals, and tactics should be somewhat compatible with the dominant political culture. The group should be seen as having public support. There should also be sympathy for the issue and for the advocacy group. Membership of the group should have relatively high status (e.g., influential people bring contacts and other resources and can gain easier access to bureaucrats and politicians). The group should have a budget that is adequate to achieve and maintain ongoing access to policy-makers. A permanent, united organizational structure should be in place. The group should also be flexible and willing to compromise on one demand in order to achieve another. Finally, the group should be committed to collaboration.

Ezell (2001) argues that policies are built on assumptions and that successful advocacy involves identifying those assumptions and countering them with alternative ideas. Sometimes the beliefs and attitudes that underpin policies and programs are based on misinformation and negative stereotypes that can be successfully challenged through educational efforts, such as social marketing.

SOCIAL MARKETING

In any communications effort, it pays to think about the people you want to reach, how you will reach them, and what you will say. These three elements are known as the *market*, *medium*, and *message* (Horton, 1990). The **market** is the audience (e.g., local residents, funders, corporations, general public). The **medium** is the approach (e.g., television, word-of-mouth, newsletter). The **message** is the content (e.g., economic, social, family values, safety, fear, anger, justice).

Social marketing is the application of marketing principles for social change. Goals of social marketing in community development may be to create awareness of an issue or of a group's work, build credibility, attract support, enhance connections, or change attitudes, practices, or behaviour. In marketing, there are "five *P*'s": *product, price, place, promotion,* and *participation.* Fishbein & Middlestadt (1997) apply these elements to the concept of social marketing. The **product** is the idea, belief, or habit you want the target audience to accept, adopt, or change. The **price** is what the target audience will have to bear, such as beliefs, time, or money, to meet its needs. The **place** is the medium through which the audience will receive the message. The **promotion** is the message that attracts interest in your product. And **participation** is the input the target audience has in planning, developing, or implementing the product it needs. For example, a community group may want to draw attention to positive aspects of its neighbourhood, which only gets media attention for issues of crime and violence. The group may want to show that the community is a safe place to live, learn, and earn a living. The price is the fear about going into the community (e.g., being a victim of crime), which the target audience would have to give up in order to go there. The place might be a showcase of community art by local residents, open to the public. The promotion could be through public service ads, or radio interviews with community leaders. Participation may be through consultation with people from other communities on their concerns about safety in the neighbourhood.

Media Relations

There are two types of techniques that community groups may use: 1) create and send a message they control, and 2) send a message created and controlled by someone else (Locke, 2001). Groups who create and deliver their own message have several options at their disposal, such as word of mouth, meetings, newsletters, brochures, position papers, guest speakers, fliers and posters, as well as Internet and online resources (Homan, 2003). Other techniques that use the services of others to help create and deliver the message are through groups and organizations (e.g., annual reports by funders such as the United Way, profiling the programs they have contributed to), public service advertising (e.g., professionally produced billboards, newspaper advertisements, or electronic bulletin boards), entertainment and public affairs programs (e.g., a radio or television host broadcasting on-site at a community event), and the news media (Homan, 2003). The media can be a valuable resource to a community group on a low budget. If there is an outlet that reaches the appropriate audience (e.g., community newspapers or community section in a major newspaper, local or general radio or television), little cost is involved. A relatively small investment, in terms of time to do advance research and preparation, can have a big payoff. Written news releases, video and radio news releases, media advisories, public information packets, fact sheets, news conferences, individual meetings with reporters, letters to the editor, public service announcements, as well as appearances on radio and television programs, are all ways of communicating through the media (Aldridge, 1994; Blohowiak, 1987; Dozier, Grunig & Grunig, 1995; Harris, 2004; Locke, 2001).

Communicating Effectively

Several factors facilitate effective communication through the media. It is important to make the story new, interesting, relevant, understandable, and memorable (Canadian Psychological Association, 1995). When constructing written media releases, keep the message clear, clean, concise, and correct (Association for Supervision and Curriculum Development, 2005).

It is a skill to craft a well-written and -received press release. Some tips for writing effective press releases include the following (Welch, 2003):

- Ensure that the information is newsworthy. For example, a story about a group of citizens concerned about crime may not attract attention. But if a prominent figure, like the director of an agency, makes a statement about a program giving youth job training and opportunities to repair homes in their community, the information might be more attractive.
- Tell the audience that the information is for them, and give them a reason to continue to read it. For example, this story matters because all citizens should be concerned about solving youth crime.
- Begin first with a description of the news, then who announced it (not the other way around). A headline reading "Solutions To Crime" may be more newsworthy than the spokesperson who announced it.
- Ask yourself, "How are people going to relate to this, and will they be able to connect to the ideas?" Crime and safety are concerns for everyone.
- Emphasize the first 10 words of your release; they are the most important.
- Avoid using a lot of adjectives and fancy language. Be clear and get to the point.
- Stick to the facts. Have information available. A written report is helpful.
- Provide contact information; include a name, fax number, telephone number, and e-mail and Internet address. It is important that there is a contact person who is able to do interviews, or connect media with those who can do interviews.
- Make sure you have something with enough substance before you issue a release.
- Make it as easy as possible for media staff to do their jobs. The more difficult it is for a reporter to find a location or a person to be interviewed, the less likely it is for an interview to happen.

There are several matters to consider in preparation for being interviewed. Remember that you are selling your activity, and talking to a reporter is an opportunity to do that:

- Practise three positive points you want to make, and stick to them.
- Speak in short sentences.
- Use plain language.
- Show you enjoy what you're doing.
- Call reporters by name.
- Look interested.
- Tell a positive story.
- Keep your cool.
- Dress simply and modestly.
- Tell the truth.
- If you don't know an answer, say, "I don't know."

Remember, your group does a lot of good things, so keep talking after you have answered a yes or no question; this is a chance for you to elaborate. However, you should always stop talking when you've made your point, and not ramble or speculate. It is also important to assume that you are always on the record, and not to say anything you do not want to be quoted as saying. Finally, always come back to your main points (Fearn-Banks, 1996; Grunig, Dozier, Ehling, Grunig, Repper & White, 1992; Federal Communicator's Network, 2001).

NETWORKING

A **network** is a group of people who exchange information, contacts, and experience for professional or social purposes. Community workers are urged to "network," although they are often given little guidance about how to do it. There are three overlapping networks in which community-oriented human service professionals are likely to operate: service user networks (including family members and other caregivers), multi-professional networks, and work groups (Payne, 2000). Typically, service participants have to negotiate through three distinct networks, which may not necessarily communicate effectively within their own systems, let alone with others.

A good understanding of these networks prepares community workers to help people get involved with the services they need. Although it may be relatively easy to find information about what different groups are doing in a community, there are challenges to developing or entering into established networks.

Many cities maintain lists of human service agencies. In smaller communities, lists may be available through local organizations. While these directories serve as useful starting points for new community workers beginning to assemble information and identify networks, they are not complete. They quickly become out of date, reflecting relatively high rates of employee attrition and changes in the priorities of funding bodies. These listings do not address issues such as the quality of the service being provided, or requirements for access (e.g., long waiting lists, exclusive eligibility).

Sometimes, agencies are reluctant to collaborate too openly with each other, particularly when they perceive themselves to be in competition with each other for scarce funds. Human service agencies may also be wary of working too collaboratively with other agencies for fear that those organizations will "dump" work on them, without providing the funds and support to do it. A further complicating factor is that of confidentiality, when people are unsure about what they can and cannot divulge to each other about others. As well, different professionals may view situations in different ways, and this can complicate the problem-solving process. The development of effective relationships, covered in Chapter 5 of this text, promotes collaborative work between agencies and requires some level of trust. This is developed over time, and takes a lot of effort.

Most important, effective networking involves a lot of face-to-face contact between community workers and other personnel. Although this can be a time-consuming process, networking can be extremely beneficial in the long term.

SUMMARY

- Community workers will come into contact with bureaucracies in some development efforts. The values and practices of bureaucracies often run counter to those of professional community workers.

- Effective meetings balance task and relationship needs of members. Community workers should pay attention to meeting planning, set-up, as well as running the meeting, and follow-up after.
- Fundraising efforts may focus on getting grants, selling something, seeking donations from the general public or from major donors.
- Effective teams have a clear goal and work together to achieve it. They develop in a series of stages, including forming, storming, norming, performing, and adjourning.
- Conflict is inevitable in community work. Effective conflict management starts with sound relationship development.
- Advocacy in community work occurs within and outside of organizations.
- Effective media relations are one important strategy community workers may assist groups in developing. There are also many ways to get the word out that the group itself controls.
- Face-to-face contact is crucial for effective networking. Effective networking is integral to community work.

DISCUSSION QUESTIONS

1. Have you worked or volunteered in a large organization? Did it function like Weber's version of bureaucracy? What was it like to work there? If you have not worked or volunteered in a large organization, reflect instead on your experience as a student, at a secondary or post-secondary institution.

2. How would you go about organizing a meeting for a group of seniors in your neighbourhood? What would you do to make it a success, and why?

3. Which kinds of fundraising activities are you most familiar with or most comfortable with? What are the pros and cons of each one described in this chapter?

4. Think about the last time you were involved in a disagreement. Was it resolved? How could it have been resolved, or resolved more effectively?

5. How would you go about finding out about local agencies and services in your community for a particular population (e.g., young adults looking for work)? If you were interested in doing community work with this population, how would you begin to develop a network? Who would you approach and how?

WEBLINKS

www.dwatch.ca/ Democracy Watch

http://charityvillage.ca/cv/guides/guide3.asp Charity Village: Fundraising

www.ccednet-rcdec.ca/en/pages/learningnetwork.asp Pan-Canadian Community Development Network

www.cedworks.com/index.html Centre for Community Enterprise

www.mediationworks.com/canada/ Mediation Training Institute of Canada

http://media.socialchange.net.au/planning_comms/guides.html Social Change Media

KEY TERMS

Adjournment stage, p. 104

Advocacy, p. 108

Bureaucracy, p. 94

Catch-22, p. 96

Challengers, p. 104

Collaborators, p. 104

Communicators, p. 104

Conflict, p. 105

Contributors, p. 104

Direct marketing, p. 101

Effective teams, p. 103

Forming stage, p. 103

Groupthink, p. 95

In-kind, p. 100

Institutional grants, p. 101

Interpersonal conflict, p. 106

Major individual donors, p. 101

Market, p. 109

Mediating conflict, p. 99

Medium, p. 110

Message, p. 110

Network, p. 112

Norming stage, p. 103

Overspecialization, p. 95

Participation, p. 110

Performing stage, p. 104

Place, p. 110

Price, p. 110

Probing and questioning, p. 99

Product, p. 110

Promotion, p. 110

Providing support, p. 99

Reflecting feelings, p. 99

Relationship dimensions, p. 98

Rigidity, p. 95

Social marketing, p. 110

Special events and product sales, p. 101

Storming stage, p. 103

Task dimensions, p. 98

Team building, p. 103

c h a p t e r   e i g h t

Canadian Case Studies

LEARNING OBJECTIVES

After reading this chapter, you will be able to:

1. Recognize a range of community development practices.
2. Understand the connections between a community's history, development process, structure, and outcomes.
3. Describe similarities and differences in community development practices across Canada.
4. Apply principles of effective community development practice to case studies.

Community development practice takes different forms depending on the local environment and local people. In different communities throughout Canada, development efforts address a range of issues with a variety of groups. Features of each community set the context for local change, with those living in the community assessing both the strengths and challenges, and deciding on a course of action that takes a particular form. In this chapter, we look at a case study of community development from each province and territory. The cases have been selected to reflect different community geographies and demographics. Each case begins with some background about the community, and goes on to identify key factors in the process of change, the structure of the effort, as well as its impact. Because each is based on local issues, it is unique. However, taken together, these cases illustrate promising approaches to contemporary community practice in Canada, including the principles of integration, partnership, grassroots involvement, and development based on local strengths.

CHAPTER OUTLINE

HUPACASATH FIRST NATION, VANCOUVER ISLAND, BRITISH COLUMBIA

Hupacasath First Nation is located just north of Port Alberni on the west side of Vancouver Island, British Columbia. The community is made up of about 300 people. High rates of unemployment and poor social conditions prompted local leaders to take new actions that would lead to the restoration of wealth to the once rich and self-sustaining community. The community decided to take control of its own resources, and embarked on an ambitious plan to bring prosperity to members.

The decision was made to move ahead without a treaty and without blame, and go back to early teachings for guidance about how to proceed (Kekinusuqs, 2005). A fundamental teaching was the concept of *Hishukishtswalk*: "Everything is one. Everything is interconnected. You cannot do one thing without affecting something else. We are all inextricably linked through Mother Earth, and everything that walks on her, grows from her, or runs through or above her" (p. 6). The economy of Hupacasath was related to the economy of Port Alberni. And in the 1980s, because of a downturn in forestry and fishing, the economy was declining. Both communities felt that there was a need for diversification.

Process

First, good working relationships needed to be developed. The community began building positive connections with neighbours in Port Alberni. Members of Hupacasath hosted and attended functions for Port Alberni residents, requested membership on local boards, and joined the local chamber of commerce. Writing letters to editors of local papers and getting to know local reporters also proved helpful in promoting a more positive image of the Hupacasath community.

The community embarked on its first economic development project in the 1990s. The lands surrounding the community included the richest forests in the world. To benefit from the forest industry, the community needed to be significantly involved in it. And in order to be involved, community members needed to know how the industry worked. Members of the community learned about the legislation and standards of governance for forest practices. These same members started their own woodlot, and ran it themselves profitably for several years.

The next steps were determined by the community, who used surveys and workshops to gather input from members on reserve as well as those living off reserve. As well, the community hired outside consultants so that the process would be seen as unbiased. The vast majority (95 percent) of members gave their input (Kekinusuqs, 2005). This information was used to develop a mission statement and goals. Two key components of the community development strategy were to (1) create jobs for members, and (2) diversify the activities.

Structure

Tourism, mining, and energy were the three areas of focus. In tourism, a project called Choo-Kwa Ventures began offering guided cultural canoe excursions, and opened a gift shop in Port Alberni (Hupacasath, 2006). The community then opened a second tourism project, and interpretive centre. In mining, three communities, including Hupacasath, Ucluelet, and Tseshaht, as well as a mining company, started a business together called Eagle Rock Materials, to train and employ local people (Eagle Rock Materials, 2006). In energy, the Upnit (meaning "calm place") Power Corporation formed to generate electricity from a local dam on the China Creek (Social Economy Showcase, 2006).

Impact

The diversification of initiatives will contribute to greater stability in the job market for residents of the community for years to come. As these projects are early in their growth, more opportunities are expected for residents to gain skills and expertise through training. Over the longer term, it is anticipated that the youth of the community will stay in the community and lead these initiatives. Because the efforts are closely tied to important cultural values, this success also serves to reinforce and strengthen local wisdom and traditions.

Effective Community Development Practice The community development process taken by the community of Hupacasath highlights several principles of effective practice. A first step was to develop partnerships with the Port Alberni community, whose economy was closely tied to Hupacasath (partnership). The initiatives taken were based on broad-scale input of members, who together decided how to move forward (grassroots involvement). The efforts taken in economic development showed a strong connection to the history, traditional teachings, and values, as well as current needs of the community—in terms of respect for the land—so that what was done would be sustainable and available for future generations (integration). A crucial component of community development in

Hupacasath was to emphasize the strengths of the community, including the peoples and the location, both of which made tourism, logging, and minerals industries logical choices (strengths-based).

THE YUKON ARTS CENTRE, WHITEHORSE, YUKON

Whitehorse is both the capital and largest city in the Yukon, with a population of approximately 23 000 (Yukon Bureau of Statistics, 2006). About 70 percent of the total Yukon population lives in the Whitehorse area. Many government offices (First Nations, federal, and the territory) are located in the city. The economic climate of the city has varied, due to highs and lows in the mining industry and in highway construction. However, because of the strong presence of government agencies and headquarters for major Yukon businesses, utility companies, and many other services, the economic climate is relatively stable (Yukon Bureau of Statistics, 2006).

Process

In the 1980s a group of volunteers from the local community set out to create a space for the visual and performing arts in Whitehorse. Members of this group were from the arts community, the government, as well as local business. Pooling resources and connections, they were able to garner the money needed to build a facility. This facility opened in 1992, operating as a non-profit organization, with a board of directors possessing diverse backgrounds and experiences.

Structure

Today, the centre is funded by an annual operating allocation from the Yukon government, as well as by donations from a variety of local businesses and individuals. Members are appointed by government to the Yukon Arts Centre Corporation Board, based on nominations from the arts, the community, and business organizations, as well as from First Nations and municipalities (Yukon Government, 2005).

The Yukon Arts Centre is open year-round, holding ticketed theatre and music events on a regular basis. There is a public art gallery, which hosts several exhibits each year. There is also a children's art gallery, where work of the youngest artists in the territory are on display, and the Centre hosts no-cost drop-in art classes for children, as well as short-term and more intensive artistic training for a fee. Moreover, the Centre works with schools to promote the arts and access to its facilities, by means of tours, matinees, after-school art clubs, and opportunities to work with professional artists-in-residence. It is also involved with community arts organizations, providing research and administrative support (Yukon Arts Centre, 2006).

Impact

Annual attendance for ticketed events now exceeds 21 000. Over 100 events are held each year, as well as many gallery exhibitions, which attract close to 10 000 people. The centre has paid staff, as well as 130 volunteers, and has continued to show increases in demand for community, education, and outreach activities (Yukon Government, 2005).

Effective Community Development Practice The development of the Yukon Arts Centre illustrates principles of effective community development practice. The origins of the Centre were with the individuals and groups from the local community who came together to promote the creative arts, and local residents are still involved on the Centre's Board of Directors (grassroots involvement). The founding members represented diverse interests and expertise, including local artists and business and government representatives who have continued to be involved in the facility's maintenance costs (partnership). The Centre encourages the strengths of local people, through efforts to involve children and youth from the community, in a way that recognizes and values their creative talents (strengths-based). The expression of culture, through the arts, is itself an integrative effort requiring physical talent and creative thinking, with a spiritual connection (integration).

THE ALBERTA CEREBRAL PALSY SPORTS ASSOCIATION, EDMONTON, ALBERTA

Edmonton is Alberta's capital city. It has an approximate population of over 650 000 (Statistics Canada, 2006), and significant rates of childhood disability. Close to 20 000 of Alberta children have some form of a disability (Statistics Canada, 2003). Cerebral Palsy (CP) is a group of conditions that affect brain functioning related to physical tasks. Typically, it is present at birth and manifests during early childhood. However, onset can also occur later in life in response to brain injury. A primary effect of CP is difficulty with muscle coordination, which occurs at a rate of 2.8/1000 (Robertson, Svenson, & Joffres, 1998), suggesting that thousands of Alberta families are affected.

Process

The Cerebral Palsy Association of Alberta (CPA) is an organization that partners with local community groups and delivers its own services; it also provides information about CP. In the early 1980s, a subgroup of individuals involved in the CPA identified a need for additional support for parents of children and youth who were interested in pursuing competitive sports at the highest levels (Benko, 2001).

Many members were professional physiotherapists, who saw sport as a form of therapy for individuals with CP. Many had contact with potential participants through their professional practice, and referred those individuals with CP to the CPA. Through the CPA, those individuals were then referred to what became the Alberta Cerebral Palsy Sports Association (ACPSA). The organization officially became less rehabilitative in emphasis, and more sports-minded. In 1984, it became an association under the Society's Act of Alberta.

Founding members met on many occasions to develop an organizational structure, including policies and procedures. They raised funds through bingo and casino revenue and membership drives. Though the opportunity came to hire paid staff, recruitment of volunteers continued throughout. Sponsorships became available for some of the member athletes, which assisted with costs of equipment and travel.

Structure

The Alberta organization is a member organization of the Canadian Cerebral Palsy Sports Association (CCPSA). The mission of the CCPSA is "an athlete focused national organization administering and governing sport opportunities targeted to athletes with CP and related disabilities. CCPSA and its provincial partners cooperate as a proactive force to facilitate the development of equitable and fair sporting opportunities for our athletes" (CCPSA, 2006). Currently, the Alberta Association works to support the efforts of athletes with CP who aspire to the level of world-class competition or Paralympics club athletes. The activities of the Alberta organization are consistent with those of the national group, which include promotion, representation, eligibility standards and rules, as well as the selection and sponsorship of athletes (CCPSA, 2006a).

Impact

More athletes participating in a wider range of events, in international competitions, both in Canada and abroad, are some of the outcomes that the organization has facilitated. A significant change to the organization's administrative structure is imminent. A National Council, Provincial Council, Athletes Council, as well as a Technical Advisory group, and a Governance Committee, will replace the existing structure (CCPSAb, 2006). The organization is enhancing an already strong national body comprised of provincial associations.

Effective Community Development Practice The Cerebral Palsy Sports Association of Alberta shows a commitment to several principles of effective community development practice. Those who were involved at the beginning of this organization came from diverse backgrounds, including professionals as well as parents and children affected by the disability (grassroots involvement). Their membership with the provincial Cerebral Palsy Association in Alberta, initially, gave the organizers an opportunity to refine their needs for a provincial sports-specific organization, which has become strongly connected to a national sports-specific group (partnerships). Participation in sports at the highest levels is physically, socially, and emotionally demanding for athletes and their families; in providing supports in this way, the organization is holistic (integration). The organization exists for the promotion of opportunities and support for athletes with CP who compete against others on the basis of their abilities (strengths).

SASKATOON COMMUNITIES FOR CHILDREN, SASKATOON, SASKATCHEWAN

Saskatoon is Saskatchewan's largest city, with a population of over 200 000 (Statistics Canada, 2006b). Agriculture and mining are major industries, with value-added food processing becoming a significant influence and strength of the local economy (City of Saskatoon, 2006). However, like other Canadian cities, the child poverty rate is unacceptably high. In Saskatoon, 26 percent of children under the age of 18 years live in poverty (Community-University Institute for Social Research, 2003). This problem has prompted the development of several new partnerships between community and government to address common concerns.

Process

In 1997 the Saskatoon Communities for Children was established to bring together government and community representatives to make Saskatoon a safer and healthier place to grow up. The organization is holistic in its approach, including physical, mental, spiritual, and emotional well-being of children, families, and communities (SCC, 2006). A major purpose of the organization was to bring people together and share resources, so that meaningful change could occur. The focus was to be on enhancing interagency collaboration.

The organization was incorporated as a non-profit corporation, managed by an executive committee, with equal representation from government and community, as well as one Aboriginal and one government representative as co-chairs.

Structure

Currently, the SCC has six paid staff members, and many local partners in government and the community. The agency receives project funding from the federal government, as well as national and provincial organizations, to coordinate collaborative community-based projects in youth addictions, sexual exploitation of youth, child poverty, and early childhood development (SCC, 2006). The organization is also a member of several working groups on related issues with multiple partners. The SCC also conducts community-based research, and has worked in partnership with a local community-university institute on human services research.

Impact

The impact of this organization can be seen in several areas: development of partnerships, information gathering and dissemination, and targeted social policy change. In each of these areas, the SCC has had a significant effect. Partnerships between government and community agencies take time and effort to develop and sustain. The presence of the agency in multiple partnerships suggests that this has worked well. The success of this agency in securing project funding demonstrates ability to both propose and produce a useful product. The research and advocacy activities are oriented to policy change in areas related to youth safety and family poverty at local as well as national levels.

Effective Community Development Practice Saskatoon Communities for Children exemplifies effective practices in Canadian community development. The development of this organization required the strengths of community and government partners to come together and recognize common areas of interest (grassroots involvement). The founding partners and current board of directors each bring particular experience and expertise to the organization (strengths-based). This organization also looks holistically at children's well-being, including physical, social, emotional, and spiritual dimensions (integration). Partnerships were and continue to be a focus; the organization is making connections between government, academic, and community groups (partnership).

SCHOOL OF COMMUNITY GOVERNMENT, YELLOWKNIFE, NORTHWEST TERRITORIES

Yellowknife is the capital and largest city in the Northwest Territories, with a population of approximately 18 000 (Statistics Canada, 2006c). One-third of all residents of this territory reside outside the city. Rich with minerals, Yellowknife's mining and oil industries are strong contributors to the local economy (City of Yellowknife, 2006).

Due to large-scale resource development across the region, local communities faced increases in activity and effects on infrastructure, such as deteriorating roads, expansion of water and sewer services, and housing shortages. Smaller communities faced the challenge of trying to maintain traditional ways, which were threatened by increasing pressures from the wage economy (Municipal and Community Affairs, 2003). Due to expanded powers and accountabilities, land agreements and self-government agreements with Aboriginal communities also increased demands for local skills training. There was a need for community governments to enhance their human resource capacities, through training, development, and hiring of quality local staff.

Process

In 1999, the School of Community Government began operations. The School is a division within the Department of Municipal and Community Affairs, Northwest Territories. It was founded on partnerships between community governments, federal and territorial governments, Aboriginal, territorial, and professional organizations, as well as educational institutions and the private sector (Government of Northwest Territories, 2006).

Structure

The school was designed to assist local governments with their capacity-building priorities by providing training that met the needs of leaders and decision makers, government staff, housing authorities, and Aboriginal organizations at the community level. It offers training and credentials for individuals already working in the community, in the areas of community governance, operations, finances, infrastructure, management, lands and public safety (School of Community Government, 2006).

The training provided is based on occupational standards. It is customized and delivered according to the needs of the community. For example, training opportunities range from a workshop series on decision making for local community leaders, or a series of courses for an entire staff in technical areas like finance or administration (INAC, 2004).

Impact

Participant satisfaction surveys of the School of Community Government consistently report high scores. But for many who participate, the benefits are also found in opportunities to network with others, learning from one another by sharing successes and challenges. Since it has opened, the School has offered 370 courses to over 3000 participants. Enrolment has climbed from 100 in its first year, to almost 900 three years later (INAC, 2004).

Effective Community Development Practice The School of Community Government is an important contributor to community development in the north. The school was developed on the basis of local knowledge and strengths, which serve as the starting points for all education offered (strengths-based). The training is offered in partnership with local leaders and communities, who together deliver programs that are useful for training in areas of community need (grassroots involvement). The school came together as the result of financial and political contributions, as well as indigenous knowledge from different government agencies, and from local people (partnership). Given that the range of training desired is broad in scope, including ways to enhance physical, social, and economic community health, the nature of the training is holistic as well (integration).

ANDREWS STREET FAMILY CENTRE, WINNIPEG, MANITOBA

Winnipeg is Manitoba's capital and largest city, with a population of approximately 650 000 (Statistics Canada, 2006d). The core area of Winnipeg includes some of the highest family poverty levels in Canada. Close to half of the city's Aboriginal population live in the core area (Loewen et al., 2005). While Winnipeg's North End neighbourhoods face considerable challenges due to an aging and inadequate housing stock, they are rich in social networks.

Process

In the early 1990s, a local drop-in centre for youth lost funding. Community residents worked to bring new life to a vacant building at 220 Andrews Street. The goal was to form a community centre in the local area. The new centre brought several community programs into one facility, and combined them with new programs that together offered a broad range of family supports (Canadian Association of Family Resource Programs, 2005). Andrews Street Family Centre (ASFC) opened its doors in 1994 and was incorporated in 1995. It is a family resource centre that builds on its community's strengths and encourages its individuals, children, elders, families, and youth to reach their full potential through support, friendship, and positive experiences (ASFC, 2005).

Through surveys distributed to local residents, the agency received an overwhelmingly positive response from the community. Surveys were conducted by community members who went door-to-door asking residents about their needs and strengths, and talked to over 700 residents (ASFC, 2005). Even when a resident insisted that she or he had no strengths, that person was encouraged to look at a list of over one hundred abilities, and check off all those that fit. Everyone who was surveyed had something he or she was good at, and was willing to help out.

ASFC has maintained a strong connection to the community, due to the leadership by local residents on the board of directors, as well as an executive director who is a long-time resident. The agency has developed and maintained strong partnerships with other local organizations and residents' groups. Cultural knowledge is an important part of what the Centre does. Approximately 80 percent of those who come to the Centre are Aboriginal. Both western and traditional approaches are used, so that all residents have the opportunity to lean in the ways that they are most comfortable with.

Structure

ASFC hires extensively from the local community. The agency employs over 30 staff, and has an annual operating budget of over $1.5 million. There is a variety of programming available for all ages, including a drop-in centre for people to visit, get some respite child care, use the telephone, or wash clothes. Parents help other parents through outreach, support, and advocacy services. The volunteer program has over 150 participants, each contributing her or his skills to the Centre. There is also a drop-in centre for youth, which is open every day, and Oshki-Majahitowin, an Aboriginal Head Start program for Cree and Ojibway children. The agency also has an arts program, where children, youth, and adults express themselves creatively in different ways.

Impact

The impact of the Andrews Street Family Centre can be measured in numbers. The program attendance has been steadily growing and so has the budget, as well as number of staff. However, the positive experiences of families who walk through the doors show the real impact that the agency has had on the local community. These success stories are the most powerful. Two examples follow. One program at the Centre is for young women to meet and learn together. Over the past few years the girls have shared stories with experienced speakers. Since the program has started, the girls have gone from wanting to have kids just so they could go on assistance and live away from their parents, to having new aspirations for going on to post-secondary education. Another example is the experience of a local mom who, after starting work at the Centre, was able to leave social assistance. The mother was able to set a good example for her children, all three of whom got jobs when they were of working age.

Effective Community Development Practice At Andrews Street Family Centre, principles of effective community development practice are clearly evident. The agency was founded by local people, based on their individual strengths, using a survey to identify those skills and abilities that could benefit others in the community (strengths-based). Partners from across the neighbourhood were part of the original group who founded the Centre, and included people from different backgrounds, such as professionals and non-professionals, long-time residents and shorter-term residents, parents and single people (partnership). Currently, a community-based board of directors oversees the activities, and local residents are hired to provide service to gain experience, as well as provide service to other families (grassroots). The services are holistic in nature; attention is paid to physical, social, emotional, and spiritual dimensions of individual, family, and community well-being (integration).

NUNAVUT ARCTIC COLLEGE, IQUALUIT, NUNAVUT

Nunavut became a territory on April 1, 1999. The land base is almost 2 000 000 square kilometers, and includes about 29 000 residents living in 26 communities (Statistics Canada, 2006e). About 85 percent of the population is Inuit. Inuit *Qaujimajatuqangit*, which is the traditional knowledge, values, and wisdom of Nunavut's founding people, shape the territory's culture (Government of Nunavut, 2006a). Iqualuit is the capital, and has a population of approximately 6000.

The government of this territory is based on consensus, blending principles of parliamentary democracy with Aboriginal values of maximum co-operation, effective use of leadership, and broad accountability (Government of Nunavut, 2006b). In August 1999, the Bathurst Mandate was completed, which outlined key priorities for the territory, including healthy communities, simplicity and unity, self-reliance, and continuing learning.

Process

The history of Nunavut Arctic College predates the territory. In 1968, the Northwest Territories government started an Adult Vocational Training Centre in Fort Smith, which offered training in the trades as well as the first teacher-training program for Aboriginal peoples on the continent. As well, other programs were available in the 1970s, including the Eastern Arctic Teacher Educational Program and the Sanavik Housing Maintainer Program, which opened in Iqualuit late that decade (Nunavut Artic College, 2006a).

In 1982, the Northwest Territories government's Special Committee on Education recommended the establishment of Arctic College. In 1984, the College came into existence, and was a combination of the other post-secondary programs in Fort Smith and Iqualuit. Demand grew, especially at the Iqualuit campus, and several new programs were added in the next years. In 1990, the College also assumed responsibilities for adult education services and expanded, opening campuses in Cambridge Bay and Rankin Inlet. In 1995, the College was formally established with the passage of the Public Colleges Act in the Northwest Territories (Nunavut Artic College, 2006a).

Structure

The College offers over 30 different programs, developed in response to local need. These programs include the trades, career development programs, as well as certificate or diploma programs, and academic programs. Programs and courses are available in classrooms and by distance education, either full- or part-time, so that they are widely accessible. Community learning centres offer programs in educational assessment and counselling, adult basic education and literacy programming, continuing education (in certificate, diploma, and degree programs), skill development programs, home management courses, cultural and traditional education, personal development courses, support for distance education learners, and job readiness training (Nunavut Arctic College, 2006b).

Impact

Nunavut Arctic College has three main campuses in Iqaluit, Cambridge Bay, and Rankin Inlet, as well as 24 Community Learning Centres spread across the territory. The expansion was necessary to meet the needs of each community. The number of students attending the colleges' programs and courses is increasing, and more offerings are planned to meet demand.

Effective Community Development Practice The programs offered at Nunavut Arctic College illustrate principles of effective community development practice. Training is delivered in partnership with local communities, and local residents' experience and knowledge are integrated into the teachings, so that the education is relevant and useful (grassroots involvement). The school itself came about as a partnership between different government agencies, as well as local knowledge holders; cultural teachings formed a basis for the content of the first programs in teacher education (partnership). Because traditional knowledge sustained the communities for many years prior to European contact, the programs are based on local cultural teachings, (strengths-based). By offering education that is culturally appropriate, the content is holistic, and includes explicit recognition of the relationships between people, their families, and communities (integration).

THE SUSTAINABLE TORONTO PROJECT, TORONTO, ONTARIO

Toronto is Canada's largest city and the provincial capital of Ontario. The city has a population of over 3 000 000, spread along the northern shore of Lake Ontario (Statistics Canada, 2006f). As a large city, it was critically important to long-term economic and social success that measures were taken to promote environmental awareness and ecological sustainability. The Sustainable Toronto project adopted a vision from the City's Environmental Plan, called Clean, Green and Healthy: A Plan for an Environmentally Sustainable Toronto:

> In the year 2025, Toronto is a world leader in sustainable urban living. It is a city that is renowned for the quality of life experienced by its residents. Civic leaders credit the city's thriving economy to measures taken to protect the environment. Decision-makers and residents understand that long-term sustainability requires a healthy natural environment, a healthy economy, and healthy communities. Planning considers the needs of future generations, the need to build in a way that supports sustainable transportation, and the need to protect and enhance Toronto's green infrastructure. (Environmental Task Force, 2000, p. 15)

Process

The project partners included two universities, the city, and national and civic organizations, as well as local community-based non-profit groups. It was funded by the Social Sciences and Humanities Research Council of Canada's Community University Research Alliance initiative. **Sustainability**, as defined by this group, meant that economic, social, and environmental decisions needed to be made in light of each other (Sustainable Toronto, 2006a). That is, economic decisions needed to be made in light of social and environmental considerations, social decisions needed to be made in light of economic and environmental considerations, and environmental decisions needed to be made in light of social and economic considerations. Cross-sectional collaboration between local government, universities, and non-profits was required.

Structure

The partners funded 10 projects, each linking research with action (Sustainable Toronto, 2006b). Each project involved a community-based non-governmental organization or city government representative, with a university-based researcher, to identify a research topic and appropriate method. University students were heavily involved in the front-line research duties, for pay or course credit. The project topics included the following:

- Seeds of our City
- Monitoring for Sustainability
- Ontario's Community Right to Know Initiative
- Promoting Education & Awareness of the Links between Health and the Environment
- Professional Development for Sustainable Learning
- Building the Management Capacity of the Environmental Non-Profit Sector
- Understanding Shifts in Canadian Environmental Governance
- Building Effective Leadership

- Sustainability Tool-Kit for Governance Environmental Studies Program
- Understanding and Facilitating Community Based Research

Impact

The project produced several **outputs,** including scholarly publications, a directory of ethno-cultural organizations, a Web site, a report documenting the benefits of community gardens, and new garden development, as well as meetings between businesses, politicians, and educators on sustainability issues (Savan, 2004).

The impact of this project was in three primary areas, including the university, collaborations, and community development. At the university level, research, teaching, and curricula would be enhanced by new knowledge about government and community issues. Collaborations between community organizations, local government, and universities were improved. Finally, community development, based on a recognition of the contributions that universities and government can make to grassroots-level change, was enhanced (Sustainable Toronto, 2006c).

Effective Community Development Practice Principles of effective community development practice are found in the Sustainable Toronto project. The project was a partnership between different levels of government as well as universities and community groups in the Toronto area (partnership). The purpose of the project was to make long-lasting connections between different groups, to pursue a vision for sustainability (integration). The activities undertaken in this project—in particular, the community-based research activities—required a pooling of expertise on research and community issues and realities (strengths-based). The community organizations were based on grassroots representation, and their role in the project provided opportunities for these groups to influence the research and practice agendas of universities and governments (grassroots involvement).

DANS LA RUE (ON THE STREET), MONTREAL, QUEBEC

Montreal is Quebec's largest city with a population of over 1.5 million (Tourism Montreal, 2006). During the 1980s this city, not unlike other Canadian cities, experienced a rise in the popularity of political and fiscal conservatism (Karabanow, 1999). Resources for the homeless population were low, and for youth, who faced additional barriers, the problems were even more serious. A Catholic priest who lived in the downtown area noticed the increasing numbers of youth on the streets (Karabanow, 1999).

Process

The founder of Dans La Rue began by asking the youth on the street what the issues were, and what would help. Youth were concerned about clothing, food, medicine, and information about where they could go for a shower, a meal, and a place to stay. Father Emmitt Jones then purchased a used Winnebago motorhome with a personal loan, and used it to take food to youth on the street. He hired a former street-involved youth to help him meet and get to know more youth (Karabanow, 1999). In 1989, a board of directors for the agency was formed, and in 1990 someone donated a new motorhome to the agency (Dans La Rue, 2006a). The youth continued to determine the services that the motorhome would provide, and they also identified what additional residential resources were needed.

Structure

In addition to the motorhome, Dans La Rue operated a temporary emergency shelter and a day centre. The shelter, known as "the Bunker," provided a safe haven for youth aged 12–19 years and included a place to stay, clothes, showers, and meals on a short-term basis. The day centre, known as "Chez Pops," operated a variety of services, including a medical clinic, cafeteria, clothing depot, music room, dental clinic, veterinary clinic, computers, a legal clinic, as well as arts workshops (Dans La Rue, 2005). As well, the centre operated a school, provided parenting classes, and operated a work entry program (Dans La Rue, 2005).

Impact

The agency has grown to include over 65 staff, and another 135 people as volunteers. The expansion of services is a testament to the success of the agency, which has contact with thousands of youth each year. One key component of the service, which has been very difficult to estimate in numbers, was the agency's prevention efforts. Each year, agency staff and youth spoke to other youth in city schools about homelessness. They would show a film titled, *Cul-de-sac*, which was developed by 15 youth, aged 17–22, based on their experiences of life on the street. The purpose of the film was to teach youth to think through the effects of decisions they made, so that they would make healthy choices (Dans La Rue, 2006b).

Effective Community Development Practice The structure and delivery of services to homeless youth by Dans La Rue reflect a community development approach and illustrate several features of effective practice. The programs run by the agency are determined by the youth, who assist with development and delivery (grassroots involvement). The agency continues to be based on a partnership between a clergyman, the church, and the youth (partnership). The services provided include housing, clothing, and food, as well as skill and education opportunities and outreach to other youth (integration). The youth presentations to other youth about issues of homelessness are effective because the youth who have the experience and expertise on life on the streets are encouraged to share their knowledge with others (strengths-based).

THE RESILIENCY CENTRE, SAINT JOHN, NEW BRUNSWICK

Saint John is the largest city in New Brunswick. It is a port city of about 100 000 (Statistics Canada, 2006g) that serves as an economic hub for some of the smaller surrounding communities. The human services community is well established and interconnected. To establish priorities for its next year, the John Howard Society (JHS), a local community-based organization serving men with involvement in the justice system, invited members of the community to assist with identifying local issues.

Process

In 1995, over 60 individuals were invited to attend a one-day training event sponsored by the JHS to identify priorities for the organization over the next year. Participants were invited from both governmental and non-governmental agencies, in several different sectors, such as health, education, social welfare, recreation, and youth services. Community residents and retired professionals were also invited. The highest priority for action among members of this group was program development for children and families.

At the meeting, it was suggested that each person in attendance consider what she or he was willing to contribute to address the issue (Kelly & Caputo, 2005). Staff members of the JHS were also invited publicly by their director to indicate if they would be willing to donate some of their volunteer time to this issue. Twenty of the sixty said they were willing to be involved, and staff identified another twenty individuals and organizations who should be approached.

Structure

The Resiliency Centre, though it grew out of the JHS training event, was a separate organization, with its own board of directors, and a mandate to develop and deliver programs for youth and families in the community (Kelly & Caputo, 2005). The Centre has assisted other community groups with the development and delivery of their own programs, has offered its own programs that were not duplicates of existing programs by other agencies, and has solicited funding for all activities through local service clubs or the business community. Since the professional staff was all volunteers, and the building and support staff members were donated, the money goes directly into meeting community needs.

Impact

Volunteers of the Centre have come from a variety of backgrounds. Some professionals volunteering at the Centre are employed in a local community agency or a government position. Others are retired professionals. Many clients of the agency also volunteer their time and expertise, gain professional experience, and go on to school or employment in the helping professions. Many of these stories are documented (Kelly & Caputo, 2005). The agency has expanded considerably during its 10 years in existence, and has provided many services to local youth and families.

Effective Community Development Practice The development and structure of the Resiliency Centre illustrates important aspects of community development practice. The centre came about through the contributions of many individuals and groups working in government and business, as well as through the contributions of local residents (strengths-based). The operation of the Centre depends on agencies and organizations to provide staff resources (partnership). Local people also volunteer at the Centre, to assist with development and implementation of programs, which keeps the services relevant and accessible to local people and provides work experience that can lead to employment opportunities within one of the partner agencies (grassroots involvement). The Centre provides programs that are not available elsewhere, and through this conscious effort not to duplicate service or compete with other agencies, the Centre is aware and connected with the local service providers (integrated).

COMMUNITY ACCESS PROGRAM, CHARLOTTETOWN, PRINCE EDWARD ISLAND

The province of Prince Edward Island has a population of approximately 150 000 (Statistics Canada, 2006h). The use of the Internet to communicate with others who share similar interests and experiences became more formalized in the 1990s, and while Prince Edward Island did not have a community networking association, the provincial government played a significant role in access to Internet for residents via PEI Net, a local service provider (Canadian Community Networks, 1995). The Internet has affected the possibilities and practices for communication, and as such, has had an impact on community development practice in PEI (Telecommunities Canada, 2006).

Process

There are many individuals who want to use the Internet but do not have access or the know-how. To address this digital divide, the federal government launched the Community Access Program in 1995, "which aimed to provide Canadians with affordable public access to the Internet and the skills they need to use it effectively" (Industry Canada, 2006). Prince Edward Island was quick to establish community Internet sites within schools, libraries, and community centres. The CAP program in PEI is the first in Canada to evolve to the next level of development: paid, local program staff, and revenue generation centres, called Community Network Centres (Prince Edward Island CAP, 2006).

Structure

There are two levels of community-based Internet access and support services in Prince Edward Island. Internet Support Centres (ISCs) are those located in community sites that offer computer and Internet access, as well as other activities, such as summer camps for children and computer training sessions. Community Network Centres (CNCs), on the other hand, are larger access points that are staffed, have more recent and a greater variety of equipment (e.g., scanners, fax machines, and photocopying) and can, therefore, offer more services. The CNCs serve to connect two or more of the smaller support centres (ISCs), and provide connections and service to them. The mandate of CNCs is to develop training programs, support distance education, and develop software.

Impact

To meet demand, the access sites have developed and delivered many programs. Some examples include specialized computer training (for e-business), web page design for older adults and youth, and a "train-the-trainer" program. And more sites have been added. There are now 25 Internet Support Centres, with one to ten computers each, and 16 Community Network Centres with at least 15 computers each (Prince Edward Island CAP, 2006). The coverage of sites across the province is comprehensive; no resident of PEI is more than 12 minutes away from a community access site (Prince Edward Island CAP, 2006).

Effective Community Development Practice Access and knowledge about the Internet have contributed to the development of new social connections between residents. The use of technology as an assistant to the community development process illustrates several principles of effective practice. The development of access centres across the province was a partnership between governments (partnership). However, the content of communication that is facilitated by the technology is creating new relationships or strengthening them, based on contributions of local residents (grassroots involvement). The potential for sharing resources is facilitated by the use of online bulletin boards and other technology-assisted methods (strengths-based). The training for use of computer technology and Internet brings together different groups, from different generations, to learn and support each other (integration).

DEVELOPMENT ISLE MADAME, ARICHAT, NOVA SCOTIA

Isle Madame is located off the coast of Cape Breton Island. It is about 70 square miles in area, with a total population of about 4000 (Statistics Canada, 2006i), scattered among many small communities. Arichat is a small community on the southern coast, where the fishing industry has been the major economic activity for many years. However, catches have decreased, and with the closure of the largest employer on the island in 1996, the industry has been dramatically affected.

Process

Before the absolute collapse of the industry in 1992, which threatened the loss of over 500 jobs, a group of leaders met to discuss ways to deal with what they saw as a serious and inevitable problem (Development Isle Madame, 1999). The leaders included trade unionists, educators, local business members, fishing industry managers, plant workers, fishermen, youth, older adults, as well as regional and municipal government representatives. This group approached the federal government for funding to assist in planning for this major change to the local economy, and an Industrial Adjustment Service Committee (IAS) was established.

The IAS commissioned a study conducted by local people with local people, which recommended the creation of social and economic renewal committees, as well as a development company to assist local business development in several areas, including tourism, wood products, aquaculture, agriculture, crafts and small-scale manufacturing, information, and entertainment. The recommendation was also made to employ a full-time human services officer for counselling and training services (Development Isle Madame, 1999).

Structure

Because no government funding was available, several members of the IAS went on to form their own association to represent the interests of the community and the process that had been undertaken to that point. In 1995, the Development Isle Madame Association (DIMA) came into existence. The board members of this non-profit group volunteered their time and expertise. Operational funding was secured for one year, and a staff, including a general manager, development officer, and event coordinator, was hired. Several short-term projects were funded during that time, and some temporary jobs were created (Development Isle Madame, 1999). Some long-term projects were also funded, including an eco-trail, tank manufacturing, and a call centre. Projects in tourism and aquaculture development also began (DIMA News, 2006). The DIMA board did not depart completely from the fishing industry, however: in 1998, the board secured a license for 100 000 pounds of shrimp, which led to the existence of the Richmond Community Fishery Management Cooperative, owned by several local fisherman (CED Online, 2006).

Impact

This economic renewal effort has created almost 500 sustainable jobs in the areas of aquaculture, tourism, small-scale manufacturing, as well as information and communication technology. The unemployment rate for the Island is now 12.5% (from a high of 65%) and is competitive with the average rate for the province.

Effective Community Development Practice The Development Isle Madame Association exemplifies several features of effective community development practice in Canada. The efforts of local citizens from different backgrounds led to the undertaking of a strategic plan for the community (partnership). The plan for change came about as a result of surveys to local people about the opportunities and challenges they and their families were about to face with the upcoming closure of the community's largest employer (strengths-based). The broad representation of local interest groups, including business, unions, and educators, as well as youth and older adults, formed the basis for the non-profit organization, which was successful in obtaining support for several local projects (grassroots involvement). The varied sectors in which the projects took place, such as tourism, fishing, and manufacturing, are evidence of the practice of diversification as well as the interconnections between these economic and social activities in the community (integration).

SENIORS BRIDGING CULTURES CLUB, ST. JOHN'S, NEWFOUNDLAND AND LABRADOR

St. John's is the capital and largest city in Newfoundland and Labrador, with a population of approximately 100 000 (Statistics Canada, 2006j). Though slightly younger than the population of all provincial residents, the city's population has been aging. Due to migration trends and aging rural communities, the province and city will double their current number of older adults by 2020, when almost one-quarter of the total population is projected to be over the age of 65 (Newfoundland and Labrador Medical Association, 2003). The community saw the effects of this changing demographic as important to plan for in terms of health and employment issues.

Process

In 1988, a national conference on ethnicity and aging led to the development of a national coordinating committee on multiculturalism, aging, and seniors. A grant from this program funded two brainstorming meetings in St. John's in 1991. At these meetings, some of the attendees organized to form the Bridging Cultures Club, which created a place for seniors from different cultures to meet, once a week, to share friendship, stories, experiences, and recipes, as well as hear speakers (Law, 2004). The Club was supported in its early days by a local organization for older adults called the Seniors Resource Centre (SRC), and later became a formal part of the SRC.

As part of the SRC, the Seniors Bridging Cultures Club contributed to the development of a volunteer program. This program went through three developmental phases: (1) initial contact with ethnic groups to identify the needs of older adults; (2) a family fun day event to bring older adults and their families, from different cultures, together; and (3) starting the Volunteer Link program in 1999. The Volunteer Link program involved having older adults from diverse cultural backgrounds as presenters, to help their peers connect with the SRC and other organizations and services for older adults (Seniors Resource Centre, 2006).

Structure

The Seniors Bridging Cultures Club was actively involved in research and planning related to health care needs of older adults from diverse ethnocultural backgrounds. An advisory committee had funding to examine needs and develop policy recommendations. The committee included representatives from the Seniors Bridging Cultures Club, the SRC, and the university, as well as provincial and federal government and local non-profits working in the community with ethnocultural groups, such as the Chinese Association, Multicultural Women's Association, and the Sikh Society (Law, 2004).

Impact

This initiative has produced a report on health care needs for older adults from diverse cultural backgrounds (over 70 individuals from 25 different countries participated in the consultation), which led to the development of policy recommendations from the report (Seniors Bridging Cultures Club, 2004). The process brought out common experiences, and contributed to a collective voice that would influence provincial health care priorities (Department of Health and Community Services, 2006). Meetings between participants and senior administrators of local heath care boards were held to discuss problems and solutions. The boards agreed to offer information and training to their staff about health issues for older adults from diverse ethnocultural backgrounds, and to involve participants as formal members of their advisory committees (Law, 2004).

Effective Community Development Practice The Bridging Cultures Club illustrates several features of effective practice in community development. The Club itself is based on bringing people together from different backgrounds, experience, and cultures to learn from one another (integration). Local residents started the Club and have expanded it to bring in more people, to share their knowledge and skills, and to build their collective power (strengths-based). The Club continues to be administered by grassroots people (grassroots involvement). An important result of the efforts of this group, through research, has led to their partnership with the health care service system so that the needs of older adults are taken into account in planning for the future as well as current issues (partnership).

PROMISING APPROACHES TO COMMUNITY DEVELOPMENT PRACTICE

As these case studies demonstrate, there are many characteristics of effective community development practice, including integration, partnership, and grassroots involvement, as well as a strengths-based approach.

Each of the cases presented evidence of integration between the particular approach used and the social, political, and natural environments of the community at the time. Whether the community is a geographic area or a group of people in a small, isolated area, or within a large urban centre, the efforts made for change fit the realities of the people and context at that time. In some cases, the connections between natural and social environments are explicit and become the focus of development, whereas others offer a more implicit connection with the natural environment and emphasize, instead, the need for political and social change. The point is that community development practice is **holistic**. One-size-fits-all or **cookie-cutter approaches** are not successful.

All cases involved partnership. Building and maintaining trust, in fact, were crucial for the success of effective relationships. Whether the partners are members of diverse cultural, socioeconomic, or geographical communities does not matter. What is important is the **integrity** of the process of building relationships based on sharing. In all the cases we presented, the partners each brought something to contribute, ranging from personal experience, to financial resources, to technical skills, to connections to other stakeholders, to political influence. All brought time and willingness to help out, for the benefit of the collective.

In each case, the emphasis was on **grassroots** leadership. *Where* the initiative started mattered as much as who became involved. If, for example, a government started the initiative, the representatives were, in many cases, themselves members of the grassroots community (as is the case particularly in smaller communities). If they were not members of the grassroots community, they were at the table to begin a discussion that the community would take the next steps on. Without grassroots direction, community development ceases to be responsive and accountable and instead becomes a top-down effort.

Successful community development is based on strengths. There is obvious benefit to identifying a problem for funding purposes or to give a focal point for a gathering, but the definition should, as these cases illustrate, come from the community, and not be imposed from the outside. The very act of a community defining its own needs and assets is, in itself, strength. Effective solutions also come from the community, and are based on capacities. Every self-aware person knows that she or he has problems and difficulties, just as every community does. The energy for change comes from doing what one is good at; and at a community level, it means people contributing their strengths to help out others. These cases illustrate that community challenges can be addressed most effectively when the solutions are based on collective strengths.

SUMMARY

- Community development practice varies across different Canadian communities.
- Community practice depends on local history, process, and structure.
- The outcomes of community development are demonstrated in many different ways.
- Promising approaches to community development include integration, partnership, grassroots leadership, as well as following a strengths-based approach

DISCUSSION QUESTIONS

1. Think about your own community. What is the history? What are the current political, environmental, and social issues?

2. In what ways does community development begin, and what makes it progress?

3. What structures can communities use to organize community development efforts?

4. What is the difference between an output and an outcome? Why is this distinction important in community development practice?

5. Can you think of any examples of community development that you are familiar with?

WEBLINKS

www.hupacasath.ca/index.html Hupacasath First Nation

www.yukonartscentre.org/ Yukon Arts Centre

www.ccpsa.ca/ Canadian Cerebral Palsy Sports Association

www.communitiesforchildren.net/ Saskatoon Communities for Children

www.sofcg.org/about1.html School of Community Government

www.manitobacapc.org/asfc_english.htm Andrews Street Family Centre

www.nac.nu.ca/ Nunavut Arctic College

www.utoronto.ca/envstudy/sustainabletoronto/whoweare.htm Sustainable Toronto

www.danslarue.org/ Dans La Rue

www.peicaps.org/modules/news/ Prince Edward Island Community Access Program

www.islemadame.com/dima/ Development Isle Madame

www.seniorsresource.ca/sbcultures.htm Seniors Resource Centre

KEY TERMS

Cookie-cutter approaches, p. 134

Grassroots, p. 134

Hishukishtswalk, p. 116

Holistic, p. 134

Integrity, p. 134

Outputs, p. 127

Sustainability, p. 126

chapter nine

Aboriginal Community Development

LEARNING OBJECTIVES

After reading this chapter you will:

1. Recognize changes in historical relations between European settlers and Aboriginal peoples of Canada.
2. Understand a range of relationships that Aboriginal peoples have with the federal government.
3. Recognize the diversity among Aboriginal peoples, both geographically and culturally.
4. Appreciate the intent and impact of the Royal Commission on Aboriginal Peoples.
5. Recognize different forms that community development initiatives have taken within Aboriginal communities.
6. Appreciate the importance of local knowledge and customs to community workers in Aboriginal communities.

Aboriginal communities changed following the arrival of the Europeans; traditional ways of life were compromised. There were many years of attempts by the colonizers to forcibly assimilate Aboriginal peoples. The relationship with the federal government has been, and continues to be, a central issue for many communities as they work to enhance the health of members on a variety of social, economic, and environmental development initiatives. Despite facing multiple challenges, many initiatives have been developed by Aboriginal people for Aboriginal people. This chapter begins with a brief overview of historical relations between Aboriginal and non-Aboriginal peoples. We review recent demographic data to highlight diversity as well as contemporary social conditions. We also describe approaches to community development and the accomplishments of Aboriginal activists before turning to implications for community development work in indigenous communities.

CHAPTER OUTLINE

HISTORY

At the time of first contact, by the Norse in about AD 1000, Canada's Aboriginal peoples were largely hunters and gatherers who relied on knowledge as their technology. Many communities existed across a vast and diverse geography, and there were over 50 different languages spoken (Dickason, 1992). The communities were egalitarian and regulated by consensus; leaders represented the common will (Miller, 2001). Some communities were interrelated by trade. Gifts were a social and political obligation; they sealed and maintained different kinds of agreements and alliances (McMillan & Yellowhorn, 2004). And while the world views varied dramatically among both Aboriginal peoples and the Europeans, the differences between them were not as great as they were to become (Dickason, 1992).

The first English (John Cabot and Martin Frobisher) and French explorers (Jacques Cartier and Samuel de Champlain) arrived in the late sixteenth and seventeenth centuries, but did not settle permanently. The first permanent European settlements by the English were in Newfoundland in 1610, and by the French in Port Royal (Nova Scotia) in 1605. With the settlers came new diseases, such as smallpox and tuberculosis, which had a devastating effect on the Aboriginal population, who lacked immunity or resistance to the viruses. For example, the Beothuk peoples, who lived in what is now called Newfoundland, were completely wiped out by the mid-1800s due to displacement from their lands and epidemics of European diseases (Marshall, 1995).

Treaties

Formal agreements between Aboriginal peoples and Europeans, known as **treaties**, concerned the relationships between nations. The earliest agreements were about maintaining peaceful relations over a long term. They often included provisions about trade, and local resources (e.g., fishing, trapping), and land use. The phrase "as long as the sun shines and the rivers flow" first appeared in a written treaty in 1794 between the Mi'kmaq and French in Port Royal, to show the enduring nature of that agreement (Wildsmith, 1985, p. 200). Aboriginal peoples saw these agreements as reciprocal; the Europeans could share the lands as long as the rights of the Aboriginal peoples were protected (Dickason, 1998). Over 500 treaties exist between governments and over half of all Aboriginal peoples across Canada. And while many treaties were created hundreds of years ago, some treaty negotiations are ongoing (Dickason, 1998). A recent example, which we highlighted in Chapter 8, is the agreement that came into effect on April 1, 1999, creating the territory of Nunavut.

Colonization

Europeans came to Canada and established colonies. The primary purpose of the new colonies was economic development of the land and those residing on it for the benefit of the "Old World" country, such as France or England. The colonizers made assumptions about Aboriginal peoples, and decided that their way of life was "inferior." Through techniques of assimilation or extinction, the colonizers attempted to force Aboriginal peoples to adopt European ways (Long & Dickason, 1998). Scholars have described the colonization of Aboriginal peoples as occurring in several ways (Chrisjohn, Young, & Mauraun, 1997; Milloy, 1999; Thira, 2005). **Legal colonization** included legislation to control the perceived "savage" population through suppression of legal rights (e.g., denial of the right to vote until 1960). **Administrative colonization**, through the forcible relocation and confinement to a particular land base, was intended to make Aboriginal peoples easier to govern (e.g., the reserve system). **Ideological colonization** included implementing strategies to assimilate children into non-Aboriginal communities (e.g., residential schools). **Medical colonization** grouped all social and economic problems together, and reorganized them as problems stemming from individual sickness, implying the need for a Western "cure" (e.g., mental health treatment).

ABORIGINAL PEOPLES AND THE CONSTITUTION

Aboriginal peoples are recognized in the constitution (Government of Canada, 1982) to include the North American Indian, Inuit, and Metis people of Canada. A **Registered Indian** is someone recorded in the register, which is maintained by the Federal Department of Indian and Northern Affairs (Government of Canada, 2004). Under the Indian Act (1876), Canadians who were entitled to registration may have lost that entitlement if, for example, a woman married someone who was not registered, or if one chose to give it up (until 1960, people who were registered could not vote in a Federal election). Others lost the entitlement to registration after residing outside of Canada for more than five years. In 1985 this changed with **Bill C-31,** which allowed people affected in these ways to register or have their registration restored. However, many eligible people didn't register.

Metis peoples are a distinct Aboriginal nation, of Aboriginal and non-Aboriginal decent. The Inuit are Aboriginal peoples who generally resided in the Yukon, the Northwest Territories, Northern Quebec, and Labrador, north of the treeline. **First Nations** is a term that is often used to identify Aboriginal peoples who are neither Inuit nor Metis. Each group has a different relationship with the government.

First Nations peoples who are registered are entitled to provisions under the Indian Act. Most First Nations peoples who are registered with the federal government are members of a local band; most bands control their own membership (Government of Canada, 2004). **Band members** may have the right to live on reserve. Members of a band that signed a treaty are entitled to whatever terms of agreement were made between the British or Canadian governments with their band. For example, members may have a right to a share of money from oil and gas royalties or land settlements.

DEMOGRAPHICS

Aboriginal peoples are a fast-growing and diverse population. Yet health and social conditions continue to be relatively poor compared to non-Aboriginal peoples in Canada.

The 2001 Census reported that 976 305 citizens reported Aboriginal identity, that about half of those (558 175) reported registered status, and about the same proportion (554 860) reported band membership (Siggner, 2003). The majority of people with Aboriginal identity are First Nations (62 percent), the Metis make up about 30 percent, and the Inuit comprise approximately 8 percent of Aboriginal peoples in Canada.

Between 1996 and 2001, there was a 22 percent increase in self-identification as Aboriginal, including a 43-percent increase among Metis peoples. Part of this increase is due to awareness of cultural roots. However, there has also been an increase in Aboriginal birth rates and life expectancy (Guimond, 2003). Based on an annual population growth rate of more than twice the national average, the number of people self-identifying as Aboriginal is expected to increase by about 400 000 by 2017 (Statistics Canada, 2005b). The Aboriginal population will remain younger than the Canadian average, and many young adults will be entering the job market in the next few years. Although most who self-identify as Aboriginal peoples will live in Ontario, the second highest absolute number of Aboriginal peoples will reside in Alberta, and then British Columbia, Manitoba, and, finally, Saskatchewan. In provinces where the Aboriginal population represents a high proportion of the total population, the proportion of children (aged 0–14) and young adults (aged 20–29) is expected to increase. For example, by 2017, 37 percent of children in Saskatchewan could be Aboriginal, and 31 percent in Manitoba.

Diversity

There is a great deal of diversity among Aboriginal peoples. Community size and location vary considerably, from small populations on large parcels of land, to large populations in tiny areas. The communities may be First Nations' reserves or Metis or Inuit settlements, within urban centres (e.g., the Muskeg Lake Cree First Nation Urban Reserve in Saskatoon) or in remote locations (e.g., Alert, a small Inuit community on Ellesmere Island, the most northerly inhabited settlement in the world). The wealth of a community also varies, from those where the local resources and agreements have meant more money for residents, to communities with difficulties meeting basic sanitation needs (e.g., Kashechewan, Ontario).

Some Aboriginal communities have been physically relocated (e.g., see *Inuit Relocation in the Eastern Arctic*, by Tester and Kulchyski, 1994). While many Aboriginal people live on reserves, the non-reserve Aboriginal population has grown. In fact, about 70 percent of the total Aboriginal identity population in Canada lives off-reserve, and 68 percent of Aboriginal peoples live in urban areas (O'Donnell & Tait, 2003). Some reserves have signed treaties, which do not necessarily mean better economic conditions for members, and others have land tenure (i.e., own their land). There are Aboriginal peoples who have had direct experience with residential schools. Others have experienced the effects indirectly. The legacy of abuse in residential schools "includes the effects of survivors, their families, descendants and communities (including communities of interest). These effects may include, and are not limited to, family violence, drug, alcohol and substance abuse, physical and sexual abuse, loss of parenting skills and self-destructive behaviour" (Stout & Kipling, 2003, p. 7).

Indeed, there are many variations in culture, traditional ways, and current practices of traditional and Western ways among Aboriginal peoples in Canada. Some communities are united in their beliefs, values, and traditions, while others reflect greater diversity. The values may be traditional Aboriginal ways, more Western ways (e.g., Christianity), or a combination of both. The degree to which Aboriginal peoples are immersed in traditional teachings and practices varies considerably between, as well as within, communities. It is therefore absolutely crucial to understand the history and traditions as well as the current realities of any community, and Aboriginal communities are no exception.

Health and Social Conditions

The life chances for Aboriginal peoples in Canada are different than non-Aboriginal people, including a lower life expectancy, a higher frequency of illness, higher rates of social problems such as family violence and alcohol abuse, lower high school graduation rates, poor housing, inadequate water and sanitation systems, higher unemployment, and over-representation in child protection and justice systems (Government of Canada, 1996).

A recent example of problems with basic sanitation difficulties faced by a community is the Cree Nation of Kashechewan, Ontario. In 2005, this community of about 2000 people on the south shore of James Bay had hundreds of people airlifted out because of medical problems associated with the community's contaminated water supply. The location of the community, on a flood plain, was a major contributor to this long-standing problem. However, basic sanitation problems as a result of old, malfunctioning water treatment plant equipment that could not keep up with demand, had been identified as early as 2001 (in Kashechewan, as well as many other First Nations communities) (Ontario Clean Water Agency, 2001). The Ontario Clean Water Agency (OCWA) reported in 2003 that Kashechewan was a "Walkerton-in-waiting" (Canadian Television Network, 2006). It was not until after many attempts by the community to draw attention to the issue, in 2005, that the federal government began to pay attention, and the Chief and council were able to negotiate with the Department of Indian Affairs to move the community to higher ground.

Aboriginal women in Canada are relatively youthful mothers and have larger families than non-Aboriginal women do (Statistics Canada, 2003a). Their health profile is what "one would normally associate with the developing world" (Stout, Kipling & Stout, 2001, p.12), including a high rate of poverty, unemployment, and low-paying jobs, as well as high rates of mortality and disabilities. Frequencies of hypertension and diabetes are much greater than in the non-Aboriginal population in Canada (Health Canada, 1999).

Moreover, Aboriginal children are more likely to reside outside of their communities in out-of-home placements, including institutions, than are non-Aboriginal children (Blackstock & Bennett, 2003; Bennett & Blackstock, 2002). For example, the institutionalization rates for Aboriginal children with disabilities in Manitoba are significant. Aboriginal children aged 0–19 made up 6.8 percent of the general population and 18 percent of the institutionalized population (Evans, Hunter, Thompson & Ramsey, 1985, cited in Martens, 2000).

THEORY OF STAGES

Dockstator (1993), an Aboriginal scholar, described the relationship between Aboriginal and non-Aboriginal peoples as a series of stages, namely, separate worlds, contact and co-operation, displacement and assimilation, and negotiation and renewal. Before 1500, during the **separate worlds** stage, the societies developed in isolation from each other, separated by the Atlantic Ocean. Each developed and maintained its own ways of governance that met the needs of its people in their geographical and cultural context. During **contact and co-operation**, from about the 1500s to the 1700s, there was frequent contact between Aboriginal and European societies. Europeans began to settle in North America, and Aboriginal peoples assisted newcomers in adapting to the land. During this time, trade alliances were developed, and mutual respect was shown. However, as the immigrant population grew, the First Peoples' population declined because of exposure to new diseases and their treatment by the settlers.

While social, political, and cultural differences were initially maintained, tolerance of the distinctiveness of Aboriginal societies waned among the colonists. During the **displacement and assimilation** stage, from the 1700s to early 1900s, non-Aboriginals used a variety of methods to attempt to systematically destroy Aboriginal cultures (Neu & Therrien, 2003). These methods included relocations, residential schools, and making cultural practices illegal:

> Aboriginal peoples were displaced physically . . . denied access to their traditional territories and in many cases actually forced to move to new locations selected for them by colonial authorities. They were also displaced socially and culturally, subject to intensive missionary activity and the establishment of schools which undermined their ability to pass on traditional values to their children, imposed male-oriented Victorian values, and attacked traditional activities such as significant dances and other ceremonies. . . they were also displaced politically, forced by colonial laws to abandon or at least disguise traditional governing structures and processes. (Indian and Northern Affairs Canada, 1996a, Chapter 4, p. 6)

Negotiation and Renewal

These efforts at assimilation were not successful at undermining social values or a sense of distinctiveness among Aboriginal peoples. Admission of the failure of these efforts by non-Aboriginal society marks the beginning of the final stage: **negotiation and renewal**. This recognition has been fueled by national social and political organizations, court decisions on Aboriginal rights, and sympathetic public opinion, as well as developments in international law and the mobilization of indigenous peoples throughout the world. A major turning point in Aboriginal relations with the federal government came in the early 1990s with the Royal Commission on Aboriginal Peoples.

THE ROYAL COMMISSION ON ABORIGINAL PEOPLES

In 1991, a **Royal Commission on Aboriginal Peoples** was established. Its purpose was to "investigate the evolution of the relationship among Aboriginal peoples, the Canadian Government, and Canadian society as a whole" (Indian and Northern Affairs Canada, 1996b). Over four years, four Aboriginal commissioners and three non-Aboriginal commissioners conducted 178 days of public hearings, visited 96 communities, consulted numerous experts, commissioned multiple research studies, and reviewed previous reports. The final report, which was made public in 1996, proposed four principles for the development of a new relationship: recognition, respect, sharing, and responsibility.

> The commissioners made over 400 recommendations. They focused on the relationships between Aboriginal and non-Aboriginal peoples and Canadian governments (Langton, Tehan, Palmer & Shain, 2004). While there were several key recommendations, the authors emphasized the essential themes that underpinned those recommendations: First, Aboriginal nations have to be reconstituted . . .
>
> Second, a process must be established for the assumption of powers by Aboriginal nations...
>
> Third, there must be a fundamental reallocation of lands and resources...
>
> Fourth, Aboriginal people need education and crucial skills for governance and economic self-reliance...
>
> Finally, economic development must be addressed if the poverty and despondency of lives defined by unemployment and welfare are to change. (Indian and Northern Affairs Canada, 1996c, p.1–3)

In 1998, the government's report, titled *Gathering Strength: Canada's Aboriginal Action Plan,* set out a series of policy objectives called Renewing the Partnership, Strengthening Aboriginal Governance, Developing a New Fiscal Relationship, and Supporting Strong Communities, People and Economics. While the promise to create a "healing fund" to address the legacy of abuse in the residential school system has been kept, progress on measures to enhance participation and control in government and improve living conditions through infrastructure and skills training has been the subject of some debate.

In 2004, a First Minister's meeting, led by Liberal Prime Minister Paul Martin, with National Aboriginal leaders and premiers, was held in Kelowna, British Columbia. The purpose of the meeting was to discuss Aboriginal issues and key determinants of health. The report, called the **Kelowna Accord**, specified a 10-year commitment to closing the poverty gap between Aboriginal and non-Aboriginal peoples in Canada. The report focused on four key areas: health, education, housing, and relationships. With the agreement came a commitment for funding of $5 billion. However, a new Conservative government and prime minister, elected in 2006, dismissed the Kelowna Accord, and instead committed to a total of $750 million for housing and water systems in Aboriginal communities within its first budget.

ABORIGINAL COMMUNITY DEVELOPMENT

Canada's Aboriginal peoples have had a long history of engaging in community development. Some community development has reflected the tactics of the Chicago-based social activist, Saul Alinsky, whom we discussed in Chapter 3. However, many of the elements of "power politics" advocated by Alinsky were known and practised by Canadian Aboriginal peoples long before Alinsky used them. For example, Aboriginal leaders often set out to educate people about their rights, and worked to build strong coalitions with concrete objectives before engaging in a variety of nonviolent strategies to pressure the targets into meeting demands.

Typically, these pressure tactics met with strong resistance from governments, whose usual response was to suppress the activity in some way, or to discredit the Aboriginal activists and the organizations they represented. Other strategies to silence the activists included dragging out negotiations for as long as possible, or calling for more studies in the hope that the pressure for change would evaporate before a decision was to be made. The government also diverted funds to less militant organizations, or engaged in divide-and-conquer tactics to weaken a coalition.

F.O. Loft

One of the earliest Aboriginal community developers in Canada was the Mohawk F.O. Loft, from the Six Nations reserve in southern Ontario. In 1918 he founded the League of Indians of Canada (Kulchyski, 1998). Loft's goal was to form a coalition of Aboriginal groups from across Canada to put pressure on the federal government: to grant Aboriginal peoples the right to vote; for greater local autonomy; for a new system of nonreligious schools; for protected hunting rights; and for more economic development on the reserves. Within a few years, Loft's organization had 9000 members from across Canada and was able to attract up to 1500 members to its rallies.

For more than a decade, F.O. Loft was an important symbol of Aboriginal solidarity in Canada. The federal government was clearly shaken by his actions and responded in a variety of ways. For example, a vast network of spies monitored the League's activities and harassed and intimidated its members. The Department of Indian Affairs refused to release funds for Aboriginal peoples to attend the League's rallies, even though, technically, these funds belonged to the bands and were merely held in trust for them by the department. Royal Canadian Mounted Police (RCMP) officers were a threatening presence at these rallies, and disruptive questioners were sometimes planted in the crowd to cause trouble.

When these strategies failed to deter Aboriginal peoples from finding their collective voice, the federal Conservative government of the day responded by attempting to force Loft to renounce his Aboriginal status through compulsory "enfranchisement"—an attempt that failed. Enfranchisement meant that Aboriginal peoples had to surrender their status as an Indian if they wanted to become full-fledged citizens of Canada (and obtain voting rights). In 1922, the new Liberal government in Ottawa repealed the compulsory enfranchisement clause. A few years later, in 1927, the federal government passed an amendment that made it illegal for Aboriginal peoples to raise money for court actions; and when Loft attempted to organize a legal challenge to the provincial game laws in 1931, the federal government began preparations to take him to court. Soon after, in failing health, Loft abandoned his political activism.

John Tootoosis

John Tootoosis was a Cree activist and leader in Saskatchewan. He frequently suffered extreme hardship as he travelled to reserves throughout the province by horse, often pursued by the RCMP although he had broken no laws (Goodwill, 1982). From 1885, when the federal government was concerned about Aboriginal peoples joining the Riel Rebellion, until the 1950s, Aboriginal peoples were required to obtain a permit from the local Indian Agent before they could leave their reserve. In 1934, Tootoosis applied for a permit so that he could travel to various reserves to inform members about their treaty rights. His request was refused, but he set out on his journey, anyway. While passing through Edmonton on his way to Driftpile, he was apprehended by police and told to return to his reserve (Goodwill, 1982). He refused. Since the requirement for Aboriginal peoples to have a travel permit was merely a policy of the Department of Indian Affairs, but not a law enforceable by the courts, Tootoosis was eventually allowed to continue on his way. He was closely monitored by Indian Agents, and denounced by church ministers as an agent of the Devil. John was instrumental in the development of the Union of Saskatchewan Indians in 1946. Over the years he served as both president and executive member for the Union. In 1959 the Union reorganized as the Federation of Saskatchewan Indians, and he was elected its first president.

Chief Deskaheh

In the early 1920s, Chief Deskaheh, an Iroquois leader, demanded complete sovereignty for his Six Nations reserve near Brantford, Ontario. While pursuing that goal, Chief Deskaheh employed a number of strategies that would be familiar to social activists today, including organizing fundraising events such as lacrosse games, hiring lawyers, lobbying the federal government, travelling to London to lobby the British government, meeting foreign diplomats, petitioning the League of Nations (the forerunner of the UN), which refused to hear his case, and generating media coverage.

The force of the federal government's opposition to Chief Deskaheh's efforts was a testament to his superb organizing skills. The government's response to these actions was to establish a permanent RCMP detachment on the reserve, abolish the band's hereditary council, and condone acts of intimidation and harassment by the RCMP and Indian Agents. Even so, the protests continued, and the RCMP was eventually forced to hire an informer to spy on the political activities on the reserve.

Chief Deskaheh's campaign was the first attempt to bring the issue of indigenous rights to the international forum. The following is an excerpt from his last speech, via radio, in Rochester, New York, on March 10, 1925:

> I ask you a question or two. Do not hurry with your answers. Do you believe—really believe—that all peoples are entitled to equal protection of international law now that you are so strong? Do you believe—really believe—that treaty pledges should be kept? Think these questions over and answer them to yourselves." (American Indian Law Alliance, 2002, p. 1)

Post-War Activism

Since the Second World War, governments have become less crude in the techniques they have used to suppress Aboriginal activism, and sometimes have been supportive of those efforts. In 1946, Saskatchewan's NDP government, led by Tommy Douglas, became the first provincial government to fund an Aboriginal organizational meeting, and by the 1960s, the National Indian Council had become an official voice of Canada's Aboriginal peoples.

In 1969, however, a key event triggered a national outcry from Aboriginal peoples and their supporters, and led to a new form of militarism among Aboriginal peoples in Canada. In that year, the Liberal Trudeau government proposed to curtail the traditional federal obligation toward indigenous peoples by abolishing the concept of Aboriginal rights, terminating the reserve system, phasing out the Department of Indian Affairs, and making the provinces responsible for Aboriginal issues. The *Statement of Government of Canada on Indian Policy* was also known as the "White Paper" (Myers & Craig, 2002).

The plan was eventually abandoned in the face of tremendous opposition from increasingly well-organized and sophisticated Aboriginal groups, including the National Indian Brotherhood, representing Status Indians, and the Native Council of Canada, which represented Metis and non-status Indians.

Several violent clashes took place between Aboriginal activists and the police over the next few years, and in an attempt to defuse the threat to law and order, the federal government began to fund many of the more moderate Aboriginal organizations, which were then able to engage in increasingly sophisticated lobbying activities. One of their most significant successes was the amendment to the Canadian Constitution, which recognized the existing treaty rights of Canada's Aboriginal peoples. The influence of a coordinated Aboriginal presence was again felt when Elijah Harper, a (then) Aboriginal MLA in Manitoba, was able to defeat the Meech Lake Accord a few years later.

Although some Aboriginal organizations have become increasingly influential in recent years, the role of the individual social activist remains as strong as ever. Among the better known are Bernard Ominayak from Alberta and Louis Stevenson from Manitoba.

Bernard Ominayak was elected chief of the Lubicon Lake Band (northern Alberta), in 1978 at the age of 28. The federal government had promised a reserve and treaty benefits to the Lubicons in 1940, but had never acted on that promise. By the late 1970s, the land rights issue had become critical, as the Lubicon's traditional lifestyle, based on hunting and trapping, was threatened by an increased pace of oil exploration and logging in the area. When the federal and provincial governments refused to act on the Lubicons' concerns, the band embarked on a strategy of nonviolent social action, involving court cases, demonstrations, boycotts, lobbying, blockades, media campaigns, and sustained political pressure (Goddard, 1991). In carrying out these activities, the band was advised by Fred Lennarson, a non-Aboriginal social activist who had trained under Saul Alinsky in Chicago. To keep pressure on the government, the Lubicons frequently changed tactics, but continued to keep their allies well informed. Ominayak organized a boycott of the Calgary Olympics, and, since 1983, his group has received regular funding from the World Council of Churches. To date, the Lubicons have built a network of support throughout Canada and in nine foreign countries.

Louis Stevenson, chief of the Peguis Band in Manitoba, also used imaginative social action strategies to improve conditions for his people, and met with considerable success. Probably his most effective strategy was to embarrass Canada's leaders in the international community by seeking a loan from South Africa and inviting the South African ambassador in Ottawa to inspect their reserve, which the ambassador did, accompanied by the media (Boldt, 1996). Clearly, this was a political act, designed to inform the world of the hypocrisy of Canada's condemnation of South Africa's treatment of its indigenous peoples while ignoring the plight of its own Aboriginal peoples. The strategy worked, and the federal government freed up significant funds shortly after this incident for the Peguis peoples to build a shopping mall and a treatment centre on their reserve, which reduced unemployment considerably.

Other social action strategies Stevenson used included forcing the federal government to build a new bridge on the reserve by burning down an old, unsafe one; organizing demonstrations and "sit-ins" at the offices of the Department of Indian Affairs; and reunifying Manitoba Aboriginal peoples under the Assembly of Manitoba Chiefs to ensure a stronger voice for the province's Aboriginal peoples (Comeau & Santin, 1990).

In other parts of Canada, Aboriginal groups have used a variety of social action strategies to draw attention to their concerns. In British Columbia, the Haida of the Queen Charlotte Islands issued travel permits to tourists visiting the area (Horwood, 2000), while the Cree in Quebec travelled to Geneva to make submissions to the United Nations Human Rights Commission (Sanders, 1994) and were also able to negotiate an adequate compensation package to offset the negative impacts of the flooding caused by the James Bay hydro project. More recently, Six Nations demonstrators blocked access through Caledonia, Ontario, in protest of housing to be built on traditional lands (Canadian Broadcasting Corporation, 2006). Roseau River Anishinabe Chief Terry Nelson, in Manitoba, led a coalition of several First Nations bands, who gave notice that they planned to block railway traffic on Canadian National and Canadian Pacific tracks to protest delays in settling land claims (*Winnipeg Free Press*, 2006).

HOLISTIC APPROACHES

Approaches to community development in Aboriginal communities may be guided by the principles of balance, stages of change, and strength. Community development takes into account the past, present, and future of each of four dimensions, as well as the interconnections among them. The goal of development is to find balance between the physical, mental, emotional, and spiritual (McCormick, 1997). Indeed, "just as the four elements (spiritual, emotional, physical and mental) in each person's life must work in unison for the balance to be achieved, all fragmented parts of Aboriginal people's past, present and future must be re-integrated again to facilitate healing on a communal level" (Wesley-Esquimaux & Smolewski, 2004, p. 18).

Some scholars describe change within Aboriginal communities as a progression through a series of stages (Lane, Bopp, Bopp, & Norris, 2004). The first is **Winter season**, where the journey begins. In this stage, the community is in crisis. Many of its members are involved in unhealthy patterns of behaviour that together consume its energy. Yet to many members, this situation may be considered "normal." The members who want to make changes begin to talk and start to form a critical mass. The second stage is the **Spring season**, where the community is gathering momentum. The change that started with the members in stage one becomes more widely accepted, and participation in change efforts strengthens. There is a growing sense of optimism. However, this does not last, for in **Summer**, the community feels like progress has stalled. Although significant change has been made, it has not been transformational. There are still groups within the community who are experiencing the same negative situations, or new issues have arisen to strip energy away from the work that has been done. It is in the final stage, the **Fall**, where a major change in consciousness takes place. Healing becomes less about repairing what is wrong, and more about transforming systems. This stage is about building upon strengths from within the community. The community's focus changes from what government can do for them, to what they can do for each other.

It has been proposed that the development process in Aboriginal communities should be based on an understanding of people's strengths and natural ways of helping (Nwachuku &

Ivey, 1991). In some communities, ways of helping included exercise, expressing emotion, building social connections, and addressing spirits. These activities served to restore balance, strengthen interconnections, and achieve transcendence (McCormick, 1995/1996).

Outcomes

The outcomes of self-initiated community development in Aboriginal communities has ranged from developing integrated responses to crisis (such as multidisciplinary and cross-organizational teams to address critical health issues affecting a community), creating better public policy (such as community-based governance), linking economic development as well as a variety of personal wellness initiatives (such as local social enterprise activities, and businesses that trade with a social purpose) (Bopp & Bopp 2001; Four Worlds, 1989). Community development has also included integrated community healing (such as community-based programming, based on traditional, Western methods, or both) and development planning (such as setting long-range goals and activities for the physical, economic, social, and spiritual well-being of residents) (Warry, 1998).

These changes may require the development of different ways of governance, resource allocation, and social impacts, in the interest of self-determination. These changes are often a blend of the past ways, current realities, and future goals for a community. Some guiding principals for policy change include the following (Clarkson, Morrissette, & Régallet, 1992):

- Protection for the traditional way of life
- Documentation, promotion and protection of traditional knowledge and practices
- Healing programs
- Education for cultural survival
- Economic self-reliance
- The development of a communication capacity

Practice Principles

There are some principles that can be used as a guide for community development in indigenous communities (Emery, 2000):

1. Indigenous communities should be able to provide free and informed prior consent before any development project is initiated.
2. Indigenous communities should be able to choose their own representatives and not have them assigned.
3. Indigenous traditional knowledge is best acquired by engaging indigenous holders of the knowledge as active participants in the project, using traditional knowledge as part of the team of experts.
4. Indigenous peoples' participation as bearers of traditional knowledge is best achieved by observing trust, respect, equity, and empowerment as the basic principles of interaction.
5. Traditional rights to resources, self-governance, and the integrity and autonomy of indigenous peoples' cultural realities should be respected.

SUMMARY

- The first permanent European settlements in Canada were in seventeenth century Nova Scotia and Newfoundland.
- Treaties between Aboriginal peoples and the French and English were agreements about how they would peacefully coexist.
- The constitution recognizes Aboriginal peoples as the First Nations, Metis, and Inuit peoples of Canada.
- The Aboriginal population is growing in size and diversity, and is overrepresented in several categories of social and economic challenges.
- The relationships between Aboriginal and non-Aboriginal peoples have progressed through a series of stages, with the last being negotiation and renewal.
- The Royal Commission on Aboriginal Peoples led to a report that recommended multiple and major changes to the relationships between Aboriginal and non-Aboriginal peoples, and addressed serious gaps in health and economic status.
- Influential Aboriginal leaders in the early 1900s included F.O. Loft, John Tootoosis, and Chief Deskaheh.
- Self-initiated and grassroots-led contemporary community development in Aboriginal communities is typically holistic in approach.

DISCUSSION QUESTIONS

1. Consider your own values, beliefs, and customs. What do you hold onto most strongly? Why? How are these similar to and different from those of others in your family, peer group, and classmates? How can you work together?
2. How would you as a worker approach development in a community where the values, beliefs, and traditions are very different from your own?
3. What was the Royal Commission on Aboriginal Peoples, and what effects have the recommendations had on Aboriginal communities?
4. What is *healing*? Do individuals, families, and communities heal in the same way, or in different ways? Which comes first? Why?
5. What forms of community economic development have you heard of in Aboriginal communities? Why is there a wide range of ideas and approaches?

WEBLINKS

www.dwatch.ca/ Democracy Watch

www.iisd.org/7thgen/default.htm International Institute for Sustainable Development

www.aboriginaltimes.com/ Aboriginal Times

www.taiaiake.com/home/index.htm Indigenous Pathways of Action and Freedom

www.aptn.ca/ Aboriginal Peoples' Television Network

www.aboriginalcanada.gc.ca/ Aboriginal Canada Portal

www.cnpr.ca/Home.aspx Centre for Native Policy and Research

www.icah.ca/content/en/topics/subtopic/section.php?tcid=98&stcid=65 Information Centre on Aboriginal Health

KEY TERMS

Administrative colonization, p. 138

Band members, p. 139

Bill C-31, p. 138

Contact and co-operation stage, p. 141

Displacement and assimilation stage, p. 141

Fall (stage of development), p. 146

First Nations, p. 139

Ideological colonization, p. 138

Kelowna Accord, p. 142

Legal colonization, p. 138

Medical colonization, p. 138

Negotiation and renewal stage, p. 141

Registered Indian, p. 138

Royal Commission on Aboriginal Peoples, p. 142

Separate worlds stage, p. 141

Spring (stage of development), p. 146

Summer (stage of development), p. 146

Treaties, p. 138

Winter (stage of development), p. 146

chapter ten

International Community Development

LEARNING OBJECTIVES

After reading this chapter, you will be able to:

1. Appreciate the history of imperialism and early efforts in international development.
2. Understand the Human Development Index, its strengths and limitations.
3. Distinguish between the two major periods of international community development.
4. Identify the seven major foci of the United Nations Millennium Report.
5. Recognize the difference between structural and cognitive social capital.
6. Understand how social capital has an impact on human development.

Although indigenous community development has been practised for a very long time all over the world, efforts have been made throughout history by some nations to take over the lands and peoples of others. However, these dated ideas of "helping" others by force, or assimilation, are being replaced by increasing recognition of national sovereignty and the right to develop in ways that are appropriate to a people's history, culture, and current reality. Early efforts made to improve the economic conditions of nations had devastating economic, social, and environmental effects. More recent efforts have been more holistic in nature. The United Nations prepared a report on international development for the new millennium in 2000, turning attention to several focal international issues concerning poverty, education, gender issues, children's health, maternal health, disease, and the enviroment. Canadians have been very involved in international community work, and have been positively recognized for their efforts.

CHAPTER OUTLINE

IMPERIALISM

Although more often seen in positive terms today, early international development activities were undertaken to benefit one nation by taking over the resources, such as land or people, of another nation. **Imperialism** refers to a policy of taking control of foreign resources to create an empire that benefits the imperialist nation. The imperialists created **colonies**, which are territories under the political control of a foreign country. For example, Britain and France practised imperialism during the mid-1800s, creating colonies in Africa as well as North and South America, including the colonies that eventually became Canada.

The key element of imperialism is control of one nation by another. It can happen indirectly or directly, through force or negotiation. For example, the French imperialist efforts in Africa during the nineteenth century focused on turning the African peoples into French peoples, through efforts targeting their language and culture (Conklin, 1997). The British efforts, in contrast, focused on making a profit, primarily from exporting raw materials and maintaining trade routes. They left territories when they perceived an insufficient return for their efforts (Ferguson, 2002).

Scholars disagree on the outcomes of imperialism for the nation targeted for expansion. Socialist Vladimir Lenin, a follower of Karl Marx, described imperialism as a necessary outgrowth of capitalism. According to Leninist scholars, capitalism required economic growth. New sources of raw materials, and processing them into goods that could be sold for a profit, necessitated the expansion of territory for raw materials and cheap labour (Kowalik, 2003). From this perspective, the imperialists gain money and the target nation loses resources. Others argue that there were positive outcomes to the target nation, such as improvements to infrastructure—roads, waterways, and railroads—as well as medical treatment, improved sanitation systems, and new crops (Cohen, 1973; Johnson, 1985).

Modern imperialism concerns not only political and economic factors, but refers to cultural influence and impact as well. For example, in his 1963 book *The Wretched of the Earth*, about the Algerian struggle for independence from colonial rule, Frantz Fanon summarized the impact of imperialism with the following statement: "European opulence has been founded on slavery. The well-being and progress of Europe have been built up with the sweat and the dead bodies of Negroes, Arabs, Indians, and the yellow races" (Fanon, 1963, p. 45). Another more recent example is the role of the United States in the world and whether the power it exercises amounts to imperialism. Because the military strength of the United States is unparalleled and tied to its world-class economic power, recent actions in oil-rich nations (e.g., a forced change of government in Iraq, heavily funded through U.S.-led corporations with military contracts) cause some to characterize these efforts as imperialistic (Boyle, 2004). In North America, media coverage of these military actions depicts soldiers eating at U.S. fast-food restaurants and watching American movie stars and musicians, as a way of emphasizing not only political and economic success, but cultural dominance, too.

INTERNATIONAL COMMUNITY DEVELOPMENT

Community development on a global level has been defined in a variety of ways. International community development may be described as both a process and a goal (Sillitoe, Bicker, & Pottier, 2002). The initiators of development efforts can be local community leaders, local government, or other players on the international scene, including other governments and non-profits. As in Canada, international community development is long term and not emergent in nature (e.g., disaster relief). Choice allows us to distinguish between the concept of international community development and modern imperialism. To meet this criterion, nations affected by development activities must make the decisions about the processes and goals of those activities, and assume that they are also the beneficiaries of those activities. In contemporary use, international community development is not limited to improvements in economic conditions, but includes attention to health, social, and environmental conditions through an inclusive and empowering process.

In 1990, the United Nations Development Program introduced the Human Development Index, in its Human Development Report. The **Human Development Index** (HDI) is a numerical indicator ranging from 0 to 1, based on longevity, knowledge, and standard of living, by nation. Longevity is measured by life expectancy, and knowledge is measured by a combination of adult literacy rate and average years of schooling in that country. Standard of living is measured by local purchasing power. Together, these indicators yield one measure of well-being that is used to make international comparisons, and as part of the way that nations are described as developed, developing, or underdeveloped (Van Ginkel, Barrett, Court, & Velasquez, 2002).

A developed nation is one where there is a high standard of living with a diversified and industrialized economy; and the HDI is a measure of a nation's standard of living.

Those countries with an HDI above .80 would have a relatively high standard of living. A **diversified economy** has many varied components (Monti-Belkaoui & Riahi-Belkaoui, 1998).

For example, tourism, technology, and agricultural trade would constitute a relatively diverse economy. In contrast, an undiversified economy, such as what one might find where there is one industry present (e.g., a gold mine), would collapse if that industry were to fail. **Industrialization** refers to the use of technology for improved production capability (Messere, 1998). To build on the previous example, individuals panning for gold would be considered pre-industrial, but a mine utilizing heavy equipment would be considered industrial.

A total of 31 nations are considered to be developed countries (Narlikar, 2003), including most of Western Europe, Japan, Singapore, South Korea, Israel, and Iceland, as well as the United States, Canada, Australia, and New Zealand. These countries have also been referred to as countries of "the north," indicating their relative wealth and political influence compared to those of "the south." This division is known as the **north-south divide**.

A developing nation is one where there is a moderate to low standard of living and low industrialization. Those countries with an HDI between .80 and .50 would have a moderate standard of living, and those with an HDI lower than .50 would be considered to have a low standard of living. There is an implication that developing nations are progressing toward change (for example, India and Brazil). In contrast, a least developed nation, by definition, is static in terms of standard of living and industrialization progress (Gonzalez & Norwine, 1998). These nations are sometimes referred to as **Third World** or **underdeveloped**. It should be noted that the terminology used to describe relative differences between countries by rank indicates their relative status in terms of social and economic "progress." Some authors, however, caution about ranking countries based on the HDI, arguing that the measurement on universal standards of success implies an inferiority for those nations ranked relatively low on the scale (Cypher & Dietz, 1997).

Community development workers from developed nations working in developing nations need to be acutely aware of and guard against perceptions that their nation's relatively "successful" record of development gives them the "right answers" for other nations. As we have noted, there is a fine line between international community development and imperialism.

A BRIEF HISTORY

Although contemporary international development was said to have started in the 1950s when U.S. president Harry Truman called for a "bold new program" for improvement, growth, and development in developing nations (Cowen & Shenton, 1995), local indigenous efforts had been going on for years. During the 1960s and 1970s, international community development focused on economic development strategies. By the 1980s, however, the focus had shifted to human development. Most recently, sustainability has emerged as an important component of development efforts.

Economic Development (1960s-1970s)

The earliest international development activities were heavily based on economics. The major players of the time were multinational banks, development agencies, and the private sector. The purpose of the efforts was to modernize developing nations and enhance their economic output by having them follow the paths of developed nations. The impetus for change came from top-level leaders in government and business, not those at the grass-roots level.

The approach to community development was highly technical and expert-driven. Many believed that countries could achieve modernity by embracing industrialization, increasing the use of new technologies, and investing in major infrastructure projects and urbanization, and thus develop into advanced capitalist economies participating in a Free Trade global economy (Latham, 2000).

Modernization would see the transformation of technology from traditional or simple techniques to more complex techniques based on the scientific method (Latham, 2000). Modernization would also mean a change from production practices based on human and animal power, to modern mechanical practices. In agriculture, for example, the movement from subsistence farming to commercial market-driven agriculture would indicate modernization. The process of modernization would also include the movement of people from rural communities to urban communities (Smelser, 1968).

Some economists thought that once nations were given appropriate levels of capital investment from both internal (private and government) and external (international aid and investment) sources, countries would move through a series of economic stages of growth: from the *traditional society*, to the *preconditions for take-off*, the *take-off*, the *drive to maturity*, and the age of *high mass-consumption* (Rostow, 1960).

A **traditional society** was characterized by a subsistence economy, within which people obtained their food, shelter, and clothing, directly through their own efforts. Barter, or the trading of goods, was how surplus was handled and how necessary items were obtained by others who did not have them. High levels of agricultural activity characterized traditional societies, and this activity was typically labour intensive (e.g., seeding fields by hand).

A society in the **preconditions for take-off stage** had begun to show expansion into other areas of activity (e.g., the development of mining practices as well as agricultural). There was an increase in size and complexity of agricultural activities, to the extent that external funding was needed, for example, to plant or harvest a crop. Societies in this stage also saw some growth in savings and investment (e.g., individuals putting money up to plant a large crop, with the hope that their share of the yield sales would return them more than they originally put forward). A society in this stage had a monetary value attached to surplus goods.

In the **take-off stage**, a society showed increased savings and investment and a greater degree of industrialization, combined with regional economic growth. A key feature of this stage was the reduction of individuals employed in the agriculture industry, because the economy had become more diverse. As well, due to the beginning use of technology (e.g., machinery for seeding), fewer labourers were needed in order to produce a surplus of goods.

In the **drive to maturity** stage, the use of technology by a society increased in sophistication and extent. A more diverse industrial base made the economy more stable and self-sustaining. For example, a heavy equipment company would be able to produce the machinery required by the agricultural, mining, and forestry industries to refine and add value to the product (e.g., trees harvested are turned into lumber suitable for building). The machinery company would require both raw materials, such as metals, as well as engineering technology and conditions (e.g., an assembly line) to produce the equipment it sells. When there is a surplus of product in the society that is sold for a profit, that profit can be invested in another industry.

High output levels and mass consumption by consumers of goods and services characterized the final stage of growth, called **high mass consumption**. In this stage, the service industry (e.g., focus on the distribution of goods, not the creation of goods) was a major employer. Some examples of service-industry jobs include banking, insurance, finance, marketing, entertainment, and recreation services. At this point, it was thought that this modernized society would be actively involved in the global economy, where all citizens would receive the benefits of a modern state. This economic development strategy involving these stages tended to be focused primarily on the urban sector.

The late 1960s saw the emergence of the **Green Revolution,** a development strategy aimed at the rural sectors of developing countries to significantly improve agricultural yields by introducing new crops and cultivars, irrigation, chemical fertilizers and pesticides, and modern mechanized practices (Simon, 1975).

The goal was to increase the capacity of the rural sector to feed the steadily increasing urban sectors and to eliminate both urban and rural hunger (Wu & Butz, 2004).

The impact of the economic development model was significant. Economic indicators suggested that exports from the developing nations had increased. There was an increase in gross national products (i.e., the total value of all goods and services produced in a nation). There was the development of a modern, mostly urban sector, accompanied by an increase in transportation networks, the utilization of more modern agricultural techniques (many for export-based commodities), and the movement to democracy and the expansion of mass media. While some people (mostly urban) benefited from the modernization process, it was also painfully clear that most people were not receiving the benefits of modernization and that, in fact, most people had become poorer (Seligson, 1979)

As a result, the gap between rich and poor often increased in developing nations (Farmer, 2003).

Out of these facts came the conclusion that economic indicators were poor indicators of development. Economic indicators could not measure the problems that development was meant to address, such as poverty, hunger, and health. Rural and urban poor did not benefit from traditional development (Johnston & Low, 1995).

Then, during the 1960s the imperialist system broke down significantly, with former colonies becoming independent states. Between 1960 and 1969, 46 countries gained independence while another 26 did so between 1970 and 1979 (Roupp, 1997). Of those countries becoming independent between 1960 and 1979, 17 were former French colonies and 37 were former British colonies. A condition of independence was to take on significant debt loads to repay their former colonial masters. Added to this debt load was the debt incurred from lending institutions in developed nations.

Third World Debt Crisis By the 1980s, many developing nations were not in a position to pay their debts (George, 1992). In 1982, Mexico could no longer service its debt, and defaulted on its payment, which caused commercial banks to stop lending to South American nations. There were several causes to this problem and its consequences (Attfield & Wilkins, 1992). Overspending in the U.S. required the printing of more dollars in the early 1970s, which weakened the value of the dollar. Then, in 1973, oil-producing countries raised the price of oil to offset the loss of revenues due to the U.S.-dollar devaluation.

Developing countries often had **soft currencies**—that is, currencies that are subject to significant value fluctuations—but had to pay back their debt in **hard currencies**, or currencies less likely to dramatically fluctuate in value (such as the U.S. dollar or British pound). As a result, developing countries were forced to generate hard currencies. Often this happened through the export of goods. But because many countries were placed in the position of needing to increase their exports, competition between those countries drove prices down. Lower values on exports decreased their ability to generate hard currency. Many developing countries refinanced their debts, taking on new loans solely to pay off old ones (Vásquez, 2000).

To avoid a pending global debt crisis, the International Monetary Fund and World Bank (created in the mid-1940s to help with rebuilding efforts in Europe after World War II, which has since lent money for the purpose of enhancing global trade) began to prescribe terms and conditions for lending to developing countries. They commonly required developing countries to make several significant structural adjustments (Pastor, 1987; O'Brien, Goetz, Scholte & Williams, 2000):

- Reduce social spending, such as in education and health. This came at a high cost to the welfare of the general population.
- Reduce the size of government bureaucracies. This led to a significant increase in unemployment, because in many cases, the government was a major national employer.
- Cut government subsidies on basic goods. In many cases, countries had provided subsidies for basic food, such as corn and flour, causing the price to rise significantly and make it difficult or impossible for the poor to buy these basic commodities. In some cases, this led to domestic food riots.
- Reduce or remove import tariffs. As in Canada, import tariffs are often in place to protect local industries from foreign competition.
- Remove foreign ownership rules. As a result, free zones appeared, which attracted multinational corporations by offering tax incentives, removing import taxes, and offering lower wage prices. Many industrial and assembly jobs in developed nations started to move to the less developed nations, displacing many skilled and semi-skilled positions in the developed world.

Human Development (1980s–1990s)

International trade and development only benefited wealthier, capitalist nations and contributed to underdevelopment among developing nations. One explanation for this was found in dependency theory (Chilcote, 1994). The basic premise of the theory, developed by the director of the United Nations Economic Commission for Latin America, was that economic activity in richer countries led to serious economic problems in poorer countries (Lindstrom, 1998). Poor countries exported raw materials to richer countries, which manufactured products out of them and sold them back to the poor countries. Because the cost of manufacturing was always greater than the raw materials, poor countries could never earn enough from exports to pay for their imports (Taétreault & Able, 1986). The wealthier capitalist nations were at the centre of the global system, and the developing nations at the periphery (Novak, 1987). Interestingly, there were parallels between this centre/periphery concept at the international and national levels. Indeed, urban centres had more often benefited from development, while rural communities remained underdeveloped.

Dependency theorists argued for import substitution as a solution to these problems. In effect, this called on nations to stop buying from the countries to which they exported raw materials because the products cost them more to buy than to make themselves. The general consensus however, was that this solution was unworkable (Yeager, 1998), in part, because of a combination of limited local market size and the ongoing need to import technology and resources, such as petroleum.

An alternative approach slowly developed. Rather than focusing on economic indicators, this approach concerned quality of life and the ability of individuals to meet their basic needs. As well, the focus shifted from economic development to human development or social development, which has also been referred to as people-centred development, basic needs development, and human-needs centred development (Lewis, 2001).

The 1995 World Summit for Social Development, which was the first UN conference dealing specifically with Social Development, included over 100 heads of state/government and over 800 non-government organizations (Schechter, 2001).

The resulting approach to development was more holistic, taking into account factors related to life expectancy, general health, child mortality, access to education, and gender equity. Poverty, a severe and persistent global problem, was not seen exclusively in terms of material conditions; rather, it was characterized as a lack of opportunity, which included individual choice and capacity. So, merely alleviating the material conditions of poverty would not constitute development unless accompanied by increased human capacity. In short, development was equated with "empowerment." **Empowerment**, in this sense, refers to the ability of individuals to take control over their lives and, therefore, over their own development, both individually and collectively.

Movement on these issues also saw the devolution from large, state-controlled development projects to more local community-based projects. In some nations, development work was downloaded from the state to local communities. There was a corresponding rise in non-governmental organizations working directly with grassroots communities worldwide (Gallopín & Raskin, 2002).

Sustainability At the same time that development was being redefined, there was also a growing awareness of the impact of human activity on the environment. The first major conference, called the UN Conference on the Human Environment, occurred in Stockholm, Sweden, in 1972, which looked at both human impact on the environment and the extent to which human activity was also putting humanity at risk (Chasek, 2001). In 1983, the UN commissioned Dr. Gro Harlem Brundtland (who would go on to become the Norwegian prime minister), the chair of the World Commission on Environment and Development (WCED), to prepare a report. After three years of consultation the report, titled "Our Common Future," was released.

The report suggested that the critical environmental problems the world was facing had two sources at its roots (Adams, 2001). First was the enormous poverty of the developing nations. Second was the unsustainable consumption and production pattern of the developed nations. The report suggested that there was a need to change the focus of human activity to fit within natural ecological restraints. It also concluded, however, that economic development should not stop.

The commission has often been credited with popularizing the term **sustainable development**, which can be defined as the ability to meet current human needs without threatening future generations from doing the same. "Our Common Future" was debated at the

UN in 1989, and the result was a decision to organize a Conference on the Environment and Development, which occurred in 1992 in Rio de Janeiro—and was more commonly referred to as the Earth Summit or the Rio Summit. The Secretary General of the Summit was Canadian Maurice Strong. While the summit itself attracted over 150 heads of state, there was a parallel forum that attracted over 17 000 individuals, representing over 2000 non-government organizations (Hough, 2004).

INTERNATIONAL DEVELOPMENT IN THE NEW MILLENNIUM

The United Nations Millennium Declaration passed at the General Assembly on September 18, 2000. The Declaration established a series of development goals to be met by the year 2015 on issues of reducing poverty, promoting universal primary education, promoting gender equality, reducing child mortality, improving maternal health, combating serious disease (e.g., HIV/AIDS and malaria), as well as ensuring environmental sustainability (Black & White, 2003).

Poverty

World poverty was a focal issue of the Declaration. Indeed, of the approximately 5 billion people living in the developing world, over one billion live in dehumanizing conditions of extreme, abject poverty. The report's goals (United Nations, 2005) were to reduce by half the proportion of people living on less than a dollar per day, as well as the proportion of people suffering from hunger.

There is much work to be done relative to correcting huge income gaps. In 2001, over 1 billion people in developing nations lived on less than US $1.00 a day; if the criteria for poverty was adjusted to less than US $2.00 a day, the estimated number living in poverty would be close to 3 billion (half the world's population). In Sub-Saharan Africa, for example, the proportion of people living on $1.00 per day increased from 44.6 percent in 1990 to 46.4 percent in 2001; the average daily income dropped from $0.62 to $0.60; and the number of poor rose from 227 million to 314 million (Anderson, 2004).

Chronic hunger, defined as inadequate food to meet daily needs, dropped from 20 percent in the years 1990–1992 to 17 percent in the years 2000–2002 among developing nations. This change is modest, however. In 2002, there were 815 million hungry people in the developing nations (Gonzalez-Pelaez, 2005), only 9 million fewer than in 1990. Most of those who were hungry were rural people, who grew crops both for subsistence and sale (Herman, Pietracci, & Sharma, 2001). Chronic hunger is most severe among those who have no land, and among farmers with small land holdings. There are 150 million children in developing nations under the age of five who are underweight. In fact, child malnutrition contributes to over 50 percent of all child deaths (Derose, Messer, & Millman, 1998).

Education

There is a need for universal primary education. The report's goal was to ensure that all boys and girls complete primary education. According to "The State of the World's Children" (1999), UNICEF estimated that there were close to one billion individuals who were illiterate, worldwide (Andrews & Kaufman, 1999). "The Millennium Development

Goals" report for 2005 indicated that there were still 115 million children not enrolled in primary education. Most of these children were the poorest of the poor, whose mothers had also received no primary education. Often, these families were also rural residents. While many regions of the developing world are now close to universality, Sub-Saharan Africa, Oceania, and Southern Asia still have a significant way to go. In fact, 80 percent of children who are not in school live in Sub-Saharan Africa, where the HIV/AIDS crisis has had a major impact. It is estimated that close to a million schoolchildren in the region have lost their teachers to HIV/AIDS (Moulton, Mundy, Walmond, & Williams, 2002).

Gender Equality

Another goal of the Declaration is to eliminate gender disparities in education. Gender equality is a human right, as well as a prerequisite to overcoming hunger, poverty, and disease. Gender equality needs to be addressed at all levels of education and in all areas of work, leading to equal control over resources and equal representation in public and political life (Kramarae & Spender, 2000). One important indicator of progress in this area is the number of women involved in nonagricultural labour. Currently, this ranges from a low of 13 percent in Southern Asia to a high of 49 percent in the CIS (Commonwealth of Independent States—i.e., former Soviet republics, such as Kazakhstan, Kyrgyzstan, Ukraine, and Armenia).

Women in rural communities, in particular, face greater challenges. For example, in many rural communities, students wishing to go on to secondary education must leave their home communities, resulting in greater family expenses (cost of room and board) in addition to the loss of family labour. As well, opportunities for paid employment are almost always in urban or semi-urban locations. However, one program that attempts to provide women with the opportunity to increase their incomes in rural areas is the Grameen Bank, which provides small loans for women in Bangladesh (Todd, 1996). In 2004, the Grameen Bank had over 3 000 000 borrowers, and of them 96 percent were women (Grameen Bank, 2006). There are similar micro-credit programs in many other regions.

Child Health

The health of children is also a significant issue identified in the UN report. The Development Goal (United Nations, 2005) was to reduce the mortality rate among children under five by two-thirds. Worldwide, just under 1 billion children younger than five years of age died (9 900 000) in 2002 (Black & White, 2003),which is equivalent to 27 120 deaths daily. In Sub-Saharan Africa, 172 of every 1000 live births will die before the age of five, and in southern Asia the rate is 90 of 1000 (Belshaw & Livingstone, 2002).

About three-fifths of all child deaths in developing regions (United Nations, 2006) occurred within the first four weeks of life; such child deaths are due to infections such as tetanus, sepsis (severe infection of the bloodstream), and diarrhea (Black & White, 2003). Together, malaria, measles, and AIDS account for about 15 percent of all child deaths (United Nations, 2006).

Low-cost solutions, such as insecticide-soaked mosquito nets for malaria prevention, a rehydration mixture of salt, sugar, and potable water for diarrhea, and low-cost immunization programs for measles could have prevented many of these deaths (Livi-Bacci & Santis, 1998).

Maternal Health

Maternal health is a serious concern in developing nations. The Declaration (United Nations, 2005) reported a goal for a reduction in maternal mortality by three-quarters. Worldwide, over 500 000 women died in childbirth in 2000 (Bloom, Canning, & Sevilla, 2003). However, this varied considerably between nations. For example, in 2000 the likelihood of a woman dying during childbirth in the developed world was 20 in 100 000 (2500 deaths), while in Sub-Saharan Africa it was 920 per 100 000 live births (247 000 deaths) (Forman & Ghosh, 2000). In contrast, the risk of death during pregnancy or childbirth in Sweden was 1 in 29 800; in Angola, Malawi, however, it is 1 in 7 (Black & White, 2003). According to the 2005 Millennium report, only 37 percent of all births in Sub-Saharan Africa were attended by a health care professional.

Disease

Disease is a leading cause of death in developing nations. In countries most affected, the average life expectancy has plummeted by 20 years (Stanton, 2004). The report specifically targeted as critical the reduction of HIV/AIDS. In 2005, there were 40.3 million adults and children living with HIV/AIDS, and 3.1 million deaths due to AIDS, and close to 5 million new cases were reported. About half of those living with AIDS are women, aged 15 to 49. About 65 percent of all people in the world living with and dying of AIDS are in Sub-Saharan Africa (25.8 million people, 2.4 million deaths). As well, over 60 percent of new cases are in Sub-Saharan Africa. By the end of 2004 it was estimated that there were 15 million AIDS orphans (children who had lost one or both parents to AIDS). This was equivalent to the total population of children in Britain and Germany (UNICEF, 2006). In Botswana, one child in five is an AIDS orphan, while regionally the percentage of AIDS orphans is 15 percent.

Malaria kills approximately 1 000 000 children a year—one every 30 seconds in Africa alone. And tuberculosis increased from 145 per 100 000 to 153 per 100 000 between 1990 and 2003 (UNICEF, 2006). According to UNICEF's "State of the World's Children" report, 2.2 million children died because they were not immunized for common preventable diseases, such as measles (UNICEF, 2006).

Environment

In relation to the environment, the report (United Nations, 2005) specified a goal to reduce, by half, the proportion of people without sustainable access to safe drinking water. Access to safe drinking water means significant improvements to sanitation and hygiene. Indeed, sanitation and hygiene improvements are as important for health and poverty reduction as is safe water. This issue has been recognized in the United Nations Convention on the Rights of the Child (United Nations, 1990): "the right of the child to the enjoyment of the highest attainable standard of health . . . through the provision of . . . clean drinking water, taking into consideration the dangers and risks of environmental pollution" (p. 57).

For example, handwashing alone (with clean water), in severely affected areas, could lead to a 40 percent reduction in the risk of infectious intestinal diseases. Each year, this could prevent between 0.4 to 1.5 million deaths from such diseases. And in fact, the total number of deaths from infectious intestinal diseases appears to have fallen from 4.6 million in 1980, to 3.3 million in 1990 and 2.94 million in 1997 (Curtis & Cairncross, 2003).

SOCIAL CAPITAL

In Chapter 1, we introduced the concept of *social capital* and looked historically at how changes to social networks have affected the health of families and individuals. Then, in Chapter 6 we discussed social capital as one component of functioning that the worker should be aware of when entering a community. In this chapter, we expand on the concept to include both the assessment and mobilization of social capital in the context of international development.

The concept of social capital has been receiving increasing attention in the international development community. In its most simple form, social capital refers to those components/aspects of a community that foster co-operation between its members for the betterment of the community as a whole. Communities with significant amounts of social capital are more capable of meeting their individual and community needs. Conversely, communities lacking social capital are less likely to be able to meet their individual or collective needs internally and must rely on external resources for the amelioration of community problems. The World Bank has developed a Social Capital Assessment Tool (SCAT). It attempts, in part, to understand why some communities are more able to address and resolve their issues, while others are not (Grootaert & Van Bastelaer, 2002).

Social capital becomes another dimension along with financial capital (monies available for investment), physical capital (buildings and land), and human capital (the skills people have) in defining a community's health. Within a community social capital can be broken down into two categories, structural and cognitive social capital (Uphoff, 1999).

Structural Social Capital

Structural social capital is viewed by most theorists as the degree of linkage between community members and the formal and informal social institutions in the community. Informal social organizations are groups of individuals who might meet on a regular basis but without any formal organizational structure. Formal organizations would include village/neighbourhood councils, school associations, religious groups, women's groups, and farmers' groups.

A distinction should be made between internal formal institutions and those that are often imposed by outside agencies and organizations as a condition of receiving assistance. Often, the criteria imposed by external agencies, such as literacy, numeracy, religious, and land ownership groups, exacerbates social inequality within communities. Social capital of one group is used for their collective benefit and to shut out other community members. For example, in one community, about half the houses had cement floors, while the other half had dirt floors. The material for cement floors was donated by an international, religiously based organization, which required the local community to organize a local committee to bring forward the names of those who would be recipients. All of the recipients, as well as the committee, were members of the same religious group because the agent for the international organization sought out co-religionists in the community.

There are several components of structural social capital, such as decision making, and participation, as well as levels of and motives for involvement, diversity, and leadership. Each has implications for work in that community, including the following:

- How are community decisions made? Their degree of transparency depends, among other factors, on the nature of local leadership (achieved or ascribed) and their relationship to the community, as well as the nature and history of collective action within the community.

- Who is involved? It is often assumed that rural communities in developing countries are homogeneous. Yet these communities are often divided between landless and-land owning farmers, new arrivals/migrants, and original families, religious groups, caste or clan or other social categories. Is community leadership reflective of that diversity?

- How are people involved? Another way of viewing structural social capital is by looking at the levels of involvement of individuals in community life. More specifically, who is involved and who is not? Is community involvement broad based or is it limited to a group of local elite?

- Is the community socio-economically diverse? While often not apparent to outsiders (since everyone seems poor), local individuals often divide their communities into rich and poor, based on criteria such as the construction materials of their homes (cement block walls vs. abode walls; thatched roofs vs. tin roofs; cement floors vs. dirt floors); access to latrines and water sources; the size of their land holdings or lack of land; the number of chickens, pigs or beasts of burden. Development workers must be aware and sensitive to the fact that in socio-economically diverse communities there may be competing needs or demands.

- Do local decision makers represent the interests and needs of the whole community or just one group within the community? Does local leadership tend to reflect the needs and issues of only one socio-economic group? Are there opportunities for local leadership development, or are leadership opportunities monopolized?

In one sense, structural social capital refers to the existing mechanisms, relationships and institutions within the community that could be mobilized. However, if those relationships and institutions only reflect a part of the community, the issues and concerns of the other community members may be overlooked or ignored. In this situation we could have one part of the community with relatively high levels of structural social capital and one part of the community with very little structural social capital, with the sector of the community with high structural capital the primary beneficiary of the development process. This in turn could erode what limited social capital exists in the marginalized group.

Cognitive Social Capital

The second component of social capital, cognitive social capital, is more problematic to discern but in many ways the most important for development purposes. Cognitive social capital (Uphoff, 1999) refers to the social norms, values, beliefs, attitudes, and social behaviours people hold that impact on the ability of the community to take collective action. It is crucial to include local knowledge as well as the community's social history, particularly as it relates to previous development projects, since both impact on both individual and community actions (Krishna, 2002).

What follows is part of a questionnaire that has been used to assess cognitive social capital:

❑ Most people are basically honest and can be trusted.

❑ People are interested only in their own welfare.

❑ Some members are always more trustworthy than others.

❑ I have to be aware or someone may take advantage of me.

❑ If I have a problem there is always someone to help.

❑ Most people are willing to help if you need it.

❑ I feel accepted.

❑ *Rural*: If you lose an animal, someone in the village would help look for it or would return it to you.

❑ *Urban*: If you drop your pocketbook in the neighborhood, someone will see it and return it to you. (Hjollund & Svendson, 2006)

In the 1950s the psychologist Abraham Maslow, whom we briefly discussed in Chapter 5, suggested that people satisfy their needs hierarchically. He further asserted that lower-level basic needs, such as food, shelter, security, and access to water, must be met before individuals can move on to higher social needs (Tomer, 1999). According to Maslow, the needs start with those to sustain life (e.g., food, water, clothing), and move to safety and security needs (e.g., security from exploitation of others as well as physical security and health security). The social needs, in contrast to the first two stages, are externally oriented and are a precondition for converting individual capital to social capital (e.g., acceptance by others, need for belonging, friends, and associates). The esteem needs, the fourth stage, is the stage at which social capital can be mobilized (e.g., need to achieve, trust in one's own abilities, trust in others, self-respect, and respect for others).

Social Capital in Marginalized Communities

One goal of international development is to facilitate the community's ability to meet its basic human needs. However, before this can reasonably occur collectively, individual households must have moved beyond basic survival modes. However, most marginalized rural and urban communities in developing countries struggle to meet the most rudimentary basic needs of food, shelter, clothing, and minimal material goods to sustain life. Few community members will be involved in community activity while they are struggling to meet their basic survival needs. When everyone's crop in the village has failed because of lack of rain or disease infestation, or almost everyone in the neighbourhood is jobless, collective action will take a back seat to personal survival strategies. It is difficult to be concerned for one's neighbour when your children are starving. With very few exceptions this is the norm in marginalized communities in developing countries. Thus, the mobilization of social capital for the common good is contingent on the ability of individuals to have their most basic needs met.

All individuals possess individual capital: skills, knowledge, experience, and time. And all have the potential for being brought to the community table as social capital. However, as with all other forms of capital, there must be a perceived surplus before individuals are prepared to invest this capital in external endeavors. If people believe all their individual capital must be invested in the struggle to meet their elemental needs, minimal investment will be made in voluntary communal activity. Some communal activity may well take place, but this is often compulsory activity, such as road maintenance and activities required to maintain the school, particularly if this is a condition for allowing their children to attend.

To effectively begin to mobilize social capital in marginalized communities, development activities must address the most basic needs, which are currently unmet in the community. Meeting the food, shelter, clothing, and other basic material needs required to meet families' consumptive needs should be addressed before working to address secondary needs.

Community Assessment and Action A good community assessment is critical in the era of results-based evaluations, so that a community baseline is established against which results can be compared. Community members should be active participants in the community assessment process, not solely subjects of the assessment, and the assessment process should include both an evaluation of community strengths and unmet needs. Community members should not only identify their unmet needs but should also be actively involved in prioritizing those needs. Community workers must identify local individuals prepared to work on the project, which must be completely voluntary, and generally in small groups with some form of basic structure. These individuals should be actively involved in both the design and implementation of the project. Indeed, numerous studies have found that one of the critical factors that separates successful development initiatives from less successful ones is the degree of local decision making in the development process.

The project must be transparent. Local community members not directly involved must be updated on progress on a regular basis. For agriculturally based projects in particular, it is beneficial to have a project site in an area that is readily accessible to the community. While the basic goal of the development activity may be specific (e.g., increased food security), the project should also incorporate activities and processes that will allow the community participants to do the following:

- increase their knowledge base through a variety of methods, including active demonstration
- develop problem-solving skills
- develop basic management skills needed to run projects, such as bookkeeping and recording skills
- enhance group work skills, such as consensus building, conflict management, and team building
- capitalize on and build local leadership and facilitation skills.

The goal of the work is to increase the social capital, which can then be mobilized to increase community capacity and reduce reliance on outside agents. The projects should also, whenever possible, link local community projects with other communities engaged in similar activities, with the goal of developing inter-community linkages/exchanges that have the possibility of creating broader associations between like-minded groups and communities. These associations also have the potential to become formal regional or national associations, which become direct stakeholders in the development agenda.

Factors Known to Inhibit Mobilization of Social Capital

Learned powerlessness. Just as in the developed world, many people believe that they are unable to change their basic social condition. They may believe that they have neither the skills nor the power to change. Indeed, it was Paulo Freire, whom we discussed in Chapter 3, who suggested in his book, *Pedagogy of the Oppressed*, that self-depreciation was a characteristic of marginalized people, often articulated by fatalistic statements, such as "Whatever God brings, God brings," and indicative of a belief that a community's fate is beyond its immediate control. Thus, if the crops failed it was God's will, or if a child dies it, too, is God's will. The locus of control (over their daily existence), therefore, is external to them.

In some extreme cases some people even consider it sinful (against God's will) to attempt to intervene to improve one's condition. In one community, for example, developers were told that all development projects were the product of the anti-Christ and therefore people could not become involved for fear of not reaching the kingdom of heaven on Judgment Day. In another case, some farmers stopped attending to their crops planted in the fall because they were told by their local lay pastor that the Judgment Day was January 1 of the next year so they would not need food after that date. January came and went, and the farmers were unable to feed their families.

Lack of trust in government. One of the greatest barriers to development is the level of corruption that exists in some developing countries. This corruption can permeate every level of society, from the highest political office down to the lowest-level government functionary. Many communities have a history of being defrauded collectively or individually by government functionaries or their agents or have received reprisals for not co-operating with functionaries, such as having their benefits taken away. This pattern may be replicated in the local community, where individuals in positions of responsibility use their office for personal gain and profit. In these communities, people who assume responsibilities are often perceived as self-serving and self-interested, regardless of their motivations. People who take on community leadership roles will, therefore, be viewed with suspicion.

Dependency development. Development projects that provide all of the resources from external sources do little to empower local residents. These are often expensive, beyond the means of a community, and provide technical expertise from the outside. An example would be an agricultural development project that attempts to increase food security by providing local farmers with chemical pesticides, fungicides, and fertilizer, at no cost or drastically reduced prices. As long as the project stays in the community, food security may be increased, but when the project leaves, as all eventually do, the community is unable to afford the inputs and thus food security is once again a major issue. In fact, in some cases the community is left in a worse position than when it started. When communities, and by extension people, become reliant on outside sources for their welfare, they become disempowered. In this type of project the community is often the *object* of the development process rather than a participant in it.

If a worker is working in a community with low levels of social capital, it is highly probable that a process of raising the level of social capital is necessary before any meaningful change will occur. Alternatively, communities with high levels of social capital are ideally suited for community development activities. On a cautionary note, if a part of the community has low levels of social capital one must build up that capacity before starting any development process that is meant to benefit the whole community.

CANADIAN CONTRIBUTIONS

There are many Canadian organizations involved in international development initiatives. In this section, we briefly present three agencies that have made a significant contribution, by way of local partnerships with grassroots groups in developing nations on both broad and more specific issues. These organizations include the Canadian International Development Agency (CIDA), Inter Pares (IP), and the Stephen Lewis Foundation (SLF).

CIDA was formed in the late 1960s as the administrative agency responsible for Canada's humanitarian aid programs in Africa, the Middle East, the Americas, and Asia. In the 1990s, aid programs to Central and Eastern Europe were added, to assist countries in transition by supporting democratic development and equitable economic policies. CIDA has five priorities currently guiding its work: governance; health; private sector develop-ment; environmental sustainability; and gender equality (Canadian International Development Agency, 2006).

IP was formed in the mid-1970s to provide humanitarian assistance and human rights protection for people caught in civil conflict, including displaced peoples and refugees (Inter Pares, 2006). The name *Inter Pares* means "among equals," and relationships are the basis for work done in partnership to address social and economic injustice, improve the planet, and promote sustainability. Private donors, as well as CIDA, fund the agency.

The SLF was launched in 2003 to contribute to efforts made to address the HIV/AIDS pandemic in Africa. The founder, Canadian Stephen Lewis, is the United Nations special envoy for HIV/AIDS in Africa. The foundation funds grassroots projects in Africa and works primarily with small groups and charities on the front lines. Priority areas for the foundation include working with women with HIV/AIDS, orphans and HIV/AIDS-affected children, grandmothers of affected women and children, as well as associations of people living with HIV/AIDS (Stephen Lewis Foundation, 2006).

SUMMARY

- We can view the earliest attempts to develop poorer nations by the richest nations through an imperialist lens. Such efforts had a variety of negative effects on the world's poorest nations.
- The economic development emphasis in the 1960s and 1970s actually widened the gap between the world's richest and poorest peoples.
- The United Nations has developed a Human Development Index, which looks more broadly at the determinants of well-being and the impact of international development efforts.
- In 1990, the United Nations identified several major areas for international develop-ment, including poverty, education, gender issues, child health, maternal health, dis-ease, and the environment.
- *Social capital* refers to the networks among people in a community, which are both structural (e.g., organizations) and cognitive (e.g., belief that change is possible).

DISCUSSION QUESTIONS

1. What do imperialism and colonization have to do with international community devel-opment, historically and in the present? Why?

2. What are the benefits and challenges associated with a focus on economic development?

3. What is the Human Development Index? Look up the current value for Canada and compare it to the United States and one other nation. What does it tell you about these nations? What are some similarities and differences? What are the strengths and limi-tations of using this measure to make comparisons?

4. How much progress has been made on the seven focal areas for international develop-ment identified by the United Nations? What remains to be done? What initiatives should be undertaken or enhanced to make more progress in these areas?

5. What is *social capital*? How would you define it for your own community? What ques-tions would you ask? Compare your definition to questionnaires from the Internet.

WEBLINKS

www.idrc.ca/index_en.html International Development Research Centre (Canada)
www.worldbank.org/ The World Bank
www.cgdev.org/ Center for Global Development
www.publicprivatedialogue.org/ PublicPrivateDialogue
www.goshen.edu/soan/soan96cd.htm Links to International Community Development
www.iacdglobal.org/ International Association for Community Development
www.un.org/ United Nations
www.unicef.org/ United Nations Children's Fund
www.acdi-cida.gc.ca/index-e.htm Canadian International Development Agency
www.interpares.ca/ Inter Pares
www.stephenlewisfoundation.org/ Stephen Lewis Foundation

KEY TERMS

Colonies, p. 151
Diversified economy, p. 153
Drive to maturity, p. 154
Empowerment, p. 157
Green Revolution, p. 155
Hard currencies, p. 156
High mass
  consumption, p. 155

Human Development
  Index, p. 152
Imperialism, p. 151
Industrialization, p. 153
North-south divide, p. 153
Preconditions for
  take-off, p. 154
 Soft currencies, p. 156

Sustainable development,
  p. 157
Take-off stage, p. 154
Third World, p. 153
Traditional society, p. 154
Underdeveloped, p. 153

chapter eleven

Social Welfare and the Future of Community Development

LEARNING OBJECTIVES

After reading this chapter, you will be able to:

1. Recognize the range and complexity of social welfare services in Canada.
2. Describe how the Canadian welfare state developed.
3. Contrast different perspectives and critiques of social welfare service provision in Canada.
4. Distinguish between residual, institutional, and developmental approaches to social welfare.
5. Identify the main components of a community development approach.

Community development has the potential to improve the current situation of the Canadian welfare state. Social welfare in Canada began as a collection of private philanthropic efforts by wealthy citizens to help the poor in their local communities. Following World War II, at a time of prosperity and optimism, several major national programs, including national pensions, employment assistance, and medicare were introduced. However, the sustainability of these programs, as well as the extent of their achievements, have been criticized. The future of social welfare in Canada will require new ways of administration and delivery that are sensitive to the realities of local communities. As a result, community development processes are integral to promoting the levels of local social structures necessary to support the administrative and delivery functions of a redeveloped social service.

CHAPTER OUTLINE

SOCIAL WELFARE

Although the term *welfare* is usually used in a negative or pejorative way, it actually refers to "wellness." But most people view welfare recipients as being poor and needing financial assistance from government. As such, there is a great deal of stigma surrounding the term. However, all Canadian residents are contributors to as well as recipients of government assistance, whether they acknowledge it or not.

The view that some individuals benefit more than others from government assistance (that is, they put in less money or get more out) remains prevalent. Although much media attention is paid to the poorest recipients of benefits—specifically, stories about those who appear to take advantage of social assistance (a.k.a. "welfare fraud")—relatively little attention is paid to the tax advantages that Canada's richest individuals enjoy through a variety of creative efforts. Most of us ignore the fact that the richest individuals "are able to disguise some of their personal expenses as business expenses, and that some of them engage in aggressive tax avoidance strategies, such as income-splitting schemes and tax shelters, and tax evasion strategies, such as secret offshore bank accounts and legal entities" (Brooks, 2005, p. 2). In fact, all Canadian citizens contribute to and benefit from welfare services or government assistance in some way.

Social welfare is a broader term that is slightly less negative than *welfare*, and refers to the variety of measures taken by government and non-government agencies to provide minimum standards and create particular opportunities, for humanitarian reasons (i.e., help people who have less than you), religious reasons (i.e., charity as a religious duty), mutual self-interest reasons (i.e., grassroots-led activities, which may also be in receipt of government or non-government funding support), democratic reasons (services developed alongside of democratic rights), and practical reasons (i.e., economic and social benefits outweigh costs).

Contemporary social welfare efforts in Canada are multiple, interrelated, and complex. Many social welfare services exist through both public agencies (government-funded) and private (non-profit, philanthropic organizations, religious charities). Government-funded social welfare programs include, for example, federal pension programs and employment insurance. Provinces are responsible for the delivery of health care, education, and social services. In many cases, federal, municipal, and band governments also have roles in these services. In some cases (e.g., law enforcement, justice and corrections systems), responsibility is divided among all levels of government. In practice, however, these roles and responsibilities may seem blurred. There are also combinations of community-led, government-funded social welfare initiatives. In Manitoba, for example, child welfare services for First Nations and Metis families are administered through First Nations and Metis community organizations, which are funded and mandated to provide services.

Purposes of Social Welfare

Minimally, social welfare may be seen as a means to assist citizens in meeting basic or emergency income needs as well as providing social services. Despite variation from province to province, there is remarkable consistency in income assistance program benefits, for example, which are for the purpose of meeting basic food, clothing and shelter needs. The levels of these benefits sit below the poverty line in every Canadian jurisdiction. The Low Income Cut-Off (LICO) is a measure developed by Statistics Canada to indicate the point at which an individual or family spends 20 percent more of their income on basic necessities (food, clothing, and shelter) than the average family (Fellegi, 1999). The National Council of Welfare, in its report on welfare incomes across Canada for 2005 (National Council on Welfare, 2006), pointed out that typical welfare incomes in all Canadian jurisdictions were well below the LICO. For example, single people in New Brunswick were the worst off, with a social assistance rate equivalent to 19 percent of the poverty line, and single-parent families in Newfoundland and Labrador fared best in Canada with a social assistance rate equivalent to about 70 percent of the poverty line.

Emergency needs are met through either federal employment insurance or provincial income assistance programs. One purpose of emergency assistance is to aid individuals and families with meeting basic income needs for food, clothing, and shelter, at a time when some new circumstance arises, such as unemployment, illness, or injury. Other changes in an individual's situation, such as normal aging, marital separation, or childbirth can have significant financial impact on families with limited or no access to additional financial resources. All Canadian employees pay employment insurance premiums, and the benefits of this program are intended to cover changes to employment status (looking for a new job after being laid off by an employer, for example) for a limited period of time.

Social services emphasize support and training needs of individuals and families. The range of offerings and access to them vary from jurisdiction to jurisdiction. For example, large urban centres typically offer a larger range of social services, such as family support and respite workers, which are more difficult to come by in smaller or more remote communities.

A variety of barriers to accessing social services do exist, including availability, accessibility, acceptability, affordability, appropriateness, and adequacy. *Availability* refers to the presence or perceived presence of a service. *Accessibility* refers to potential participants' ability to use services. *Acceptability* refers to the degree to which participants feel that they can use the services. *Affordability* of services includes both tangible and intangible costs to participants, for use. *Appropriateness* of services refers to whether the assistance is the right kind for the participants. And finally, *adequacy* of service refers to the quality and completeness of service according to the level of diversity and need.

DEVELOPMENT OF THE CANADIAN WELFARE STATE

During World War II, the British archbishop William Temple, to contrast against the development of a German "warfare state" at the time, coined the term *welfare state* (Crane, 1994). A **welfare state**, in general terms, refers to a government that is committed to assume responsibility for the welfare of its citizens (Pierson, 2001). In Canada, the welfare state developed through a series of stages (Moscovitch, 2006): the early period (1840–1890), the transitional period (1891–1940), the interventionist period (1941–1974), and the erosion period (1975 to the present).

The Early Period

During the mid to late nineteenth century, welfare services in Canada were based on charity. Whether they were offered at all depended on the level of wealth among those with the most money in a community, and their willingness to spend it on charitable causes. Major challenges during these early days of capitalism included poverty and disease, and local relief efforts were piecemeal, because they required a commitment by the wealthiest of a community to provide for those who were poor and sick in that community (Dixon & Scheurell, 2002).

And while social welfare in Canada remained a private matter toward the end of this period, it did become slightly more formalized. Some government assistance was available, coming by way of funding to established charitable organizations and in the form of emergency food and shelter, and by legislation to protect children and the public, (e.g., housing of children in need of protection, and incarceration of lawbreakers first appeared during this time). As well, regulations concerning marriage and labour developed, as did compulsory education and public health regulation (Bothwell, 1996).

The Transitional Period

During the transitional period of the early twentieth century, social welfare expenditures by governments grew, and greater levels of taxation to fund delivery of these services were introduced. The first compulsory social insurance program was introduced to protect workers in Canada, and came as a result of passing the Ontario Workmen's Compensation Act of 1914 (Grant, 1988). In 1916, the first mother's allowance legislation appeared in Manitoba, with benefits for widowed or deserted women; other provinces passed their own versions of mother's allowance, following Manitoba's lead (Kamerman & Kahn, 1997).

At the federal level, the first old-age pension was introduced in 1927, which involved cost-sharing with the provinces to provide pensions to those who were both poor and over the age of 70 years. Federal unemployment relief, introduced in 1930, came in the form of grants to provinces to help the many people who were out of work during the Depression, and in 1935 the federal government passed the first public housing legislation. In 1940, the Unemployment Insurance Act was passed, which gave the federal government authority to collect income and corporate taxes (Crichton, Robertson, Gordon & Farrant, 1997).

The Interventionist Period

The Canadian welfare state did not emerge until the Second World War. It was during this time that the government made many provisions to assist Canadians involved in the wartime effort. As well, there was a great deal of government expansion into Canadian economic and social life, and the government introduced many new pieces of legislation and new programs, including federal housing programs, rent control, and wage legislation, as well as regulations on industry, the creation of veterans' pensions, land settlement, rehabilitation and training, and child care measures. The magnitude of change accompanied a great sense of optimism about post-war economic growth and social security in Canada and Britain. The need for increasing government expenditures on social programs was reflected in the national Beveridge (Britain) and Marsh (Canada) reports on social security in 1942 and 1943, respectively (Banting, Hoberg, & Simeon, 1997). The economist John Keynes, who argued that full employment would come as a result of government assistance to private enterprise and not through social welfare efforts, was influential among the critics of government expenditures on social services at the time (Runde & Mizuhara, 2003).

The early 1960s was a prosperous time for economies in North America. In the United States, new initiatives and expenditures were introduced as part of the "war on poverty" (Zarefsky, 1986). In Canada, the government passed three pieces of major legislation that, today, are considered the basis of the welfare state (Blane, Brunner & Wilkinson, 1996): the Canada Pension Plan (national and compulsory pensions), the Canada Assistance Plan (social assistance for individuals who became unemployed or experienced a disability as well as services for single parents, including day care), and medicare (national personal health care system).

The Erosion Period

From the mid-to late 1970s and into the 1980s, there was a downturn in the Canadian economy, which had serious consequences for welfare state programs because they required contributions from taxpayers, many of whom were struggling to make ends meet. Initial responses to the increasing rates of unemployment were to put more money into the unemployment insurance system. This, however, was not sustainable. Inflation grew, and expenses increased to the point that reductions in social program spending were necessary on the part of both the federal and provincial governments. Downsizing has continued through all levels of government since the mid-1980s, eroding the welfare state (Ismael & Vaillancourt, 1988). It has become common for governments to change eligibility and benefits, privatize services through contracts, raise premiums and user fees, decrease program budgets, and, in some cases, end programs (Castles, 2004). Certain terminology we use today, such as "facing cutbacks" and "doing more with less," combined with increasing waiting lists for services, have contributed to the public's lack of confidence in social welfare.

In 2001, the proportion of gross domestic product that Canada spent on welfare-state activities ranked the country 25th among the 30 members of the Organization for Economic Co-operation and Development (OECD, 2006). This translated into US$27,130 per Canadian in social benefits for one year. Today, different opinions continue to exist regarding the range and cost of welfare-state services, as well as the nature and extent of returns. One obvious problem is that it is precisely during times of highest demand for service that the economy is weakest. Indeed, the welfare state is most needed when it is least affordable.

Criticisms of the Canadian Welfare State

Criticisms of the contemporary welfare state are found on both sides of the political spectrum. Modern conservatives tend to favour tax reductions and reductions in social spending, arguing that increased business revenues ultimately benefit workers, who could then pay for their own social services, privately. Modern socialists, on the other hand, emphasize efforts to promote social change and social equality, and the maintenance of minimum standards, toward the outcomes of social cohesion and collective responsibility. However, socialist writers have argued that the welfare state has not, and probably will not, lead to these outcomes (Ife, 2002). They have argued instead that the welfare state, because of its structure and function, cannot contribute to social change and, rather, perpetuates economic and social disparities by maintaining class distinctions. That is, the relatively rich provide services to clients who are relatively poor and who receive benefits that do not elevate them out of poverty.

THE FUTURE OF CANADIAN SOCIAL WELFARE

There are three major perspectives on social welfare. These perspectives are known as residual, institutional, and developmental. The first two perspectives, to a large extent, describe the competing forces apparent in the development of social welfare. However, it is the third perspective—development—that holds the greatest promise for the future of social welfare in Canada.

A residual perspective on social welfare is that the market and family provide all the essential social and economic support necessary to citizens. An institutional perspective on social welfare holds that a system of social welfare services, distinct from the market and family, is necessary to meet social and economic needs. The residual perspective is based on the premise that it is exceptional when the individual cannot manage contingencies effectively. The institutional perspective, however, is based on the premise that *all* contingencies are, by definition, exceptional. The discussions about the future of medicare, for example, and the debate over private versus public funding illustrate some differences. From a residual perspective, privatization of medicare is desirable. From an institutional perspective, a publicly funded health care system is desirable. Residualists see social welfare as being for the poor, or as being selective, while institutionalists see social welfare as being for everyone, or universal.

In contrast, a developmental perspective is based on two significant departures from both the residual and institutional approaches. According to a developmental approach, social welfare is neither a personal nor a governmental responsibility. Rather, it is a collective responsibility that is founded on reciprocal, personal relationships among individuals. The developmental approach emphasizes strengths and capacities rather than weaknesses and problems.

A developmental approach, therefore, works from a particular set of assumptions. People are seen as generally healthy; they want to be healthier; and they are capable of becoming healthier. Service provision starts with capacity inventory and asset identification, as opposed to needs assessment and problem identification. Balance in relationships is sought. Everyone involved has something to contribute and something to gain. The resources for change, then, come from within the individual, family, and community. The effect of change is something new and not a predetermined standard outcome.

A Community Development Alternative

Defenders of the welfare state argue that it needs to be re-established, with a new emphasis on public expenditure. Opponents argue that these services are not cost-effective, and if they are to be delivered at all, they should be by the voluntary sector (charities).

We propose a third option: local governance and delivery of social welfare. Community development offers the means to strengthen local structures that support the administration and delivery of social service. As we have presented in this textbook, there are several features of community development activities that serve to enhance community health, including an emphasis on strengths, well-being, social change, power within, bottom-up process, and preventive, holistic, and relationship-based service.

Strengths

From a community development approach, service provision is based on abilities, not deficits. That is, abilities determine, to a large extent, capacity to cope and move forward. Deficit- or weakness-based approaches imply that abilities have either not been inherited or developed, and that the most one can hope for is a steady state—not sick, but not well, either. Community development approaches are based on the recognition that all people and communities have strengths that may be blocked from expression, are underutilized, or unrecognized. Finding and using these strengths are crucial.

Well-Being

From a community development perspective, the goal is maximization of collective well-being. The welfare of a community determines, to a large extent, the well-being of its residents. Wellness depends on the community; individuals make up the community. Therefore, the welfare of individual and community are interconnected and mutually reinforcing. Community development approaches emphasize the interconnections between people and emphasize wellness.

Social Change

Change is inevitable. In community development, it is understood and expected that change will occur as the process unfolds. The change may be modest or revolutionary, depending on the community and those involved. However, the activities themselves emphasize change at the level of community. While the immediate targets for change may be individuals or families, the desired level of impact is broader.

Power Within

The concept of power, as the ability to influence, is an important force in community development. Power is seen as value-neutral. That is, it becomes good or bad, depending on one's perspective of the circumstances in which it is used. Community development approaches are based on the power within, not on power from outside. That is, those within the community assess the influence of forces inside and out, and determine how best to use the power within to make change. The target for change may be either within or outside of the community.

Bottom-Up Process

Grassroots participation and indigenous leadership are crucial in community development. The impetus for change comes from the grassroots community, and people from within the community lead the process. The approach is bottom-up, and not top-down in direction. That is, the people in the community, not those outside, determine the purpose and direction of change.

Preventive Service

A major emphasis of community development is to act proactively, not reactively. Local development efforts may indeed begin in response to a particular issue. The process of community change is inclusive and the outcomes broad enough to include not only the resolution of a focal issue, but also the overall strengthening of local social structures. Internal social structures can then turn to the business of creating the future that the community wants, instead of organizing, as needed, to attend to crises.

Holistic Service

The nature of community development is holistic—the interconnections between physical, social, emotional, and spiritual are assumed. Any change that is pursued, therefore, will impact the community in many ways. This makes it difficult to resolve certain issues—for example, finding a trade-off between environmental protection and local jobs that may be created by the building of a local lumber mill. Successful development efforts, as we have seen in Chapter 8, find a balance between these areas. Such efforts might involve, for example, creating a local environment protection committee with a mandate to ensure that the business practices are sustainable.

Relationship-Based Service

In the end, it is the relationships among community members as well as relationships between communities that determine progress. The communities define customs and rules about how relationships work, which must be respected as legitimate ways of operation.

FUTURE OF COMMUNITY DEVELOPMENT

Our argument here has not been in support of the welfare state as it exists, nor to inject massive resources into its preservation, nor to advocate its complete dismantling. Our argument is, rather, a practical one. As the state continues to reduce its commitment to social welfare, communities will be increasingly expected to carry out those functions. However, structures necessary for local governance have been severely damaged through years of distant control. Communities need time, therefore, to develop their capacities to the point when they can be meaningfully involved in their own administration and delivery of services, which have been imposed on them by mainstream health, education, social, and justice systems.

There are two significant challenges remaining: mobilizing social *and* economic capital. It is a daunting task for communities to develop local internal structures that can contribute to self-government. We propose, however, that community development principles can be used to develop the structures necessary to meet the human service responsibilities, which are increasingly being downloaded onto communities from government. Another challenge is ensuring that financial resources accompany this transition of service to a point of stabilization. There is ample evidence to indicate that external financial resources are necessary for community development to happen, and that the timelines for development must be determined by the community and not imposed from outside.

SUMMARY

- Social welfare includes efforts made by government or private means to ensure that a minimum level of financial support for basic or emergency needs is met and that social support is provided to citizens.
- The welfare state in Canada has evolved through a series of stages. The stages include early, transitional, interventionist, and erosion.
- Conservative critics of the welfare state today argue that is has created an unnecessary burden on the economy.
- Socialist critics of the Canadian welfare state argue that the welfare state has not led to social equity.
- Community development offers a method of restoring accountability and sustainability to social welfare services in Canada, by restoring local administration and delivery.
- Community development includes an emphasis on strengths, well-being, social change, power within, bottom-up process, prevention, and holistic and relationship-based human services.

DISCUSSION QUESTIONS

1. What do you think of when you hear the term *welfare*? What other definitions are there for this term?
2. What purposes for social welfare services are most and least important to you? How would you make an argument in favour of your position to your critics?

3. Do you agree or disagree with the following statement: "Social welfare services owe their existence to a strong Canadian economy"? Why or why not?

4. Is the Canadian welfare state sustainable? What improvements could be made to make it stronger economically?

5. Why do some argue that the welfare state has become an agent of social control that perpetuates the oppression of the poor by the rich?

6. Is local control and administration of social welfare services desirable and possible?

7. In your own professional work, what aspects of community development would be easiest for you? Which practices would be most difficult to adhere to?

WEBLINKS

www.reformmonitor.org/ International Reform Monitor

www.un.org/rights/ Human Rights (United Nations)

www.ncwcnbes.net/index.htm National Council on Welfare (Canada)

www.statcan.ca/ Statistics Canada

www.hrsdc.gc.ca/en/gateways/topics/cyd-gxr.shtml Community Development in Canada (Human Resources and Development Canada)

KEY TERMS

Social welfare, p. 169   Welfare state, p. 171

Bibliography

Abram F., & Hoge, J. (2003). Doing justice: Women ex-offenders as group facilitators, advocates, and community educators. *Social Thought, 22,* 159–176.

Adams, W.M. (2001). *Green Development: Environment and Sustainability in the Third World.* London: Routledge.

Adamson, N., Briskin, L., & McPhail, M. (Eds.). (1989). *Feminist Organizing for Change: The Contemporary Women's Movement in Canada.* New York: Oxford University Press.

Addams, J. (1930). *The Second Twenty Years at Hull-House.* New York: Macmillan.

Adler, R.B., & Towne, N. (1999). *Looking Out/Looking In. Interpersonal Communication* (9th ed.). Orlando, FL: Harcourt Brace.

Aldridge, M. (1994). *Making Social Work News.* New York: Routledge.

Alexander, A. (1997). *The Antigonish Movement: Moses Coady and Adult Education Today.* Toronto, ON: University of Toronto Press.

Alinsky, S.D. (1969). *Reveille for Radicals.* New York: Random House.

Alinsky, S.D. (1972). *Rules for Radicals. A Practical Primer for Realistic Radicals.* New York: Vintage.

American Indian Law Alliance (2002). *In Our Own Voices.* New York, NY: author.

Anderson, R.E. (2004). *Just Get Out of the Way: How Government Can Help Business in Poor Countries.* Washington, DC: Cato Institute.

Anderson, R., Carter, I., & Lowe, G. (1999). *Human Behavior in the Social Environment: A Social Systems Approach.* New York: Aldine De Gruyter.

Andrews Street Family Centre (2005). *Andrews Street Family Centre and Community Development in the William Whyte Neighborhood.* Winnipeg, MB: author.

Andrews, A.B. & Kaufman, N.H. (Eds.). (1999). *Implementing the U.N. Convention on the Rights of the Child: A Standard of Living Adequate for Development.* Westport, CT: Praeger Publishers.

Armour, N. (1998). *Specialist and generalist cultures (Social Work 555 course handout).* Calgary, AB: University of Calgary. Assembly of First Nations. (2006). *Assembly of First Nations—the story.* Retrieved March 2, 2006, from **www.afn.ca/ article.asp?id=59**

Assembly of First Nations. (2006). Retrieved October 16, 2006, from **www.afn.ca/**

Association for Supervision and Curriculum Development (2005). *Working with the media.* Retrieved August 9, 2005, from **www.ascd. org/advocacykit/ working_media.html**

Atal, Y. (Ed.). (1999). *Poverty in Transition and Transition in Poverty: Recent Developments in Hungary, Bulgaria, Romania, Georgia, Russia, Mongolia.* New York: Berghahn Books.

Attfield, R. & Wilkins, B. (Eds.). (1992). *International Justice and the Third World: Studies in the Philosophy of Development.* New York: Routledge.

Aureli, F., & Waal, F.B. (2000). *Natural Conflict Resolution.* Berkeley, CA: University of California Press.

Baldhead, E., Campbell, M., & Members of Saskatchewan's Commission on First Nations and Metis Peoples and Justice Reform (2004). *Legacy of Hope: An Agenda for Change.* Saskatoon, SK: Province of Saskatchewan.

Banks, K. (2002). Community social work practice across Canada. In F. Turner (Ed.), *Social Work Practice: A Canadian Perspective (2nd ed).* (p. 301–314). Toronto, ON: Pearson Education.

Banting, K., Hoberg, G., & Simeon, R. (1997). *Degrees of Freedom: Canada and the United States in a Changing Global Context.* Kingston and Montreal: McGill-Queen's University Press.

Barbuto, D. (1999). *The American Settlement Movement: A Bibliography.* Westport, CT: Greenwood Press.

Barker, L., Wahlers, K., Watson, K., & Kibler, R. (1987). *Groups in Process: An Introduction to Small Group Communication* (3rd ed.). Englewood Cliffs, NJ: Prentice Hall.

Barker, R.L. (1999). *The Social Work Dictionary* (4th ed.). Washington, DC: NASW Press.

Barnsley, P. (2006). *Georges Erasmus: Fighting for his people's rights began at an early age.* Retrieved March 2, 2006, from **www.ammsa.com/achieve/AA 98-G.Erasmus.html**

Barr, N. (2001). *The Welfare State As Piggy Bank: Information, Risk, Uncertainty, and the Role of the State.* Oxford, England: Oxford University Press.

Bar-Siman-Tov, Y. (Ed.). (2004). *From Conflict Resolution to Reconciliation.* Oxford: Oxford University Press.

Bartle, P. (2006). Culture and Social Animation. Retrieved October 16, 2006, from **www.scn.org/ cmp/modules/ emp-cul.htm**.

Baxter, B. (2002). *Ecologism: An Introduction.* Toronto, ON: Scholarly Book Services.

Beairsto, B. (1999). *The Education of Educators: Enabling Professional Growth for Teachers and Administrators.* Tampere, Finland: University of Tampere.

Bell, B. et al. (1990). *We Make the Road by Walking: Conversations on Education and Social Change. Myles Horton and Paulo Freire.* Philadelphia, PA: Temple University.

Bella, L. (1978). The Origins of Alberta's Preventive Social Service Program. Unpublished manuscript. Edmonton, AB: U of A Dept. of Rec. Admin.

Bella, L. (1980). Alberta's Preventive Social Service Program: A Study of Goal Effectiveness. Unpublished manuscript. Edmonton, AB: U of A Dept. of Rec. Admin.

Belshaw, D. & Livingstone, I. (Eds.). (2002). *Renewing Development in Sub-Saharan Africa: Policy, Performance, and Prospects.* London: Routledge.

Benko, T. (2001). The Formation of Voluntary Sport Associations. M.A. Thesis, University of Alberta, Edmonton.

Bennett, M. & Blackstock, C. (2002). *First Nations fact sheet: a general profile on First Nations child welfare in Canada.* Ottawa: First Nations Child & Family Caring Society of Canada.

Benson, J. F. (2001). *Working More Creatively With Groups.* London: Routledge.

Berton, P. (2001). *The National Dream: The Great Railway 1871–1881.* Toronto, ON: Random House.

Bettis, N. (2006). Jane Addams. Retrieved March 2, 2006, from **www.webster.edu/ ~woolflm/janeadams.html**

Bhattacharyya, J. (1995). Solidarity and agency: Rethinking community development. *Human Organization, 54,* 60–69.

Biddle,W.W., & Biddle, L.J. (1965). *The Community Development Process: The Rediscovery of Local Initiative.* New York: Holt, Rinehart & Winston.

Biddle, W.W., & Biddle, L.J. (1979). The community development process. In F.M. Cox et al., *Strategies of Community Organization.* Itasca, IL: F. E. Peacock.

Black, R. & White, H. (Eds.). (2003). *Targeting Development: Critical Perspectives on the Millennium Development Goals.* New York: Routledge.

Blackstock, C. & Bennett, M. (2003). *National children's*

alliance: Policy paper on Aboriginal children. Ottawa: First Nations Child & Family Caring Society of Canada.

Blane, D., Brunner, E., & Wilkinson, R. (Eds.). (1996). *Health and Social Organization: Towards a Health Policy for the Twenty-First Century.* New York: Routledge.

Blohowiak, D. W. (1987). *No Comment! An Executive's Essential Guide to the News Media.* New York: Praeger Publishers.

Blondin, M. (1969). *Social Animation: As Developed and Practised By le Conseil des Oeuvres de Montreal.* Ottawa: Community Funds and Councils of Canada.

Bloom, D.E., Canning, D., & Sevilla, J. (2003). *The Demographic Dividend: A New Perspective on the Economic Consequences of Population Change.* Santa Monica, CA: Rand.

Boldt, M. (1996). Surviving as Indians: The Challenge of Self-Government, *Ethnic and Racial Studies, 19* (2), 503–522.

Boothroyd, P. (1990). In B. Kirwin, *Development and Social Welfare: Canadian Perspectives.* Toronto, ON: Canadian Scholars Press.

Bopp, M. & Bopp, J. (2001). *Recreating the World: A Practical Guide to Building Sustainable Communities.* Ottawa: Four Worlds Press.

Bothwell, R. (1996). *History of Canada Since 1867.* Washington, D.C.: Association for Canadian Studies in the United States.

Bouwen, R., & Taillieu, T. (2004). Multi-party collaboration as social learning for interdependence: developing relational knowing for sustainable natural resource management. *Journal of Community and Applied Social Psychology, 14,* 137–153.

Boyle, F. A. (2004). *Destroying World Order: U.S. Imperialism in the Middle East Before and After September 11.* Atlanta: Clarity Press.

Briggs-Myers, I., & Myers, P.B. (1980). *Gifts Differing.* Palo Alto, CA: Consulting Psychologists Press.

Brooks, A.C. (2004). Evaluating the effectiveness of nonprofit fundraising. *Policy Studies Journal, 32,* 363–370.

Brooks, N. (2005). The share of income tax paid by the rich. *Behind the Numbers, 7*(5), 1–7.

Brown, J., Higgitt, N., Wingert, S., Miller, C., & Morrissette, L. (2004). *Shared Responsibility: Building Communities in Winnipeg's North End.* Winnipeg, MB: Winnipeg Inner City Research Alliance.

Brown, N. (2005). *Robert Park and Ernest Burgess: Urban Ecology Studies 1925.* Chicago, IL: CSISS Classics.

Brown, R., & Cook, R. (1974). *Canada 1896–1921: A Nation Transformed.* Toronto: McClelland and Stewart.

Brown, S., Foye, C., Nawagesic, V., & Welch, T. (2000). *The community action plan on homelessness in Hamilton-Wentworth.* North Hamilton, ON: Social Planning and Research Council of Hamilton-Wentworth.

Burns, R. (2002). *The Adult Learner at Work: The Challenges of Lifelong Education in the New Millennium.* (2nd ed.). Crows Nest, N.S.W.: Allen & Unwin.

Cahn, D.D. (Ed.). (1994). *Conflict in Personal Relationships.*

Hillsdale, NJ: Lawrence Erlbaum Associates.

Calder, J. (1993). *Disaffection and Diversity: Overcoming Barriers for Adult Learners.* London: Falmer Press.

Caley, P. (1983). Canada's Chinese Columbus, *The Beaver,* 313:4.

Cameron, J. G., & Kerans, P. (1985). Social and political action. In S.A. Yelaja, *An Introduction to Social Work Practice in Canada.* Scarborough, ON: Prentice-Hall.

Canada Revenue Agency (2005). *Charities directorate.* Retrieved July 13, 2005, from **www.cra-arc.gc.ca/tax/ charities/menu-e.html**

Canadian Association of Family Resource Programs (2005). *Case Studies of Family Resource Programs: Andrews Street Family Centre.* Ottawa, ON; author.

Canadian Association of Social Workers (2005). *Code of Ethics.* Ottawa, ON: CASW.

Canadian Broadcasting Corporation. (2006a). *Caledonia blockade coming down on Monday, reporter says.* Retrieved June 23, 2006. from **www.cbc.ca/story/ canada/national/2006/05/21/ caledonia.html?ref=rss**

Canadian Broadcasting Corporation. (2006b). *Georges Erasmus: Native rights crusader* [Electronic Version]. Retrieved March 2, 2006, from **archives.cbc.ca/ ACT-1-74-516/people/ erasmus/educational_ activities/.**

Canadian Cerebral Palsy Sports Association. (2006a). *Objectives.* Retrieved September 4, 2006, from **www.ccpsa.ca/en/aboutus/ objectives.aspx**

Canadian Cerebral Palsy Sports Association. (2006b). *February 2006 newsletter.* Ottawa, ON: Author.

Canadian Community Networks. (1995). *Canadian community networks directory.* Retrieved May 8, 2006, from **www. tc.ca/directories.html**

Canadian Heritage. (2005). *Six-point action plan.* Retrieved June 26, 2005, from **www.pch.gc.ca/multi/plan_a ction_plan/tous_all/part_two _2_e.cfm?nav=2**

Canadian International Development Agency. (2006). *What is CIDA?* Retrieved June 24, 2006 from **www.acdi-cida.gc.ca/index-e.htm**

Canadian Nurses Association. (2002). *Code of ethics for registered nurses.* Ottawa, ON: CNA.

Canadian Psychological Association. (1995). *Working with the media: A guide for psychologists.* Retrieved September 4, 2006, from **www.cpa.ca/cpasite/userfiles /Documents/publications/Wo rking%20with%20the%20 Media.pdf**

Canadian Psychological Association. (2000). *Canadian Code of Ethics for Psychologists.* Ottawa, ON: CPA.

Canadian Television Network. (2004). *Election 2004.* Retrieved September 6, 2006 from **www.ctv.ca/ servlet/HTMLTemplate/!ctv/ Search?query= election+2004&x=0&y=0&si te_codename=ctv**

Canadian Television Network. (2006). *Concerns over water on reserve ignored for years.* Retrieved June 23, 2006, from **www.ctv.ca/servlet/ ArticleNews/story/CTVNews/20 051027/aboriginal_water_**

feature_051027?s_
name=&no_ads=

Carson, M. (1990). *Settlement Folk: Social Thought and the American Settlement Movement, 1885–1930.* Chicago: University of Chicago Press.

Cartright, J. (2004). Cities and strategies for progressive politics. *Canadian Dimension, 38*(6), 25–32.

Castles, F.G. (2004). *The Future of the Welfare State: Crisis Myths and Crisis Realities.* Oxford: Oxford University Press.

Cawsey, R., Little Bear, L., Brtolin, C., Cooper, C., Franklin, J., Galet, A., et al. (1991). *The Criminal Justice System and Its Impact on the Indian and Metis People of Alberta.* Edmonton: Government of Alberta.

CED Online. (2006). *The transformation of Isle Madame.* Retrieved May 8, 2006, from ced.gov.ns. ca/main/cedin_ns/region/ counties/richmond/ islemadame.htm

Center for Community Organizations. (2005). *Board handbook.* Retrieved July 14, 2005, from www.coco-net. org/publications.html

Cerebral Palsy Association of Alberta. (2006). *About CP Alberta.* Retrieved May 4, 2006, from www. cpalberta.com/about.htm

Chalmers, K., & Bramadat, I. (1996). Community development: theoretical and practical issues for community health nursing in Canada. *Journal of Advanced Nursing, 24*, 719–26.

Chambers, E. & Cowan, M. (2003). Roots for Radicals. New York, NY: Continuum Publishing.

Chapman, D. (2005). *Chronology of Canadian adult education.* Retrieved July 11, 2005, from www. ucfv.bc.ca/aded/encyclopedia/chronology.htm

Charity Village. (2006). Main Street. Retrieved April 25, 2006, from www. charityvillage.com/CV/main. asp

Chasek, P.S. (2001). *Earth Negotiations : Analyzing Thirty Years of Environmental Diplomacy.* New York: United Nations University Press.

Checkoway, B. (1997). Core concepts for community change. *Journal of Community Practice, 4,* 11–29.

Chilcote, R.H. (1994). *Theories of Comparative Politics: The Search for a Paradigm Reconsidered.* Boulder, CO: Westview Press.

Chomsky, N. (1987). *Chomsky Reader.* New York, NY: Pantheon.

Chrisjohn, R., Young, S., & Mauraun, M. (1997). *The Circle Game: Shadows and Substance in the Indian Residential School Experience in Canada.* Penticton, BC: Theytus Books.

Christenson, J.A., & Robinson, J.W. (1980). *Community Development in America.* Ames, IA: State University Press.

City of Saskatoon. (2006). *Quick facts.* Retrieved May 4, 2006, from www.city.saskatoon.sk. ca/org/quick_facts/ index.asp

City of Whitehorse (2004). *Local action plan to reduce energy and greenhouse gas emissions.* Whitehorse, UK: author.

City of Yellowknife (2006). *About Yellowknife.* Retrieved May 4,

2006, from www.yellowknife. ca/Visitors/About_Yellowkni fe.html

Clague, M., Dill, R., Seebaran, R., & Wharf, B. (1984). *Reforming Human Services: The Experience of the Community Resource Boards in B.C.* Vancouver, B.C.: University of British Columbia Press.

Clarkson, L., V. Morrissette, and G. Régallet. 1992. *Our responsibility to the seventh generation: Indigenous peoples and sustainable development.* Winnipeg, MB: International Institute for Sustainable Development.

CLSC. (2006). Retrieved October 16, 2006, from www.clscmetro.qc.ca/en/.

Coady International Institute. (1986). *Annual report 1985/86.* Antigonish, NS: St. Francis Xavier University.

Coady, M.M. (1939). *Masters of Their Own Destiny.* London: Harper and Brothers.

Coady, N. (2002). The helping relationship. In F. Turner (ed.), *Social Work Practice: A Canadian Perspective.* (pp. 116–130). Toronto: Prentice-Hall.

Cockshott, W.P., & Cottrell, A. (1993). *Towards a new socialism.* Nottingham: Spokesman, Bertrand Russell House.

Cohen, B.J. (1973). *The Question of Imperialism: The Political Economy of Dominance and Dependence.* New York: Basic Books.

Coley, S., & Scheinberg, C. (2000). *Proposal Writing* (2nd ed). Thousand Oaks: Sage.

Collins, D.E. (1971). *Paulo Freire–His Life, Works, and Thought.* New York: The Paulista Press.

Comeau, P. & Santin, A. (1990). *The First Canadians: A Profile of Canada's Native People Today.* Toronto, ON: Lorimer.

Community-University Institute for Social Research (2003). *Child Poverty in Canada, Saskatchewan and Saskatoon: A Literature Review and the Voices of the People.* Saskatoon, SK: author.

Community Toolbox (2005). *Outline for developing strategic action plans.* Retrieved July 16, 2005, from **ctb.ku.edu/tools/ tk/en/tools_tk_content_ page_193.jsp**

Conklin, A.L. (1997). *A Mission to Civilize: The Republican Idea of Empire in France and West Africa, 1895–1930.* Stanford, CA: Stanford University Press.

Consulting Psychologists' Press. (2005). *Myers-Briggs Type Indicator.* Retrieved June 26, 2005, from **www.cpp.com/ products/mbti/index.asp**

Coombs, C.H., & Avrunin, G.S. (1988). *The Structure of Conflict.* Hillsdale, NJ: Lawrence Erlbaum Associates.

Corporation Centre. (2005). *Non-profit incorporation.* Retrieved September 4, 2006, from **www. corporationcentre.ca/docen/ home/faq.asp?id=incnp#q4**

Cowen, M., & Shenton, R. (1995). The Invention of Development. In *Power of Development*, Crush, J. (Ed.) (pp. 27–43). London: Routledge.

Cox, M.J. & Brooks-Gunn, J. (Eds.). (1999). *Conflict and Cohesion in Families: Causes and Consequences.* Mahwah, NJ: Lawrence Erlbaum Associates.

Cox. F.M., Erlich, J.L., Rothman, J., & Tropman, J.E. (1979). Strategies of Community

Organization. Itasca, IL: F.E. Peacock.

Crane, J.A. (1994). *Directions for Social Welfare in Canada: The public's View.* Vancouver, B.C.: University of British Columbia Press.

Crichton, A., Robertson, A., Gordon, C., & Farrant, W. (1997). *Health Care: A Community Concern?* Calgary, AB: University of Calgary Press.

Cross, E.Y. (2000). *Managing Diversity: The Courage To Lead.* Westport, CT: Quorum Books.

Curtis, V., & Cairncross, S. (2003). Effect of washing hands with soap on diarrhea risk in the community: A systematic review. *The Lancet Infectious Diseases, 3*(5): 275–281.

Cypher, J.M., & Dietz, J.L. (1997). *The Process of Economic Development.* London: Routledge.

Dans La Rue (2005). *2004 annual report.* Montreal, QC: author.

Dans La Rue (2006a). *History.* Retrieved May 6, 2006, from **www.danslarue.com/**

Dans La Rue (2006b). *Prevention.* Retrieved May 6, 2006, from **www.danslarue.com/**

Davies, L., & Shragge, E. (1990). *Bureaucracy and Community.* Montreal, PQ: Black Rose.

Deep, S., & Sussman, L. (1998). *Power Tools: 33 Management Inventions You Can Use Today.* Reading, MA: Perseus Publishing.

Delaney, I. (1985). *By Their Own Hands. A Fieldworker's Account of the Antigonish Movement.* Hantsport, NS: Lancelot Press.

Demick, J., & Wapner, S. (1988). Children-in-environments: Physical, interpersonal, and sociocultural aspects.

Children's Environments Quarterly, 5, 54–62.

Department of Health and Community Services. (2006). *Healthy aging for all.* St. John's, NL: Government of Newfoundland and Labrador.

Derose, L., Messer, E., & Millman, S. (1998). *Who's Hungry? And How Do We Know? Food Shortage, Poverty, and Deprivation.* New York: United Nations University Press.

Development Isle Madame. (1999). *Our story: Past, present and future.* Arichat, NS; author.

Dew, J.R. (1997). *Empowerment and Democracy in the Workplace: Applying Adult Education Theory and Practice for Cultivating Empowerment.* Westport, CT: Quorum Books.

Dickason, O. (1992). *Canada's First Nations: A History of Founding Peoples from the Earliest Times.* Toronto: McClelland & Stewart.

Dickason, O. (1998). Toward a larger view of Canada's history: The native factor. In D. Long and O. Dickason (Eds.). *Visions of the Heart: Canadian Aboriginal Issues* (2nd ed.) (pp. 11–30). Toronto, ON: Thompson Nelson.

DIMA News (2006). *Development Isle Madame Association, Vol. 1.* Retrieved May 8, 2006, from **www. islemadame.net/ newsletter/Newsletter-Winter.pdf**

Dixon, J. & Scheurell, R.P. (Eds.). (2002). *The State of Social Welfare: The Twentieth Century in Cross-National Review.* Westport, CT: Praeger.

Dockstator, M. (1993). *Towards an understanding of Aboriginal self-government: A proposed theoretical model an illustrative factual analysis*, Doctor of Jurisprudence dissertation, Toronto: York University.

Dozier, D.M., Grunig, J.E., & Grunig, L.A. (1995). *Manager's guide to excellence in public relations and communication management.* Mahwah, NJ: Lawrence Erlbaum Associates.

Draper, J. & Carere, J. (1998). Selected chronology of adult education in Canada. *Canadian Journal for the Study of Adult Education, 12,* 44–75.

Driscoll, J. (1996). Reflection and the management of community nursing practice. *British Journal of Community Health Nursing, 1,* 92–96.

Drover, G., & Kerans, K. (1993). (Eds.). *New Approaches to Welfare Theory.* Andershot: Edward Elgar.

Dubuc, A., Erasmus, G., & Saul, J. (2002). *Lafontaine Baldwin Lectures.* Toronto: Penguin.

Durkheim, E. (1964). *The Division of Labour in Society.* New York, NY: Free Press.

Dyer, S., Buell, T., Harrison, M., & Weber, S. (2002). Managing public relations in nonprofit organizations. *Public Relations Quarterly, 47,* 13–19.

Dyer, W. (1995). *Team Building: Current Issues and New Alternatives* (3rd ed.). Toronto, ON: Pearson.

Eagle Rock Materials. (2006). *About us.* Retrieved May 3, 2006, from **www. eagleaggregates.ca/ about.html**

Egan, G. & Cowan, M. (1979). *People in Systems.* Monterey, CA: Brooks/Cole.

Emery, A. (2000). *Integrating indigenous knowledge in project planning and implementation.* Ottawa: The International Labour Organization, The World Bank, The Canadian International Development Agency, and KIVU Nature Inc.

Environmental Task Force. (2000). *Environmental plan, clean, green and healthy, A plan for an environmentally sustainable Toronto.* Toronto, ON: author.

Erasmus, G. (2006). Healing the legacy of the residential schools. Retrieved March 2, 2006, from **www. wherearethechildren.ca/en/ about.html**

Estlund, C. (2003). Working Together: How Workplace Bonds Strengthen a Diverse Democracy. New York: Oxford University Press.

Ewen, R. (1998). Introduction to Theories of Personality. Mahwah, NJ: Lawrence Erlbaum.

Ezell, M. (2001). *Advocacy in the Human Services.* Stanford, CT: Brookes Cole.

Fanon, F. (1963). *The Wretched of the Earth.* New York, Grove Weidenfeld.

Farazmand, A. (2002). *Modern Organizations: Theory and Practice.* Westport, CT: Praeger.

Farmer, P. (2003). *Pathologies of Power: Health, Human Rights, and the New War on the Poor.* Berkeley, CA: University of California Press.

Fearn-Banks, K. (1996). *Crisis Communications: A Casebook Approach.* Mahwah, NJ: Lawrence Erlbaum Associates.

Federal Communicator's Network, 2001. *Communicator's Guide.* Gainesville, FL: Author.

Fellegi, I. (1999). *On poverty and low income.* Ottawa, Statistics Canada.

Ferguson, N. (2002). *Empire: The Rise and Demise of the British World Order and the Lessons for Global Powers.* New York, NY: Basic Books.

Fessler, D.R. (1976). *Facilitating Community Change. A Basic Guide.* La Jolla, CA: University Associates.

Finks, D.P. (1984). *The Radical Vision of Saul Alinsky.* New York: Paulist Press.

Fishbein, M., & Middlestadt, S.E. (1997). *Social Marketing: Theoretical and Practical Perspectives.* Mahwah, NJ: Lawrence Erlbaum Associates.

Fisher, C.M. (1998). *Resource Allocation in the Public Sector: Values, Priorities, and Markets in the Management of Public Services.* New York: Routledge.

Foley, G. (2004). *Dimensions of Adult Learning: Adult Education and Training in a Global Era.* Crows Nest, N.S.W.: Allen & Unwin.

Forman, S. & Ghosh, R. (Eds.). (2000). *Promoting Reproductive Health: Investing in Health for Development.* Boulder, CO: Lynne Rienner.

Four Worlds. (1989). *Developing Healthy Communities: Fundamental Strategies for Health Promotion.* Ottawa: Four Worlds Press.

Francisco, V, & Schultz, J. (2005). *Conducting public forums and listening sessions.* Retrieved September 4, 2006, from **ctb.ku.edu/tools/en/sub_section_main_1021.htm**

Frank, F., & Smith, A. (1999). *The Community Development Handbook: A Tool to Build Community Capacity.* Ottawa,

ON: Human Resources Canada.

Freire, P. (1970). *Pedagogy of the Oppressed*. New York: Herder & Herder.

Freire, P. (1973). *Education as the Practice of Freedom* in *Education for Critical Consciousness*. New York: Continuum.

Freire, P. (1985). *The Politics of Education*. South Hadley, MA: Bergin & Garvey.

French, J. & Raven, B. (1959). The bases of social power. In D. Cartright (Ed.). *Studies in Social Power* (pp. 150–167). Chicago, IL: Institute for Social Research.

Fry, D.P. & Björkqvist, K. (Eds.). (1997). *Cultural Variation in Conflict Resolution: Alternatives to Violence*. Mahwah, NJ: Lawrence Erlbaum Associates.

Galbraith, M.W. (1990). The nature of community and adult education. In M.W. Galbraith (Ed.), *Education Through Community Organizations* (pp. 3–11). San Francisco: Jossey-Bass.

Gallopín, G.C., & Raskin, P. D. (2002). *Global Sustainability: Bending the Curve*. London: Routledge.

Galper, J.H. (1975). *The Politics of Social Services*. Englewood Cliffs, NJ: Prentice-Hall.

Garner, H.G. (1988). *Helping Others Through Teamwork*. Washington, DC: Welfare League of America.

George, S. (1992). *The Debt Boomerang: How Third World Debt Harms Us All*. Boulder, CO: Westview Press.

Germain, C., & Gitterman, A. (1995). Ecological perspective. In R.L. Edwards (Ed.), *Encyclopedia of Social Work*

(19th ed.) (pp. 816–824). Washington, DC: National Association of Social Workers Press.

Gerth, H. & Mills, C.W. (1946). *Max Weber: The Theory of Social and Economic Organization*. Oxford: Oxford University Press.

Gibbon, M., Labonte, R., & Laverack, G. (2002). Evaluating community capacity. *Health and Social Care in the Community, 10,* 485–491.

Gilchrist A. (2003). Community development in the UK—possibilities and paradoxes. *Community Development Journal, 38,* 16–25.

Gitterman, A. (1994). Editor's note. In J.B. Mondros & S. M. Wilson (Eds.), *Organizing for Power and Empowerment* (pp. ix–x). New York: Columbia University Press.

Glassman, R.M., Swatos, W. H., & Rosen, P.L. (Eds.). (1987). *Bureaucracy Against Democracy and Socialism*. New York: Greenwood Press.

Goddard, J. (1991). *Last Stand of the Lubicon Cree*. Toronto, ON: Douglas & McIntyre.

Godwin, W. (1993). *Enquiry Concerning Political Justice and Its Influence on Modern Morals and Happiness*, New York, NY: Viking Press.

Gonzalez, A. & Norwine, J. (Eds.). (1998). *The New Third World* (2nd ed.). Boulder, CO: Westview Press.

Gonzalez-Arizmendi, L. & Ortiz, L. (2004). Neighborhood and community organizing in Colonias: A case study in the development and use of pro-motoras. *Journal of Community Practice, 12,* 23–35.

Gonzalez-Pelaez, A. (2005). *Human Rights and World*

Trade: Hunger in International Society. London: Routledge.

Goodwill, J. (1982). *John Tootoosis : Biography of a Cree leader*. Ottawa, ON: Golden Dog Press.

Government of Canada. (1982). Constitution Act. Ottawa: Queen's Printer.

Government of Canada. (1996). *Royal Commission on Aboriginal Peoples*. Ottawa: Indian and Northern Affairs Canada.

Government of Canada. (2004). *Status: Most often asked questions*. Ottawa: Indian and Northern Affairs Canada.

Government of Northwest Territories. (2006). *The school of community government*. Retrieved May 4, 2006, from **www.maca.gov.nt.ca/ school/index.html**

Government of Nunavut. (2006a). *Our land*. Retrieved May 5, 2006, from **www.gov.nu.ca/ Nunavut/English/about/ ourland.pdf**

Government of Nunavut. (2006b). *Consensus government*. Retrieved May 5, 2006, from **www. gov.nu.ca/Nunavut/ English/about/cg.pdf**

Governor General of Canada. (2006). Order of Canada. Retrieved March 2, 2006, from **www.gg.ca/honours/ nat=ord/index_e.asp**

Grameen Bank. (2006). Bank for the Poor. Retrieved May 29, 2006, from **www.grameen-info.org/bank/**

Grant, J. (1984). *Moon Over Wintertime: Missionaries and the Indians of Canada in Encounter Since 1534*. Toronto: U of T Press.

Grant, S.D. (1988). *Sovereignty or security? Government policy in the Canadian north, 1936–1950.* Vancouver, B.C.: University of British Columbia Press.

Greene, J.O. & Burleson, B.R. (Eds.). (2003). *Handbook of Communication and social Interaction Skills.* Mahwah, NJ: Lawrence Erlbaum Associates.

Greene, R. (1999). *Human Behavior Theory and Social Work Practice.* New York: Aldine De Gruyter.

Grootaert, C. & Van Bastelaer, T. (Eds.). (2002). *The Role of Social Capital in Development: An Empirical Assessment.* Cambridge, England: Cambridge University Press.

Grunig, J.E., Dozier, D.M., Ehling, W.P., Grunig, L.A., Repper, F.C., & White, J. (Eds.). (1992). *Excellence in Public Relations and Communication Management.* Hillsdale, NJ: Lawrence Erlbaum Associates.

Grunig, L.A., Grunig, J.E., & Dozier, D.M. (2002). *Excellent Public Relations and Effective Organizations: A Study of Communication Management in Three Countries.* Mahwah, NJ: Lawrence Erlbaum Associates.

Guimond, E. (2003). Fuzzy definitions and population explosion: Changing identities of Aboriginal groups in Canada. In *Not Strangers in These Parts: Urban Aboriginal Peoples*, edited by D. Newhouse and E. Peters. Ottawa: Policy Research Initiative.

Hafen, B.Q., Karren, K.J., Frandsen, K.J., & Smith, N.L. (1996). *Mind/Body Health: The Effects of Attitudes, Emotions and Relationships.* Boston: Allyn and Bacon.

Hagan, L. & Garon, G. (1998). CLSC's Info-Sante: An effective service? *Canadian Journal of Public Health, 89* (2), 125–128.

Hall, B., & Kidd R. (Eds.). (1978). *Adult Learning: A Design for Action.* Oxford: Pergamon.

Hannis, D. (1988). *The social impact of major energy projects* (unpublished). Edmonton, AB: Alberta Social Services and Community Health.

Hannis, D. (2003). *Community Practice Methods.* Department of Social Work, Edmonton, AB: Grant MacEwan College.

Hanvey, C. & Philpot, T. (Eds.). (1996). *Sweet charity: The Role and Workings of Voluntary Organizations.* New York: Routledge.

Hardcastle, D.A., Powers, P.R., & Wenocur, S. (2004). *Community Practice: Theories and Skills for Social Workers.* New York: Oxford University Press.

Hardina, D. (2002). *Analytical Skills for Community Organization Practice.* New York: Columbia University Press.

Hardina, D. (2004). Guidelines for ethical practice in community organizations. *Social Work, 49*, 595–604.

Hare, A.P. (1992). *Groups, Teams, and Social Interaction Theories and Applications.* New York: Praeger Publishers.

Harris, R.J. (2004). *A Cognitive Psychology of Mass Communication.* Mahwah, NJ: Lawrence Erlbaum Associates.

Harvey, J.H. & Wenzel, A. (Eds.). (2002). *A Clinician's Guide to Maintaining and Enhancing Close Relationships.* Mahwah, NJ: Lawrence Erlbaum Associates.

Hawkins, C. (1997). First aid for meetings. *Public Relations Quarterly*, 42(3), 33–38.

Health Canada. (1999). *The health of Aboriginal women.* Ottawa: Women's Health Bureau.

Health Canada. (2003). *A Statistical Profile on the Health of First Nations in Canada.* Ottawa, Ontario: Health Canada.

Hearn, G. (1969). *The General Systems Approach: Contributions Toward an Holistic Conception of Social Work.* New York: Council on Social Work Education.

Heaven, C. (2005). *Developing a plan for identifying local needs and resources.* Retrieved September 4, 2006, from **ctb.ku.edu/tools/en/sub_section_main_1019.htm**

Heller, J. (1961). *Catch-22.* New York: Simon & Schuster.

Herman, B., Pietracci, F., & Sharma, K. (Eds.). (2001). *Financing for Development: Proposals from Business and Civil Society.* New York: United Nations University Press.

Heskin, A.D. (1991). *The Struggle for Community.* Boulder, CO: Westview Press.

Hessel, D.T. (1972). *A Social action primer.* Philadelphia: Westminster Press.

Hjollund, L., & Svendson, G. (2006). *Social capital: A Standard method of measurement.* Retrieved May 30, 2006, from **www.hha.dk/nat/WPER/00-9_gts.pdf**

Homan, M. (2003). *Promoting Community Change: Making It Happen in the Real World.* Belmont, CA: Brooks/Cole.

Hook, S.W. (Ed.). (1996). *Foreign Aid Toward the Millennium.* Boulder, CO: Lynne Rienner.

Horton, M. (1990). *The Long Haul. An Autobiography.* New York: Doubleday.

Horwitt, S.D. (1992). *Let Them Call Me Rebel. Saul Alinsky: His Life and Legacy.* New York: Vintage.

Horwood, D. (2000) *Haida Gwaii: The Queen Charlotte Islands.* Toronto, ON: Heritage House.

Hough, P. (2004). *Understanding Global Security.* New York: Routledge.

Huitt, W. (2003). *A systems model of human behavior.* Educational Psychology Interactive, Valdosta, GA: Valdosta State University.

Hull House. (2006). Jane Addams' Hull House. Retrieved March 2, 2006, from **www.hullhouse.org/**

Hunter, F. (1969). *Community Power Structure: A Study of Decision Makers.* Raleigh, NC: North Carolina Press.

Hupacasath. (2006). *Choo Kwa ventures.* Retrieved May 3, 3006, from **www.chookwa.com/**

Hutchinson-Crocker, R. (1992). *Social Work and Social Order: The Settlement Movement in Two Industrial Cities, 1889–1930.* Urbana: University of Illinois Press.

Ife, J. (2002). *Community Development: Community-Based Alternatives in an Age of Globalization.* (2nd ed.). Frenchs Forest, NSW: Pearson Education Australia.

Indian and Northern Affairs Canada. (1996). *Royal Commission on Aboriginal Peoples.* Retrieved March 2, 2006, from **www.ainc-inac.gc.ca/ch/ rcap/index_e.html**

Indian and Northern Affairs Canada (INAC). (1996a). *Royal Commission on Aboriginal Peoples.* Retrieved April 5, 2005, from **www.ainc-inac.gc.ca/ ch/rcap/sg/cg_e.html**

Indian and Northern Affairs Canada. (1996b). *Royal Commission on Aboriginal Peoples, Vol. 1, Part 3, Appendix A.* Retrieved August 31, 2005, from **www.ainc-inac.gc.ca/ch/ rcap/sg/sga1_e.html**

Indian and Northern Affairs Canada. (1996c). *Royal Commission on Aboriginal Peoples. Report Highlights. Looking forward, looking back.* Retrieved August 31, 2005 from **www. ainc-inac.gc.ca/ch/ rcap/rpt/lk_e.html**

Indian and Northern Affairs Canada. (1997). *Gathering Strength: Canada's Aboriginal Action Plan.* Retrieved October 16, 2006, from **www.ainc-inac.gc.ca/gs/ chg_e.html**.

Indian and Northern Affairs Canada (INAC). (2004). School of community government: Building capacity for a changing territory. *Plain Talk, Summer,* 1–4.

Indian and Northern Affairs Canada. (2006a). *Aboriginal people profiles: Georges Erasmus* [Electronic Version]. Retrieved September 2, 2006, from **http://www. ainc-inac.gc.ca/ks/ 3108_e.html**

Indian and Northern Affairs Canada. (2006b). *Neechi foods co-operative limited.* Retrieved August 16, 2006, from **www. ainc-inac.gc.ca/pr/ra/ coo/neec2000_e.html**

Indian Residential Schools Resolution Canada. (2006). *The residential school system overview.* Retrieved September 4, 2006, from **http://www.irsr-rqpi.gc.ca/**

Industrial Areas Foundation. (2005). *International affiliates.* Retrieved September 4, 2006, from **www. industrialareas foundation.org/**

Industry Canada. (2006). *What is CAP?* Retrieved May 8, 2006, from **cap.ic.gc.ca/ pub/about_us/whatiscap. html**

Inter Peres. (2006). *Who we are.* Retrieved June 24, 2006, from **www. interpares.ca/en/who/ index.php**

International Institute for Sustainable Development. (2005). *About IISD.* Retrieved July 1, 2005, from **www.iisd.org/ about/**

Ismael, J.S. & Vaillancourt, Y. (Eds.). (1988). *Privatization and Provincial Social Services in Canada: Policy, Administration, and Service Delivery.* Edmonton, AB.: University of Alberta Press.

Jacks, L.P. (1986). The process of planning. In *Handbook of Strategic Planning for Nonprofit Organizations* (pp. 42–56). New York: Praeger Publishers.

Jackson, R.J. & Jackson, D. (2006) *Politics in Canada* (9th ed.), Scarborough, ON: Prentice-Hall.

Jarrett, R., Sullivan, P., & Watkins, N. (2005). Developing social capital through participation in organized youth programs: Qualitative insights from three programs. *Journal of Community Psychology, 33,* 41–55.

Jewkes,Y., & Letherby, G. (2001). Insiders and outsiders: Complex issues of identification, difference and distance in social research.

Auto/Biography Studies, 16, 41–50.

Johnson, G.W. (1985). *Double Impact: France and Africa in the Age of Imperialism.* Westport, CT: Greenwood Press.

Johnston, F.E., & Low, S.M. (1995). *Children of the Urban Poor: The Sociocultural Environment of Growth, Development, and Malnutrition in Guatemala City.* Boulder, CO: Westview Press.

Jordan C., & Franklin C. (1995). *Clinical Assessment for Social Workers: Quantitative and Qualitative Methods.* Chicago: Lyceum.

Kahn, A.J. (1969). *Theory and Practice of Social Planning.* New York: Russell Sage Foundation.

Kalbfleisch, P.J. (Ed.). (2004). *Communication Yearbook.* Mahwah, NJ: Lawrence Erlbaum Associates.

Kamerman, S.B. & Kahn, A. J. (Eds.). (1997). *Family Change and Family Policies in Great Britain, Canada, New Zealand, and the United States.* Oxford: Clarendon Press.

Karabanow, J. (1999). Creating community: A case study of a Montreal street kid agency. *Community Development Journal, 34,* 318–327.

Kaye, G. & Berkowitz, B. (2005). *Conducting effective meetings.* Retrieved August 4, 2005, from **ctb.ku.edu/tools/en/sub_section_main_1153.htm**

Kekinusuqs. (2005). A Nation's economic catalyst. *Making Waves, 4,* 5–10.

Kelly, K. & Caputo, T. (2005). Case study of grassroots community development: Sustainable, flexible, and cost-effective responses to local needs. *Community Development Journal, 2,* 234–245.

Kelly, K.S. (1991). *Fund Raising and Public Relations: A Critical Analysis.* Hillsdale, NJ: Lawrence Erlbaum Associates.

Kelly, K.S. (1998). *Effective Fund-Raising Management.* Mahwah, NJ: Lawrence Erlbaum Associates.

Kelly, P. (2005). Practical suggestions for community interventions using participatory action research. *Public Health Nursing, 22,* 65–73.

Kenny, M. (2001). *Learning To Serve: Promoting Civil Society Through Service-Learning.* New York: Kluwer.

Kettner, P., Daley, J. & Nichols, A. (1985). *Initiating Change in Organizations and Communities: A Macro Practice Model.* Pacific Grove, CA: Brooks/Cole.

Khinduka, S.K. (1979). Community development: Potentials and limitations. In F.M. Cox et al., *Strategies of Community Organization.* Itasca, IL: F.E. Peacock.

Kirst-Ashman, K., & Hull, G. (2001). *Generalist Practice with Organizations and Communities* (2nd ed.). Chicago: Nelson-Hall.

Klodawsky, F. (May, 2002). *Community-centered evaluation.* Paper presentation at First International Seminar on Women's Safety, Montreal, QC.

Kouzes, J., & Posner, B. (1996). *The Futurist, 2,* 14–19.

Kowalik, T. (2003). *The Accumulation of Capital.* New York: Routledge.

Kozeny, G. (2000). In community intentionally. In *Communities directory: A guide to intentional communities and cooperative living.* Rutledge, MO: Fellowship for Intentional Community.

Kramarae, C. & Spender, D. (Eds.). (2000). *Routledge International Encyclopedia of Women: Global Women's Issues and Knowledge* (Vol. 2). New York: Routledge.

Kramer, R., & Specht, H. (1983). *Readings in Community Organization Practice (3rd ed.).* Englewood Cliffs, NJ: Prentice Hall.

Krebs-Hirsh, S. (1985). *Using the Myers-Briggs Type Indicator in Organizations.* Palo Alto, CA: Consulting Psychological Press, Inc.

Kremarik, F. (2000). *Canadian Social Trends.* Ottawa, ON: Government of Canada, StatsCan.

Krishna, A. (2002). *Active Social Capital: Tracing the Roots of Development and Democracy.* New York: Columbia University Press.

Kruger, E. (2005). *Diversity Training Program.* Calgary, AB: Cultural Diversity Institute.

Kulchyski, P. (1998). A considerable unrest: F.O. Loft and the League of Indians, *Native Studies Review, 4* (1–2), 107–120.

Kuyek, J.N. (1992). *Fighting for Hope. Organizing To Realize Our Dreams.* Montreal, PQ: Rose Black.

Kwiatkowski, L.M. (1998). *Struggling with Development: The Politics of Hunger and Gender in the Philippines.* Boulder, CO: Westview Press.

Lane, P., Bopp, M., Bopp, J., & Norris, J. (2004). *Mapping the Healing Journey.* Ottawa: Solicitor General.

Langton, M., Tehan, M., Palmer, L., & Shain, K. (2004). *Honour Among Nations? Treaties and Agreements with Indigenous Peoples.* Melburne: Melburne University Press.

Lasch, C. (1966). *Beloved Lady: A History of Jane Addams' Ideas on Reform and Peace.* Baltimore: Johns Hopkins Press.

Lasch-Quinn, E. (1993). *Black neighbors: Race and the limits of reform in the American settlement house movement, 1890–1945.* Chapel Hill: University of North Carolina Press.

Latham, M.E. (2000). *Modernization as Ideology: American Social Science and "Nation Building" in the Kennedy Era.* Chapel Hill, NC: University of North Carolina Press.

Lauffer, A. (1979). Social planning in the United States: An overview and some predictions. In F.M. Cox et al., *Strategies of Community Organization.* Itasca, IL: F.E. Peacock.

Law, R. (2004). *Effecting changes in elder care based on identified healthcare needs of ethnic seniors.* Paper presentation at 3rd International Conference on Elder Care, Registered Nurses Association of Ontario, Toronto, September.

League of California Cities. (1979). Social needs assessment: A scientific or political process. In F. M. Cox et al., *Strategies of Community Organization.* Itasca, IL: F. E. Peacock.

Lee, B. (1992). *Pragmatics of Community Organization* (2nd ed.). Mississauga, ON: Commonact Press.

Lee, J. (2001). *The Empowerment Approach to Social Work Practice: Building the Beloved Community.* New York: Columbia University Press.

Lewis, D. (2001). *The Management of Non-Governmental Development Organizations: An Introduction.* New York: Routledge.

Lim, T. (1994). Personality types among Singapore and American students. *Journal of Psychological Type, 31,* 10–15.

Lindstrom, N. (1998). *The Social Conscience of Latin American Writing.* Austin, TX: University of Texas Press.

Linn, J. (1935). *Jane Addams: A Biography.* New York: Appleton-Century.

Livi-Bacci, M. & Santis, G. D. (Eds.). (1998). *Population and Poverty in the Developing World.* Oxford: Clarendon Press.

Locke, C. (2001). *Gonzo Marketing: Winning Through Worst Practices.* Cambridge, MA: Perseus Publishing.

Loewen, G., Silver, J., August, M., Bruning, P., MacKenzie, M., & Meyerson, S. (2005). *Identifying Employment Opportunities for Low-Income People Within the Manitoba Innovation Framework.* Winnipeg, MB: Manitoba Research Alliance, p. 13.

Long, D., & Dickason, O. (1998). *Visions of the Heart: Canadian Aboriginal Issues* (2nd ed.). Toronto, ON: Thompson Nelson.

Lotz, J. (1977). *Understanding Canada. Regional and Community Development in a New Nation.* Toronto, ON: NC Press.

Lotz, J. (1988). *The Quest for Community Development in Canada.* Sydney, NS: UCCB Press.

Lotz, J., & Welton, M. (1997). *Father Jimmy–The Life and Times of Jimmy Tompkins.* Wreck Cove, NS: Breton Books.

Lotz, J., & Welton, M.R. (1987). Knowledge for the people: The origins of the development of the Antigonish movement. In M. Welton (Ed.), *Knowledge for the People: The Struggle for Adult-Learning in English-Speaking Canada* (pp. 97–111). Toronto, ON: The Ontario Institute for the Study of Education Press.

Lovell, M. (1991). *The Friendship Group: Learning the Skills To Create Social Support.* Vancouver, BC: University of British Columbia.

MacDonald, A.A. (1987). *The Coady International Institute. A Contemporary Program Perspective.* Antigonish, NS: St. Francis Xavier University Press.

MacLellan, M. (1985). *Coady Remembered.* Antigonish, NS: St. Francis Xavier University Press.

MacNair, R., Gross, J., & Daniels, M. (1995). State promotion of community advocacy organizations: a comparative analysis of four case studies in Georgia. *Journal of Community Practice, 2,* 77–97.

Maluccio, A., Pine, B., & Tracy, E. (2002). *Social Work Practice with Families and Children.* New York: Columbia University Press.

Marsh, L. (1974). *Communities in Canada.* Toronto, ON: McClelland and Stewart.

Marshall, I. (1996). *A History and Ethnography of the Beothuk.* Montreal, QC: McGill-Queen's University Press.

Marshall, S. (1995). Confrontations and cooptations in antifeminist organizations. In M. Ferree and P. Martin (Eds.). *Feminist Organizations: Harvest of the New Women's Movement* (pp. 323–335). Philadelphia: Temple University Press.

Martens, C. (2000). *Intellectual disability and Aboriginal people: An overview of current practice and process in institutionalization.* M.Ed. thesis, University of Manitoba, Winnipeg.

Marx, J.D. (2000). Women and human services giving. *Social Work, 45,* 27.

Marx, K. (1999, reprinted). *Das Kapital.* Washington, DC: Gateway Editions.

Maslow, A. (1968). *Toward a Psychology of Being.* New York: Van Nostrand Reinhold.

Maslow, A. (1971). *The Further Reaches of Human Nature.* New York: Penguin.

Mawhinny, A. (Ed.). (1996). *Rebirth: Political, Economic, and Social Development in First Nations.* Toronto, ON: Dundurn.

Mawhiney, Anne-Marie & Pitblado, Jane. (Eds.). 1999. Boom Town Blues: Elliot Lake: Collapse and Revival in a Single-Industry Community. Toronto, ON: Dundurn Press.

Mayo, M., Pastor, J., & Wapner, S. (1995). Linking organizational behavior and environmental psychology. *Environment and Behavior, 27*(1), 73–89.

McCaleb, S.P. (1994). *Building Communities of learners: A Collaboration Among Teachers, Students, Families, and Community.* Mahwah, NJ: Lawrence Erlbaum Associates.

McCormick, R. (1997). Healing through interdependence: The role of connecting in First Nations healing practices. *Canadian Journal of Counselling* 31(3): 172–184.

McCormick, R. (1998). *Ethical considerations in First Nations counselling and research.* Canadian Journal of Counselling 32(4): 284–297.

McCormick, Rod (1995/1996). Culturally appropriate means and ends of counselling as described by the First Nations people of British Columbia. *International Journal for the Advancement of Counselling* 18(3): 163–172.

McIntyre, G. (1998). Just housing. In "Choices," a coalition for social justice. *Dynamic Communities Fighting for Our Future.* Conference proceedings. Winnipeg, MB.

McKay, E., Young, D., Chartrand, P., & Whitecloud, W. (2001). *The Aboriginal Justice Inquiry.* Winnipeg, MB: Province of Manitoba.

McKnight, J.L. (1994). Two tools for well-being: Health systems and communities. *American Journal of Preventive Medicine, 10,* 23–25.

McKnight, J.L. (1995). *The Careless Society.* New York: Basic Books.

McKnight, J.L. & Kretzmann, J. (1990). *Mapping Community Capacity.* Evanston, IL: Northwestern University.

McKnight, J.L. & Kretzmann, J. (1994). *Building Communities from the Inside Out.* Evanston, IL: Center for Urban Affairs.

McMillan, A. & Yellowhorn, E. (2004). *First Peoples in Canada.* Toronto: Douglas & McIntyre.

McQuaig, S. (2005). *The City of Red Deer: Youth community*

action plan. Red Deer, AB: Insight Advanced.

McWhorter, D. (2001). *Carry Me Home: Birmingham, Alabama, the Climactic Battle of the Civil Rights Revolution.* New York: Touchstone.

Medved, C.E., Morrison, K., Dearing, J.W., Larson, R.S., Cline, G., & Brummans, B. (2001). Paradox in community health improvement initiatives: Communication and collaboration in a managed care environment. *Journal of Applied Communication Research, 29,* 137–152.

Messere, K. (Ed.). (1998). *The Tax System in Industrialized Countries.* Oxford: Oxford University Press.

Mifflen, F. (1974). *The Antigonish movement. A revitalization movement in eastern Nova Scotia* [unpublished PhD thesis]. Boston College.

Mignone, J. (2003). *Measuring Social Capital: A Guide for First Nations Communities.* Winnipeg: Centre for Aboriginal Health Research, University of Manitoba.

Miles, M. & Huberman, A. (1994). *Qualitative Data Analysis: An Expanded Sourcebook.* (2nd ed). Thousand Oaks, CA: Sage.

Miller, J. (1982). People, berdaches, and left-handed bears, *Journal of Anthropological Research, 38,* 274–287.

Miller, J. (2001). *Skyscrapers Hide the Heavens: A History of Indian-White Relations in Canada.* Toronto: *University of Toronto* Press.

Milloy, J. (1999). *A National Crime: The Canadian Government and the Residential School System: 1879–1986.* Winnipeg, MB: University of Winnipeg Press.

Milofsky, C. (Ed.). (1988). *Community Organizations: Studies in Resource Mobilization and Exchange.* New York: Oxford University Press.

Miner, J.B. (2002). *Organizational Behavior: Foundations, Theories, and Analyses.* New York: Oxford University Press.

Minkler, M. (1990). Improving health through community organization. In: Glanz K., Lewis F.M., Rimer B.K., (Eds.) *Health Behavior and Health Education: Theory, Research and Practice.* San Francisco: Jossey-Bass Publishers.

Monti-Belkaoui and Riahi-Belkaoui, A. (1998). *The Nature, Estimation, and Management of Political Risk.* Westport, CT: Quorum Books.

Moscovitch, A. (2006). The welfare state. In J. Marsh (ed.). *The Canadian Encyclopedia*, Revised edition. Retrieved June 23, 2006, from **www.histori.ca/default. do?page=.index**

Moulton, J., Mundy, K., Walmond, M., & Williams, J. (2002). *Education Reforms in Sub-Saharan Africa: Paradigm Lost?* Westport, CT: Greenwood Press.

Mullaly, R.C. (1977). *Structural Social Work: Community and Its Counterfeits.* New York: Basic Books.

Mulroy, E.A., & Shay, S. (1997). Nonprofit organizations and innovation: A model of neighborhood-based collaboration to prevent child maltreatment. *Social Work, 42,* 515–524.

Municipal and Community Affairs. (2003). *Community action toolkit: Protecting community infrastructure and preparing for resource development.* Yellowknife, NWT: Government of the Northwest Territories.

Musil, L., Kubalcikova, K., Hubikova, O., & Necasova, M. (2004). Do social workers avoid the dilemmas of work with clients? *European Journal of Social Work, 7,* 305–319.

Myers, G. & Craig, D. (2002). *Indigenous Peoples and Governance Structures. A Comparative Analysis of Land and Resource Management Rights.* Canberra, NSW: Aboriginal Studies Press.

Myers, I. (1995). *Gifts Differing: Understanding Personality Type.* New York: Davies-Black.

Narayan, U. (1997). *Voices of the poor: Poverty and social capital in Tanzania.* Washington DC: World Bank.

Narlikar, A. (2003). *International Trade and Developing Countries: Bargaining Coalitions in the GATT & WTO.* London: Routledge.

National Aboriginal Achievement Awards. (1998). Award recepients: Georges Erasmus, Public service. Retrieved March 2, 2006, from **www. ainc-inac.gc.ca/ch/rcap/index_e.html**

National Council on Welfare. (2005). *Welfare incomes 2004.* Ottawa, ON: Author.

National Council on Welfare. (2006). *Canadian welfare incomes 2005.* Ottawa: Author.

Neu, D., & Therrien, R. (2003). *Accounting for Genocide: Canada's Bureaucratic Assault on Aboriginal People.* Halifax, NS: Fernwood.

Newfoundland and Labrador Medical Association. (2003). An open door: The Seniors Resource Centre. *NEXUS Online, Summer.* Retrieved May 9, 2006, from **www. nlma.nf.ca/nexus/issues/summer_2003/articles/article_17.html**

Newman, O. (1973). *Defensible Space: Crime Prevention Through Urban Design.* New York: Collier Books.

Nierenberg, G. (1995). *The Art of Negotiating: Psychological Strategies for Gaining Advantageous Bargains.* New York: Barnes Noble.

Nijstad, B. & Paulus, P. (2003). *Group Creativity: Innovation Through Collaboration.* New York: Oxford University Press.

Nobel Foundation. (2006). Jane Addams—Biography. Retrieved March 2, 2006, from **nobelprize.org/peace/laureates/1931/addams-bio.html**

Norlin, J., & Chess, W. (1997). *Human Behavior and the Social Environment: Social Systems Theory* (3rd ed.). Boston, MA: Allyn and Bacon.

Norlin, J., Chess, W, Dale, O., & Smith, R. (2003). *Human Behavior and the Social Environment: Social Systems Theory* (4th ed.). Boston, MA: Allyn Bacon.

Norris, M. & Clatworthy, S. (2003). Aboriginal mobility and migration within urban Canada; Outcomes, factors and implications. In Newhouse, D., & Peters, E. (Eds.)*Not Strangers in These Parts: Urban Aboriginal Peoples.* Ottawa: Policy Research Initiative.

Novak, M. (Ed.). (1987). *Liberation Theology and the Liberal Society.* Washington, DC: American Enterprise Institute.

Nunavut Arctic College. (2006a). *About the college*. Retrieved May 5, 2006, from **www.nac.nu. ca/about_the_college/ about_college.htm**

Nunavut Arctic College. (2006b). *Campuses and community learning centres*. Retrieved May 5, 2006, from **www.nac.nu. ca/about_the_college/ campus.htm**

Nwachuku, U., & Ivey, A. (1991). Culture-specific counseling: An Alternative training model. *Journal of Counseling and Development, 70*, 106–111.

O'Toole, L. & Meier, K. (2003). *Desperately seeking Selznick: Cooptation and the dark side of public management in networks*. Paper presented at the 7th National Public Management Research Association Conference, Georgetown University, October 9–11.

Oakley, D., Yu, M., Lu, H., Shang, S., McIntosh, E., Pang, D., & Van Doren, E. (2004). Communication channels to help build an international community of education and practice. *Journal of Professional Nursing, 20,* 381–389.

O'Brien, R., Goetz, A.M., Scholte, J.A., & Williams, M. (2000). *Contesting Global Governance: Multilateral Economic Institutions and Global Social Movements*. Cambridge, England: Cambridge University Press.

O'Brien, T. (1999). *The Century of U.S. Capitalism in Latin America*. Albuquerque: University of New Mexico Press.

O'Donnell, V. & Tait, H. (2003). *Aboriginal peoples survey 2001—Initial findings:*

Well-being of the non-reserve Aboriginal population. Ottawa: Statistics Canada.

OECD. (2006). Social expenditure database. Retrieved June 23, 2006, from **hermia.sourceoecd.org/vl=41 6681/cl=19/nw=1/rpsv/ statistic/s22_about.htm?jnliss n=1608117x**

O'Grady, C. (2000). *Integrating Service Learning and Multicultural Education in Colleges and Universities*. Mahwah, NJ: Lawrence Erlbaum Associates.

Ontario Clean Water Agency. (2001). *Annual report*. Toronto, ON: author.

Ontario Healthy Communities Coalition. (2005). *Effective proposal writing*. Toronto: author.

Ott, J.S. (Ed.). (2001). *Understanding Nonprofit Organizations: Governance, Leadership, and Management*. Boulder, CO: Westview Press.

O'Toole, L.J. & Meier, K.J. (2003). *Bureaucracy and Uncertainty*. In Burden, B.C. (Ed.) *Uncertainty in American Politics*, (pp. 98–117). Cambridge, MA: Cambridge University Press.

Parks, C.D., & Sanna, L.J. (1999). *Group Performance and Interaction*. Boulder, Colorado: Westview Press.

Pastor, M. (1987). *The International Monetary Fund and Latin America: Economic Stabilization and Class Conflict*. Boulder, CO: Westview Press.

Payne, M. (2000). *Teamwork in Multiprofessional Care*. Chicago: Lyceum Books, Inc.

Petras, E.M., & Porpora, D. V. (1993). Participatory research: Three models and an analysis. *The American Sociologist, 24*(1), 109.

Pierson, P. (Ed.). (2001). *The New Politics of the Welfare State*. Oxford, England: Oxford University Press.

Pittenger, D. (1993). The utility of the Myers-Briggs type indicator. *Review of Educational Research, 63*, 467–488.

Plant, R. (1974). *Community and Ideology*. London: Routledge and Kegan Paul.

Plas, J.M., & Lewis, S.E. (2001). *Leadership in Non-Profit Organizations*. Thousand Oaks, CA: Sage Publications.

Plato. (1992). *The Republic*. Indianapolis, IN: Hackett.

Popple, K. (1995). *Analyzing Community Work: Its Theory and Practice*. Buckingham: Open University Press.

Prince Edward Island CAP. (2006). *News*. Retrieved May 8, 2006, from **www. peicaps.org/modules/ news/**

Putnam R. (1995). Bowling alone: America's declining social capital. *Journal of Democracy 1,* 65–79.

Putnam, R.D. (2000). *Bowling Alone. The Collapse and Revival of American Community*. New York: Simon and Schuster.

Putnam, R.D., Leonardi, R., & Nonetti, R.Y. (1993). *Making Democracy Work: Civic Traditions in Modern Italy*. Princeton NJ: Princeton University Press.Rabie, M. (1994). *Conflict Resolution and Ethnicity*. Westport, CT: Praeger.

Rabie, M. (1994). *Conflict Resolution and Ethnicity*. New York: Praeger Publishing.

Radforth, I., & Sangster, J. (1987). The struggle for autonomous workers' education: The workers' educational association in Ontario, 1917–1951. In M.R.

Welton (Ed.), *Knowledge for the People: The Struggle for Adult Learning in English-Speaking Canada, 1828–1973* (pp. 73–96). Toronto: OISE Press.

Radtke, J. (1998). *Strategic Communications for Nonprofit Organizations: Seven Steps to Creating a Successful Plan*. New York: John Wiley.

Rahim, M.A. (1990). (Ed.). *Theory and Research in Conflict Management*. New York: Praeger Publishers.

Rahim, M.A. (2001). *Managing Conflict in Organizations*. Westport, CT: Quorum Books.

Ramos, I., May, M., & Ramos, K. (2001). Environmental health training of promotoras in colonias along the Texas-Mexico border. *American Journal of Public Health, 91*, 568–570.

Ravensbergen, F. (2004). *Key questions to think about before incorporating a non-profit organization*. Montreal, QC: Centre for Community Organizations.

Reich, M. & Lowe, J. (2000). "Of means and ends" revisited: Teaching ethical community organizing in an unethical society. *Journal of Community Practice, 7*, 19–38.

Rekart, J. (1993). *Public Funds, Private Provision: The Role of the Voluntary Sector*. Vancouver, B.C.: UBC Press.

Robb, M., Barrett, S., Komaromy, C., & Rogers, A. (Eds.). (2003). *Communication, Relationships and Care: A Reader*. New York: Routledge.

Roberts, H. (1979). *Community Development: Learning and Action*. Toronto, ON: University of Toronto Press.

Roberts, W., Macrae, R., & Stahlbrand, L. (1999). *Real Food for a Change*. Toronto, ON: Random House of Canada.

Robertson, C., Svenson, L., & Joffres, M. (1998). Prevalence of cerebral palsy in Alberta. *Canadian Journal of Neurological Science, 25*, 117–122.

Robinson, B., & Hanna, M. (1994). Lessons for academic from grassroots organizing: A case study—the industrial areas foundation. *Journal of Community Practice, 1*(4), 63–94.

Rogers, M.B. (1990). *Cold Anger: A Story of Faith and Power Politics*. Denton, TX: University of North Texas Press.

Ross, R. (1996). *Returning to the Teachings: Exploring Aboriginal Justice*. Toronto, ON: Pearson.

Rostow, W.W. (1960). *The Stages of Economic Growth: A Non-Communist Manifesto*. Cambridge, England: University Press.

Rothman, J. (1979). Three methods of community organization practice. In F.M. Cox et al., *Strategies of Community Organization*. Itasca, IL: F.E. Peacock.

Rothman, J. (1995). Approaches to community intervention. In Rothman, J., Erlich, J.L., & Tropman J.E. (Eds.), *Strategies of Community Intervention* (pp. 26–63). Itasca, IL: F.E. Peacock Publishers.

Rothman, J., & Tropman, J. (1987). Models of community organization and macro practice perspectives: Their mixing and phasing. In Cox, F., Erlich, J. Rothman J., & Tropman J., (Eds.), *Strategies of Community Organization:*

Macro Practice (4th ed.) (pp. 3–26). Itasca, IL: Peacock.

Roupp, H. (Ed.). (1997). *Teaching World History: A Resource Book*. Armonk, NY: M.E. Sharpe.

Rubin, H. & Rubin, I. (1986). *Community Organizing and Development*. Ohio: Merrill Publishing Company.

Rubin, H. & Rubin, I. (2001). *Community Organizing and Development*. Needham Heights, MA: Allyn and Bacon.

Runde, J. & Mizuhara, S. (Eds.). (2003). *The Philosophy of Keynes' Economics: Probability, Uncertainty and Convention*. New York: Routledge.

Ryff, C.D. & Singer, B.H. (Eds.). (2001). *Emotion, Social Relationships, and Health*. New York: Oxford University Press.

Sampson, E.E., & Marthas, M. (1981). *Group Process for the Health Professions* (2nd ed.). New York: Wiley.

Sanders, D. (1994). *Developing a modern international law on the rights of Indigenous peoples: executive summary*. Unpublished manuscript. University of British Columbia, Vancouver.

Sanna, L. (1999). *Group Performance and Interaction*. Boulder, CO: Westview Press.

Saskatoon Communities for Children. (2006). *About us*. Retrieved September 4, 2006, from **http:// www.communities forchildren.net/**

Savan, B. (2004). Community-university partnerships: Linking research and action for sustainable community development. *Community*

Development Journal, 39, 372–384.

Schechter, Michael (Ed.). (2001). *United Nations-sponsored World Conferences: Focus on Impact and Follow-up.* Tokyo: UN University Press

Schiele, J., Jackson, S., & Fairfax, C. (2005). Maggie Lena Walker and African American community development. *Affilia, 20,* 21–38.

School of Community Government. (2006). *About the school.* Retrieved on May 4, 2006, from **www.sofcg. org/about1.html**

Schwarz, R. (2002). *The Skilled Facilitator.* New York: Jossey-Bass.

Scottish Community Education Council. (1990). *CeVe Scotland: Preservice Training for Community Education Work.* Edinburgh: SCEC.

Selden, S.C. (1998). *The Promise of representative Bureaucracy: Diversity and Responsiveness in a Government Agency.* Armonk, NY: M. E. Sharpe.

Seligson, M.A. (Ed.). (1979). *Politics and the Poor: Political Participation in Latin America* (Vol. 2). New York: Holmes & Meier.

Seniors Bridging Cultures Club. (2004). *Building bridges: Collaborative health policy development—Final Report.* St. John's, NL: author.

Seniors Resource Centre. (2006). *Welcome to the SRC.* Retrieved May 9, 2006, from **www. seniorsresource.ca/**

Sharan, S. (Ed.). (1999). *Handbook of Cooperative Learning Methods.* Westport, CT: Praeger.

Siggner, A.J. (2003). Urban Aboriginal populations: An update using the 2001 Census results. In Newhouse, D. and Peters, E. (Eds.) *Not Strangers in These Parts: Urban Aboriginal Peoples.* Ottawa: Policy Research Initiative.

Simon, J. (1975). The positive effect of population growth on regional savings in irrigation systems. *Review of Economics and Statistics, 57,* 71–79.

Sillitoe, P., Bicker, A., & Pottier, J. (Eds.). (2002). *Participating in Development: Approaches to Indigenous Knowledge.* London: Routledge.

Sims, R.R. (Ed.). (2002). *Changing the Way We Manage Change.* Westport, CT: Quorum Books.

Smelser, N.J. (1968). Towards a theory of modernization, in Smelser, N.J. (ed.) *Essays in Sociological Explanation,* Prentice-Hall, Englewood Cliffs, NJ.

Smith, A., & Krueger, A. (2003, reprinted). *The Wealth of Nations.* Danvers, MA: Bantam Classics.

Smith, K. (2005). Conflict management in community organizations. Retrieved August 6, 2005, from **ohioline.osu.edu/ cd-fact/1701.html**

Smith, M. (2005a). *Radical adult education.* Retrieved July 9, 2005, from **www.infed.org/ lifelonglearning/ b-raded.htm**

Smith, M. (2005b). *Community education.* Retrieved July 9, 2005, from **www.infed.org/ community/b-comed. htm#Theorzing**

Social Economy Showcase. (2006). *Unpit Power Corporation.* Retrieved May 3, 2006, from **ucscoop.com/uploads/687/48 3/Hupacasath.pdf**

Stanton, T. (Ed.). (2004). *HIV/AIDS and Information.* London: ASLIB-IMI.

Starhawk. (1990). *Truth or Dare: Encounter with Power, Authority and Mystery.* New York: Harper and Row.

Statistics Canada. (2003a). *Aboriginal People of Canada: A Demographic Profile.* Ottawa, ON: Author.

Statistics Canada. (2003b). *Participation and Activity Limitation Survey.* Ottawa: author.

Statistics Canada. (2005a). *Community belonging and self-perceived health: early CCHS findings.* Ottawa, ON: Author.

Statistics Canada. (2005b). *Projections of the Aboriginal Populations, Canada, Provinces and Territories, 2001–2017.* Ottawa, ON: Author.

Statistics Canada. (2006). *Community profiles: Edmonton.* Retrieved May 4, 2006, from **www12. statcan.ca/english/profil01/CP 01/index.cfm?Lang=E** and select the city and province.

Statistics Canada. (2006b). *Community profiles: Saskatoon.* Retrieved May 4, 2006, from **www12.statcan.ca/english/pro fil01/CP01/index.cfm?Lang= E** and select the city and province.

Statistics Canada. (2006c). *Community profiles: Yellowknife.* Retrieved May 4, 2006, from **www12.statcan.ca/ english/profil01/CP01/index. cfm?Lang=E** and select the city and province.

Statistics Canada. (2006d). *Community profiles: Winnipeg.* Retrieved May 4, 2006, from **www12.statcan.ca/english/ profil01/CP01/index.cfm?**

Lang=E and select the city and province.

Statistics Canada. (2006e). *Community profiles: Iqualuit.* Retrieved May 5, 2006, from **www12.statcan.ca/english/ profil01/CP01/index.cfm? Lang=E** and select the city and province.

Statistics Canada. (2006f). *Community profiles: Toronto.* Retrieved May 6, 2006, from **www12.statcan.ca/english/ profil01/CP01/index.cfm?La ng=E** and select the city and province.

Statistics Canada. (2006g). *Community profiles: Saint John.* Retrieved May 8, 2006, from **www12.statcan.ca/ english/profil01/CP01/index. cfm?Lang=E** and select the city and province.

Statistics Canada. (2006h). *Community profiles: Charlottetown.* Retrieved May 8, 2006, from **www12.statcan.ca/english/ profil01/CP01/index.cfm? Lang=E** and select the city and province.

Statistics Canada. (2006i). *Community profiles: Richmond subdivision.* Retrieved May 8, 2006, from **www12.statcan.ca/ english/profil01/CP01/index. cfm?Lang=E** and select the city and province.

Statistics Canada. (2006j). *Community profiles: St. John's.* Retrieved May 9, 2006, from **www12.statcan.ca/english/ profil01/CP01//index.cfm? Lang=E** and select the city and province.

Stephen Lewis Foundation. (2006). *About us.* Retrieved June 24, 2006, from **www.stephenlewi-sfoundation.org/about.htm**

Stern, A.J., & Hicks, T. (2000). *The Process of Business/ Environmental*

Collaborations: Partnering for Sustainability. Westport, CT: Quorum Books.

Stoecker, R. (2001). Power or programs? Two paths to community development, *International Association for Community Development Conference.* Aukland, NZ.

Stout, M. & Kipling, G. (2003). *Aboriginal people, resilience, and the residential school legacy.* Ottawa: The Aboriginal Healing Foundation.

Stout, M., Kipling, G., & Stout, R. (2001). *Aboriginal women's health research.* Winnipeg: Canadian Women's Health Network.

Sustainable Toronto. (2006a). *Defining sustainability.* Retrieved May 6, 2006, from **www.utoronto. ca/envstudy/ sustainabletoronto/ whoweare.htm#3**

Sustainable Toronto. (2006b). *Projects and partners.* Retrieved May 6, 2006, from **www.utoronto.ca/envstudy/ sustainabletoronto/ project.htm**

Sustainable Toronto. (2006c). *Meeting our objectives.* Retrieved May 6, 2006, from **www. utoronto.ca/envstudy/ sustainabletoronto/ project.htm**

Taétreault, M.A. & Abel, C.F. (Eds.). (1986). *Dependency Theory and the Return of High Politics.* New York: Greenwood Press.

Telecommunities Canada. (2006). *A brief history.* Retrieved May 8, 2006, from **www.tc.ca/ tcbriefhistory.html**

Temme, J. (1996). *Team Power.* Missions, KS: Skill Path Publications.

Tesoriero, F. (1999). Will social work contribute to social development into the new millennium? *Australian Social Work, 52,* 11–17.

Tester, F., Kulchyski, P. (1994). *Tammarniit (Mistakes): Inuit Relocation in the Eastern Arctic, 1939–63,* Vancouver, BC: University of British Columbia Press.

Thira, D. 2005. *Through the pain: community-based suicide prevention manual.* Vancouver, BC: Thira Consulting.

Thompson, L. (2000). *The Mind and Heart of the Negotiator.* New York: Prentice Hall.

Tilstone, C., Florian, L., & Rose, R. (1998). *Promoting Inclusive Practice.* London: Routledge.

Timmreck, T.C. (2003). *Planning, Program Development and Evaluation: A Handbook for Health Promotion, Aging, and Health Services* (2nd ed.). Mississauga, ON: Jones and Bartlett.

Todd, H. (1996). *Women at the Center: Grameen Bank Borrowers after One Decade.* Boulder, CO: Westview Press.

Tomer, J.F. (1999). *The Human Firm: A Socio-Economic Analysis of Its Behavior and Potential in a New Economic Age.* London: Routledge.

Tourism Montreal. (2006). *Montreal is…Montreal,* QC: author.

Tracy, E. & Whittaker. J. (1990). The social network map: Assessing social support in clinical social work practice. *Families in Society, 71,* 461–470.

Tropman, J.E. (1980). *Effective Meetings: Improving Group Decision-Making.* Beverly Hills, CA: Sage.

Tuckman, B. (1965). Developmental sequence in small groups, *Psychological Bulletin, 63*, 384–399.

Tuckman, B., & Jensen, M. (1977). Stages of small group development revisited. *Group and Organizational Studies, 2*, 419–427.

Tuijnman, A. (Ed.) (1996), *The International Encyclopedia of Adult Education and Training*, (2nd ed). Oxford: Elsevier Science.

Turner, B. (1993). *Max Weber: From History to Modernity*. London: Routledge.

UNESCO. (1976). *Recommendation on the Development of Adult Education*. Paris: UNESCO.

Ungar, M., Manuel, S., Mealey, S., Thomas, G., & Campbell, C. (2004). A study of community guides: Lessons for professionals practicing with and in communities. *Social Work, 49*, 550–561.

UNICEF. (2006). State of the World's Children Report: Excluded and Invisible. New York, NY: Author.

United Nations. (1990). *Convention on the rights of the child*. Retrieved May 30, 2006, from **www.unhchr.ch/html/menu3/ b/k2crc.htm**

United Nations. (2005). The Millennium Development Goals Report. New York, NY: Author.

United Nations Children's Fund (UNICEF). (1990). *First Call for Children*, Convention on the Rights of the Child, New York: UNICEF.

United Nations Platform for Action Committee. (2005). *Community economic development*. Retrieved October 1, 2005, from

unpac.ca/economy/ ced.html

University of British Columbia. (2006). *Georges Henry Erasmus* [Electronic Version]. Retrieved March 2, 2006, from **www.moa.ubc. ca/Exhibitions/Online/ Sourcebooks/Honour/ photo7.html**

Uphoff, N. (1999). Understanding social capital: Learning from the analysis and experiences of participation, in Dasgupta and Seregeldin. In *Social capital: A Multifaceted Perspective*, Washington DC: World Bank.

Van Ginkel, H., Barrett, B., Court, J., & Velasquez, J. (Eds.). (2002). *Human Development and the Environment: Challenges for the United Nations in the New Millennium*. New York: United Nations University Press.

Vásquez, I. (Ed.). (2000). *Global Fortune: The Stumble and Rise of World Capitalism*. Washington, DC: Cato Institute.

von Bertalanffy, L., (1934). Untersuchungen über die gesetzlichkeit des wachstums. I. allgemeine grundlagen der theorie; Mathematische und physiologische gesetzlichkeiten des wachstums bei wassertieren. *Arch Entwicklungsmech, 131*, 613–652.

Walsh, W., Craik, K., & Price, R. (Eds.). (2000). *Person-Environment Psychology: New Directions and Perspectives* (2nd ed.). Mahwah, NJ: Lawrence Erlbaum Associates.

Wapner, S. & Demick, J. (2000). Person-in-environment psychology: A holistic, developmental, systems-oriented perspective.

(pp. 25–60). In Walsh, W., Craik, K., & Price, R. (Eds.). Person-Environment Psychology: New Directions and Perspectives (2nd ed.). Mahwah, NJ: Lawrence Erlbaum Associates.

Warren, R. (1978). *The Community in America*. Chicago: Rand McNally.

Warry, W. (1998). *Unfinished Dreams: Community Healing and the Reality of Aboriginal Self- Government*. Toronto: University of Toronto Press.

Watson, D. (2005). *The board member's companion*. Thunder Bay, ON: Volunteer Thunder Bay.

Weber, M. (1968). *Economy and Society: An Outline of Interpretive Sociology*. New York: Bedminster Press.

Weber, M., & Whimster, S. (2003). *The Essential Weber: A Reader*. Noew York, NY: Routledge.

Welch, J. (2003). *How to write powerful press releases*. Knoxville, TN; Press-Release-Writing.

Well, M.O., & Gamble, D.N. (1995). *Community practice models*. In R. L. Edwards (Ed.), *Encyclopedia of Social Work*, Vol. 1 (19th ed., pp. 577–694), Silver Spring, MD: NASW Press.

Welton, M. (2005). *Dangerous knowledge: Canadian workers' education in the decades of discord*. Retrieved September 4, 2006, from **www-distance.syr.edu/ welton.htm**

Wesley-Esquimaux, C. & Smolewski, M. (2004). *Historic trauma and Aboriginal healing*. Ottawa: Aboriginal Healing Foundation.

Wiatrowski, M. & Campoverde, C. (1996). Community policing and community organization: Assessment and consensus development strategies. *Journal of Community Practice, 3,* 1–18.

Wildsmith, B. (1985). Pre-confederation treaties. In Morse, B. (Ed.), *Aboriginal Peoples and the Law* (pp. 200–212). Ottawa, ON: Carleton University Press.

Williams, L., Labonte, R., & O'Brien, M. (2003). Empowering social action through narratives of identity and culture. *Health Promotion International, 18,* (31), 33–40.

Wilson, J.Q. (2000). *Bureaucracy: What Government Agencies Do and Why They Do It.* New York: Basic Books.

Winnipeg Free Press. (2006). Natives delay CN's injunction application. Retrieved June 23, 2006, from **www.winnipegfreepress.com**

Wollf, T. & Kaye, G. (1994). *From the ground up: a Workbook on Coalition Building and Community Development.* Amherst, MA: Community Partners.

Wright, S. (2004). Child protection in the community: A community development approach. *Child Abuse Review, 13,* 384–398.

Wrong, D. (1995). *Power: Its Forms, Bases and Uses.* New Brunswick, NJ: Transaction.

Wu, F., & Butz, W.P. (2004). *The Future of Genetically Modified Crops: Lessons from the Green Revolution.* Santa Monica, CA: Rand.

Wyman, K. (1995). *Fundraising ideas that work for grassroots groups.* Ottawa: Department of Canadian Heritage.

Yeager, T.J. (1998). *Institutions, Transition Economies, and Economic Development.* Boulder, CO: Westview Press.

Yukon Arts Centre. (2006). *Programs.* Retrieved May 3, 2006, from **www.yukonartscentre. org/yac.htm**

Yukon Bureau of Statistics. (2006). *Yukon community profiles.* Retrieved May 3, 2006, from **www.yukoncommunities.yk. ca/communities/ whitehorse/**

Yukon Government. (2005). *New board members for Yukon Arts Centre.* Retrieved May 3, 2006, from **www.gov.yk.ca/ news/2005/05-175.html**

Zachary, E. (2000). Grassroots leadership training: a case study of an effort to integrate theory and method. *Journal of Community Practice, 7,* 71–93.

Zarefsky, D. (1986). *President Johnson's War on Poverty: Rhetoric and History.* University, AL: University of Alabama Press.

Zastrow, C. (2002). *Practice of Social Work* (7th ed.). Toronto: Nelson.

Zepatos, T., & Kaufman, E. (1995). *Women for a Change: A Grassroots Guide to Activism and Politics.* New York: Facts on File.

Index